Decision Support in Organizational Transformation

IFIP – The International Federation for Information Processing

IFIP was founded in 1960 under the auspices of UNESCO, following the First World Computer Congress held in Paris the previous year. An umbrella organization for societies working in information processing, IFIP's aim is two-fold: to support information processing within its member countries and to encourage technology transfer to developing nations. As its mission statement clearly states,

> IFIP's mission is to be the leading, truly international, apolitical organization which encourages and assists in the development, exploitation and application of information technology for the benefit of all people.

IFIP is a non-profitmaking organization, run almost solely by 2500 volunteers. It operates through a number of technical committees, which organize events and publications. IFIP's events range from an international congress to local seminars, but the most important are:

- the IFIP World Computer Congress, held every second year;
- open conferences;
- working conferences.

The flagship event is the IFIP World Computer Congress, at which both invited and contributed papers are presented. Contributed papers are rigorously refereed and the rejection rate is high.

As with the Congress, participation in the open conferences is open to all and papers may be invited or submitted. Again, submitted papers are stringently refereed.

The working conferences are structured differently. They are usually run by a working group and attendance is small and by invitation only. Their purpose is to create an atmosphere conducive to innovation and development. Refereeing is less rigorous and papers are subjected to extensive group discussion.

Publications arising from IFIP events vary. The papers presented at the IFIP World Computer Congress and at open conferences are published as conference proceedings, while the results of the working conferences are often published as collections of selected and edited papers.

Any national society whose primary activity is in information may apply to become a full member of IFIP, although full membership is restricted to one society per country. Full members are entitled to vote at the annual General Assembly, National societies preferring a less committed involvement may apply for associate or corresponding membership. Associate members enjoy the same benefits as full members, but without voting rights. Corresponding members are not represented in IFIP bodies. Affiliated membership is open to non-national societies, and individual and honorary membership schemes are also offered.

Decision Support in Organizational Transformation

IFIP TC8 WG8.3 International Conference on Organizational Transformation and Decision Support, 15–16 September 1997, La Gomera, Canary Islands

Edited by

Patrick Humphreys
London School of Economics
London
UK

Sabino Ayestaran
University del Pais Vasco
San Sebastian
Spain

Andrew McCosh
University of Edinburgh
Edinburgh
Scotland

and

Bill Mayon-White
London School of Economics
London
UK

Published by Chapman & Hall on behalf of the
International Federation for Information Processing (IFIP)

CHAPMAN & HALL
London · Weinheim · New York · Tokyo · Melbourne · Madras

Published by Chapman & Hall, 2–6 Boundary Row, London SE1 8HN, UK

Chapman & Hall, 2–6 Boundary Row, London SE1 8HN, UK

Chapman & Hall GmbH, Pappelallee 3, 69469 Weinheim, Germany

Chapman & Hall USA, 115 Fifth Avenue, New York, NY 10003, USA

Chapman & Hall Japan, ITP-Japan, Kyowa Building, 3F, 2-2-1 Hirakawacho, Chiyoda-ku, Tokyo 102, Japan

Chapman & Hall Australia, 102 Dodds Street, South Melbourne, Victoria 3205, Australia

Chapman & Hall India, R. Seshadri, 32 Second Main Road, CIT East, Madras 600 035, India

First edition 1997

Printed in Great Britain by Athenæum Press Ltd, Gateshead, Tyne & Wear

ISBN 0 412 83050 7

A catalogue record for this book is available from the British Library

∞ Printed on permanent acid-free text paper, manufactured in accordance with ANSI/NISO Z39.48-1992 and ANSI/NISO Z39.48-1984 (Permanence of Paper).

CONTENTS

1
Introduction and overview

P. Humphreys
Department of Social Psychology
London School of Economics and Political Science
Houghton Street, London WC2A 2AE.
Tel +44 171 955 7711 Fax +44 171 955 7565
e-mail P.Humphreys@lse.ac.uk

W. Mayon-White
Department of Information Systems.
London School of Economics and Political Science
Houghton Street, London WC2A 2AE.
Tel: +44 171 955 7784 Fax: +44 171 955 6079
e-mail wmmw@compuserve.com

1 INTRODUCTION

This book presents a selection of contributions to the conference on *Decision Support in Organizational Transformation* held in La Gomera, Canary Islands, in September, 1997. The conference was organized by the International Federation of Information Processing's Working Group 8.3 on Decision Support Systems and the Organisational Research Group of the London School of Economics and Political Science. (LSE). The Programme Committee for the Conference comprised Patrick Humphreys, LSE, Sabino Ayestaran, Universidad del Pais Vasco, Andrew McCosh, University of Edinburgh and Bill Mayon-White, LSE. The chairperson of the organising committee was Lucia Sell, LSE. The programme committee members served also as the editors of this book.

Working group 8.3 was formally established in 1981 on the recommendation of IFIP's Technical Committee on Information Systems (TC8). The scope of the working group covers:

> "Development of approaches for applying information systems technology to increase the effectiveness of decision makers in situations where the computer system can support and enhance human judgement in the performance of tasks that have elements that cannot be specified in advance."

The principal aim of the working group is:

> "To improve ways of synthesising and applying relevant work from reference disciplines to practical implementations of systems that enhance decision support capability."

This book has its origins in ideas that have travelled within the decision support community for a number of years, and led, in 1990, the formation of the Task Group on Organisational Transformation within Working Group 8.3. Conversations at the IFIP WG8.3 conference on Decision Support System Experiences and Expectations, held at INSEAD, France, in 1992 (Jelassi and Mayon-White, 1992) led to the plan for this book. Invited and contributed papers were sought, reviewed, and presented at an WG8.3 conference held in San Sebastian (Basque Country) in 1994. The dialogue continued at the 1996 IFIP WG8.3 conference on Implementing Systems for Supporting Management Decisions held at LSE (Humphreys *et. al.,* 1996), Selected papers from the San Sebastian conference were revised and refined, and three additional, papers were specially commissioned to ensure a consistent coverage across the topics considered in the book, which has now emerged in its published form for the 1997 conference in La Gomera.

In the early 1990s, two strong themes were observable in different parts of the decision support community. The first of these themes was attention to the concept of change. In business schools across Europe and the USA there was an observable and growing pre-occupation with the theme of change. Prompted by the pace of economic and political change, academics appeared to be searching in either the organisational development (OD) literature, or to be referring work in strategic and corporate planning. Little genuinely new thinking emerged, but the literature was abundant, and the popular management texts at the airport book stalls seemed to be replete with recipes for change.

The second theme was an emerging debate within the Decision Analysis and Decision Support community which appeared to reflect a growing sense of unease with the traditional offerings of this field. Part of this debate was reflected in plenary panel discussions at the 1992 INSEAD conference. On this occasion, a polarisation of views surfaced between US speakers and those from Europe. The essence of this debate focused on the role of decision support in organisations. A "North American" view of the decision maker emerged: a positivist view of the decision maker as the rational actor, pre-disposed to use discrete decision analytic tools, and working within a rational organisational setting. This was strongly countered by the view generally held in both East and West Europe, and probably in most of the world, which considers "decisions" as merely one expression of the unfolding web of the organisation, which itself exists and operates within an irrational, unpredictable, and dynamic socio-political setting.

In this discussion, the positivist view of decision making as represented in the "rational" literature was argued to be unrealistic and narrow, perhaps representing a organisations as some managers and decision analysts might wish it to be, but patently wrong and misleading for the majority of settings. But what would the alternatives look like? How does decision making take place in a highly politicised environment? What role, if any, does the positivist view retain in such circumstances?

Such contrasting views are necessarily polarised, but they serve us well as the beginning of an exploration of the ambiguous challenge posed by the title to this volume: "Decision Support in Organisational Transformation". Two challenges set by this title are, firstly, the potential and role of decision support in the aiding and helping those in the midst of organisational change, and, secondly, the prospect of using examples of organisational change as a source of new models of decision making.

The first challenge suggests a test for our decision support tools and techniques: if they are indeed reliable sophisticated quality products, then they should be capable of helping groups and individuals to shape, structure, and manage decisions concerning the future shape of their organisations. This view then leads on to a hypothesis that if such tools were indeed appropriate and relevant we should be able to find evidence widespread use of the products of the decision support community, and to ask if this is so.

We can also examine the second challenge: do the observable processes and facts of organisational change or transformation prove to be a rich arena for research? if so they should show the student of change how groups in organisations, under the stress and pressure of change, really react to the problems of making and implementing decisions. Understanding how such groups go about decision making should, in principle, tell us a more about those characteristics which we should endeavour to build into our decision tools.

This volume is part of the response to these challenges and issues. The authors are drawn from a range of countries and cultures and reflect on their experiences of change and decision making. They are well placed to offer commentary on these trends and developments. The collection should thus be of considerable value to students and researchers from both of the traditions described above, and it is hoped that this volume will serve to mark a turning point in our views on decision making in organisations.

The is one other theme underlying this collection. It concerns the role of technology in today's organisations, both as an essential component which is itself shaping and controlling organisational form, and as a vehicle which embodies much of our thinking about decision making and about efficient decisions. For example, the credit rules used by a bank are managed and mediated via networks of computers. Customer service centres, or call centres, have emerged as the hub at the core of telephone banking in the UK and the USA. With these has come a delegation of decision making. A lending decision is now no longer made by a "bank manager", instead it is derived form a decision support system used and operated by a clerk cum telephonist dealing directly with customer queries. This new form of service replaces the old, and brings with a new organisational form with a flatter structure within which employees enjoy greater responsibility for decisions, and are supported and enmeshed within a complex technological environment.

This one example serves to illustrate the intertwining of decision support and organisational transformation. there are many others such examples and cases in the collection in this volume. They are all intended to stimulate debate and to challenge some of our pre-conceptions about decisions and about change. The contributors are all experts in the field with real-life experience and expertise in the process of organizational transformation and implementation of decision support. The frameworks presented represent a synthesis of the wide range of experience gained in practice during the 1990's. The cases are written by those people who played key roles in them. This helps to convey to the reader a (justified) sense of immediacy, richness, timeliness and reliability. The cases and examples span many countries, including Chile, France, Russia, Germany, Great Britain, Hungary, Italy, Spain, Sweden, and the USA. They are described in a consistently accessible style, providing both intrinsic interest in their variety and the possibility of inter-sectoral and inter-cultural comparisons.

2 OVERVIEW

In chapter 2, the scene is set by Osvaldo Garcia and Renato Orellana, who provide a comprehensive critique of current approaches to the design of DSS, stating from the concerns of managers within organisations, viewed as human activity systems, who must take care of the organisation in the midst of a changing environment. They describe the structural, conversational and emotional adjustments which are necessary so that DSS can be reinterpreted as conversational devices that trigger the language and emotional processes of the community sharing the concerns of the manager.

An important type of change in the environment is where a company or other organization faces a major change in the way it is perceived by the public, in a situation where the change is in the company's stance on an ethical question. In chapter 3, Andrew McCosh notes the problems companies can have with ethical episodes, (something not considered before in the DSS design literature) and makes a preliminary attempt to derive a DSS which will predict the path of an ethical episode, for the guidance of corporate transforming agents.

In chapter 4, Patrick Humphreys and Eric Nappelbaum investigate the organisational perspective generally adopted by top management, in Eastern Europe and elsewhere, and explore the consequential stresses generated throughout organizations in the attempt to implement the ensuing prescriptions for change. On the basis of the model for problem formulation and choice developed by Nappelbaum (presented in chapter 15) this situation is examined to the issue of implementation design for strategic decisions taken by the upper management. Team building is shown to be an important part of this process, involving every echelon in participative management. This imposes new requirements on organisational communications and on computer support for organisational change. DSS design guidelines conventionally assume that the Decision which the system is attempting to support will be the "right" one.

In chapter 5, Maurice Schlumberger challenges the hegemony of this assumption in the context of organisational transformation, showing how it leads to people in the organisation focusing on getting good figures for reporting, in contrast to making a "reasonable" decision, such that personnel focus on getting the deed done as well as possible, supported by mechanisms to monitor the outcome of the decision and to support the improvement of both this outcome and the decision making process itself.

In chapter 6, Gerard de Zeeuw notes that efforts to develop DSS still seem to be based on decision theory as a theory *of* rational action (hence the tendency in DSS design to focus on supporting the "right" decision), whereas, as Schlumberger also stresses, there is a need to return to the original notion of support to improve action. DSS design and can still draw profitably on decision theory, reconceptualised to provide languages that support the improvement of individual and collective actions.

In chapter 7, Liam Bannon shows how GDSS (Group DSS) design and implementation has also persevered with the rational cognitive model *of* decision making activity criticised by de Zeeuw, and extends the critique comprehensively within the context of GDSS, in the light of concerns within the field of Computer-Supported Cooperative work (CSCW). Key concerns are reframed, and topics which it might be fruitful for the CSCW and GDSS communities to jointly explore and debate are identified, i.e., pluralism in conceptual frameworks, decision making, information use in organisations, understanding groups, the role of models, (mis-)use of tools, communication or conversation?

In chapter 8, Sven Carlsson points out that the majority of DSS in organisations are no longer built by DSS professionals, but by the DSS manager-users themselves. Most of these DSS are developed using evolutionary approaches, stressing continuous development of decision tasks. This has the drawback that it can lead to the exploitation of old tasks instead of exploration of new possibilities which, in the long run, can be harmful to an organization. Two approaches to improve manager-user developed DSS Design are presented, with case studies. The first approach (strategic opportunistic design) has the aim that managers should become more strategically oriented in their secondary decisions as well as their DSS building activities. The goal of the second approach (redesign of decision processes) is to challenge and strive for radical changes in an organisation's current decision processes.

In chapter 9, Piero Migliarese and Claudio Ferioli draw on research on dynamic networks in organizations to propose a new method, the Organisational Relational model, for the analysis of innovative organisational models,. Its basic elements are nodes (organisational units or agents) and links among nodes (organisational relations, communication channels, etc.). The importance of IT, and especially GDSS, in providing tools for innovative organisations, is conceptualised in terms of extending the autonomy of nodes, and providing instruments for supporting links between nodes and illustrated in case studies.

Organisations have had links with others and have operated globally for decades. However, while previously these links were at arm's length, information systems linking organisations are now emerging with a new impetus due to developments in communications and networking, and to management initiatives, like outsourcing, joint ventures, etc. In chapter 10, Claudia Loebbecke and her colleagues discuss inter-organisational systems (IOS) and identify why managers need to consider them differently from other, internal, information systems. Different types of IOS are considered in terms of functional scope and IOS-autonomy, IOS-induced business transformation and issues of IOS planning and design. New business opportunities are outlined, afforded by combining strategies for cooperation between mutually interdependent organisations and IOS which span corporate boundaries.

In Chapter 11, Anne Davies and Trevor Campbell present a case study of a strategic partnership in outsourcing a central government computing service in Northern Ireland. The partnership was held to be successful due to mutual reliance between the organizations involved. However, the study also revealed that the wider issues of information stewardship and informatization in public administration may be undermined by outsourcing.

In chapter 12, Andrew McCosh reviews the history of DSS use by investment and merchant banks in dealing with mergers and acquisitions, finding little change in the financial models, except for database availability due to the improvements in communications technology reviewed in previous chapters. Problems of organisational fit, personnel policy and organisational structure are identified as continuing areas of serious difficulty during merger operations. These are not addressed in conventional model-based DSS design, but could receive new impetus through the alternative DSS design approaches outlined above.

In chapter 13, Zita Paprika describes results from the decision-making sub-project of the of the research programme, "In Global Competition - Microeconomics Factors of Competitiveness of the Hungarian Economy", which starts from the premise that the method of making decisions in the microsphere is one of the strategic factors of any market economy and addresses the question, on the basis of interviews with Hungarian and Spanish managers, of whether they have the proper attitudes and skills to implement the change of the economic system or not.

In chapter 14, Sabino Ayestaran and his colleagues analyse the different ways of handling conflicts within organisations in relation to the local organisational culture , analysed in terms of the degree of identification of the members with the objectives of the organisation, the degree of power distance in the organization, and whether it functions as a closed or an open system. A case study in the Basque Public Health service illustrates how transformation, from a style of resistance and process control in transactions between an organizational group and the central authorities in this institution, to one based on compromise and negotiation was achieved through cultural change involving transformation of the internal dynamic of the group, reduction in the degree of hierarchical organization of the institution by creating channels of dialogue and negotiation, and separation of the group's task from the negative emotions associated with conflict with the authorities.

In sum, this book draws on methods, approaches and theories from many disciplines and provides cases in many contexts and from many countries, but care has been taken to avoid jargon and assumptions of prior knowledge of particular methods and theories on behalf of the reader. Technical discussions have been kept to a minimum and we hope that the book will appeal easily to a wide range of academic, professional and business readers.

3 REFERENCES

Humphreys, P. C., Bannon, L., McCosh, A, Migliarese, P. and Pomerol, J-C. (1996) Implementing Systems for Supporting Management Decisions: Concepts, Methods, Experiences. Chapman and Hall, London.

Jelassi, T and Mayon-White, W. (1992) Decision Support Systems: Experiences and Expectations. Elsevier, Amsterdam.

4 BIOGRAPHIES

Patrick Humphreys is a founding member of IFIP working group 8.3. He is Professor of Social Psychology at the London School of Economics and Political Science, where he convenes graduate courses on Organisational Social Psychology, Decision Making and Decision Support Systems and the Social Psychology of the Media. He led the LSE teams on CEC ESPRIT projects on *Functional Analysis of Organisational Requirements* and on *Project Integrated Management Systems* and directed the CEC TEMPUS project *BEAMS - Business Economics and Management Support* and many other projects on decision making, organisational process modelling, networking and communication support. His books include *How Voters Decide*, *Analysing and Aiding Decision Processes*, *Effective Decision Support Systems*, *Exploring Human Decision Making* and *Software Development Project Management: Process and Support.*

Bill Mayon-White is an independent adviser on technology and change to both government and private sector organisations. Having previously worked as a scientist in government, and as a senior academic in universities in the UK and overseas, he now holds the position of Visiting Fellow at the London School of Economics. He divides his time between consultancy, writing and research into problems of innovation and change.

2

Decision Support Systems: Structural, conversational and emotional adjustments: Breaking and taking of organisational care

O. García and R. Orellana
CIGAR Ltda.
Padre Mariano Nº103, Of. 602
Providencia, Chile.
Tel +52 2 366 0172/366 0173 Fax + 52 *2 235 5383*

Abstract

Computer and communication technology has been used extensively in organisations to enhance the management process but experts and users report dissatisfaction with the design process and the support provided by technological systems. Increasing their effectiveness is not a question of more or better technology but one of re-interpretation of action and the manager's activity. According to developments in cognitive biology, human beings do not act based on a representation of the world and this contradicts the current foundation of the concern for providing information as an accurate representation of relevant reality. Therefore human understanding as an observer in language opens a new perspective of management. Language as the recursive flow of consensual coordinations of behaviour that constitutes a manner of living together, allows for the generation of the complexities that managers must cope with to take care of the viability of the Human Activity Systems under their responsibility. This continuous criss-crossing of consensual coordinations of consensual coordinations of behaviour follows the changing complexities of living together in a changing world; learning and acquiring new and more powerful languages to observe and coordinate in the domains of action that characterize the identity of the Human Activity System is a practice concerning viability. We understand conversation as the braiding between language and emotions, but emotions are changed in language, changing the disposition for action. Computer and communication technology can be reinterpreted as a conversational device that triggers the language and emotional processes of the community sharing the concerns of the manager.

Keywords

Taking care, human activity system, language and emotions, observational language, organisational learning.

1 INTRODUCTION

The main purpose of this paper is to contribute to the discussion about the design of computer and communication systems that can aid the management process.

1.1 Historical Overview

We propose that *Decision Support System* can be considered as a design conception conceived within the computer industry to facilitate the use of computer technology in organisations (Keen, 1991). This framework, built during the late 1970s, offers computer and communication technology as support to the decision process which constitutes, in this view, the core of the management process. The DSS framework offers the following capabilities:

- Access : ease of use, wide variety of data, analysis and modelling capacity.
- Technological : software generation tools.
- Development modes: interactive and evolutionary.

Within this perspective, computer and communication technologies are seen as an amplification of the human data processing capabilities which limit the decision process. Thus, the human being is understood metaphorically as a data processing machine. Mental processes are associated with the manipulation of symbols and human communication to signal transmission.

The decision taking process *à la 1970s* is based upon the assumption that there is an objective reality, independent of the human being, that is coping with organisational performance. Thus, the manager requires an accurate representation of relevant aspects of reality through data and therefore the decision taker (manager) must have the capacity to identify problem situations and define alternative courses of action. Criteria must be selected so that the alternatives can be compared under a common rule which specifies the "best alternative" to be chosen.

The recognition that it is not always possible to follow this process has originated the term "unstructured decisions": the higher the managerial level the more unstructured the decision process becomes. Flexibility in the manipulation of data, ease in the construction of models, and group participation in the resolution process have been some of the answers to the dilemma.

Within this DSS framework, "supporting the manager" means to provide a wide variety of data, to be analysed and modelled in various ways, in a friendly environment which allows for the effective use of the technological tools offered (Fick and Sprague, 1980). All this should lead to an increase in the manager's capacity to take action.

Today this view is regarded by several authors as a mistaken oversimplification of what is involved in taking action. The history of the practice of design and implementation of computer systems has shown that the assumptions regarding the management process do not always sustain an effective design and implementation process. This situation offers an opportunity to review the design assumptions of DSS.

Criticism and dissatisfaction regarding the use of computer and communications technology in the managerial process has been reported throughout the years. This situation is consistent with a community engaged in a permanent learning process. The understanding of the decision process leads to the belief that it is possible to obtain an accurate representation of reality. Signs of this is not the case are the unfulfilled promises of Operations Research about the role of mathematical models in management, and those of Artificial Intelligence, indicating the limitations of representing the underlying "cultural knowledge" present in the practices and traditions of a community.

The assumption that managers take correct decisions, based on accurate information, has lead to the belief that managers knew what information they needed, that "good" information produces "good" decisions, and that the information needed was independent of the manager (Schlumberger, 1997). In practice, this has not been found to be the case. As a result, the role of the traditional system designer or analyst, and the difficulties and limitations it entails, have been re-examined, establishing that the assumptions of an objective observer of the managerial reality must be very well qualified and that his or her role should be redefined (De Zeeuw, 1993, Humphreys and Berkeley, 1995).

Furthermore, it has also been argued that the computer and communications systems (EIS, DSS, expert systems...) will be only as good as the management processes they support. The argument implies that, to a large degree, the individual competencies of managers, are secondary to the quality of the organisational conversations underpinning their decisions.

Certainly there has been some response to this dissatisfaction. The concern for proper support for the manager has led to an effort to include the concern for human capabilities into the design process. Attempts have been made to include cognitive styles, abstraction levels, processing capacities, and ergonomic considerations, in various ways, in an attempt to improve the use of technology in organisations. Nevertheless this effort has not been fully successful and has not yet permitted a breakthrough in the full use of technology in the management process.

We would put forward the proposition that what has been lacking is an appropriate understanding of the management process, particularly regarding the structural capacities of human beings, who have the capacity of language and emotion as the grounds for action. In the following, we will attempt to present the possibilities that stem from a reinterpretation of the management process focused on the human being responsible for "taking care" of the organisation.

2 THE MANAGER REVISITED

Our starting point is to begin to question our understanding of the human being and his capacity to act, which is included in the work of Humberto Maturana (1969, 1978, 1994, Maturana and Varela, 1984) on the biology of cognition. We will summarily show what we consider the most important conclusions regarding the manager and his capacity to cope with the wide variety of situations relevant to "taking care" of the organisation.

Maturana establishes that the human being, as a living system, is determined by the structure of his nervous system. The conclusions following this statement are many:; one of them is that living beings do not perceive an objective reality. What ever we perceive is determined by our nervous system. Given the plasticity of our nervous system, this means that what we observe in a given situation is filtered by our education and experience: a situation is not perceived in the same way by a lawyer and an engineer. The set of distinctions characterised by the specific training received will be revealed by what is perceived by either of them and that this has as a direct consequence in our understanding of information. In our interpretation of what Maturana is saying, this means that information can be reinterpreted as a trigger of a the nervous system.

What triggers a particular observer into action may not be noticed by another, so that this situation will generate different behaviour by different human beings, given the fact that they have different historical paths. This is in direct contradiction with the pretence that underlies the design of information systems: the representation of an objective reality. A second conclusion is that there are domains of action in which they have no distinctions and therefore they are not able to observe action. This becomes transparent as we reflect upon our learning process as once we have learned something fresh we can observe situations we did not observe.

In Maturana's view, language shows up in human interaction, shows up among living beings as a flow of consensual coordinations of consensual coordinations of behaviour. Words appear, not as names given to objects, but as the possibility for consensual coordination of behaviour. An apple is not necessarily a description of an object but indicates the possibility of eating or baking a pie.

A human being, constitutively blind, must cope with the complexities of living by coupling with other human beings through language constituting a conversational network. By coupling in language, the nervous system is triggered, changing the disposition to act. Transformations in the dispositions to act is what we characterize as an emotional state.

Here we state a design consideration: the manager, blind and ignorant, lives in a continuous criss-crossing of language that gives rise to complexity. He copes through a conversational and emotional network of support. Within this configuration, technology can be understood as the possibility of strengthening his capacity of observation and enhancing the triggering of emotion and action.

In the understanding of the designer, the rational decision maker must be replaced by a new type of manager, emotional and limited, who despite his apparent ignorance and blindness caused by historical traditions to which he belongs is capable of observing, learning and constituting worlds in language and taking care of them.

Taking care of organisations in the midst of changing conditions is the concern of managers. We are saying that any enhancement in the design considerations of technological support for managers must be structured upon the understanding of the manager as a human being. We stress the point that we have enough technological power, we have enough "raw computer mips", "gigabytes of storage", and related indexes and pointers, to build useful and effective devices. What is lacking is a more powerful understanding of the management process generally by all concerned (Humphreys, Berkeley and Jovchelovich, 1996).

2.1 Emotions and Action

In concerning ourselves with the design of management support tools, we expect to create organisational mechanisms that support the manager in his resolution process towards committing himself and others to action. We are attempting to enhance the manager's capacity to initiate action at ground level (Argyris and Schon, 1978).

The concern for action is the concern for peoples' emotions, for provoking a transformation in the disposition to act. It is part of our daily experience that changes in emotions result in changes in our disposition to act. Nevertheless, emotions is not a subject that is often related to management except as a background for action. Such is the sense that words like "organisational climate" or "motivation" convey. From the perspective of action we are not concerned with the background mood but with focusing on a problem situation. Words such as important, urgent, threatening, opportunity or irrelevant show different dispositions to act.

DSS can be conceived then as the capacity to trigger these different states. In the extreme it can be understood as producing calm or alert states. In this sense we can say that DSS must be conceived with the perspective of opening and closing emotions.

The above does not mean that rationality has no place in our understanding of action. Action is the outcome of the braiding of language and emotion. Conversations are moments in which emotions can be changed so that action is possible. The appropriate mix of emotions and conversations makes management possible Garcia and Alvarez, 1991). From this perspective we can say that DSS can be conceived as a conversation triggering machine.

The design of an appropriate network of conversations must be tuned to the manager. The concern for his or her own stability, and the stability of the system under his or her care , is the basis for establishing what kind of conversations and which participants should be involved in the resolution process regarding a category of problem situations. From this perspective, Decision Support Systems can be understood as a subset of a family of tools designed to trigger conversations and emotions for action in the domains of concern of the manager's stability.

2.2 The Manager in the Human Activity System (HAS) or the Organizational Observer

In the domain of organizational design, of which the concern for design and implementation of DSS should be understood as a subset, the grounding for any action is distinguishing and naming a human activity system (Checkland, 1981; Checkland and Scholes, 1990). That a system is a distinction made by an observer is a fundamental fact for organizational design and intervention. Therefore, it is to our benefit as designers of technological interventions in organizations to understand what is going on as a social process when someone says "I take care of this organisation."

What are we distinguishing when we distinguish an organization? When we make the operation of distinction we bring forth a class identity. We may say that the specific human activity system under our care is a school, a distribution network, or an army. By distinguishing it as such, we are saying that it belongs to the class of organizations in which certain relations are present among the people that participate in it. This characteristic relational network of conversations and emotions is the system's organization.

The structure of the system is the specific form in which the relations exist in each case (Ashby, 1977). We may have different structures that conform to the same organization, i.e., that belong to the same class identity. When making the distinction system, we distinguish those elements that are part of the system and those that are excluded from the system and constitute the environment.

It is important for effective design to notice that two or more different observers may distinguish different organizations (Humphreys and Berkeley, 1995). The manager, the lawyer, and the engineer may use the same name "the company" and imply very different situations. For a company raider, the human activity system may be a device to generate financial flow, to its manager it may be a group of people committed to produce satisfaction to clients and to the head of the union it may be a device for the generation of dignified working conditions.

But we are not submerged in the midst of unmanageable chaos: it is important to remember that people belong to communities that have a common history and tradition and that have been coupled together in their interactions to each other (Beer, 1979). As a result of this there are shared distinctions and blindness through joint experience. becomes clear when we compare the engineer's and psychologist's views of the world.

This is a sensitive issue for an organizational intervention. We can ask then, from the perspective of design of technological interventions in an organization,

- what type of observer is the manager;
- how computer and communication systems enhances the manager's capacity to observe the system and its environment;
- how it generates conditions for collaboration with other observers in taking care of the performance of the organization; and
- how it helps to reveal blindness that characterize the community and threatens the organisation's viability.

If there is a language of distinctions, interests, and values concerned with the viability of the organization that can be triggered by using technology, in conditions of mutual respect and learning, then we have improved the capacity for action and care.

3 THE NEED FOR AN ORGANIZATIONAL FRAMEWORK IN THE DESIGN OF COMPUTER TECHNOLOGY SYSTEMS

Our exposure to the complexity of the world is increasing. There is no place to hide from the economic, technical, political, and cultural influences (Batten, 1973). Our "neighbours", people that have a daily impact in our lives, may be hidden from our view not only by geographic distance but also by "systemic distance": they may participate in other industries, they may pertain to a political party, they may be arranging some economic agreement or inventing some technological device.

From the organizational perspective, this situation is lived as a loss of stability: the future can no longer be a repetition of the past. New problem situations arise for management, flexibility to adjust, learning capacity and the will to adapt appear as a "need" for maintaining the organisation's identity (Beer, 1985).

Managers need help as the task of managing under these conditions is taking its toll. Very long hours, strained backs, insomnia, stress, drug abuse, and broken families are reported by people in management positions. This pain, or its anticipation, is the starting point for a meaningful organizational intervention: we must be able to provide a response to a situation of unbalance between human capacities and the complexity of the world. This unbalance is the main concern for design of organizational structures of which technology is one of the pillars. Thus, it is necessary to develop a DSS framework including a new understanding of the manager and the managing process.

3.1 Observing Organisations

The concern for the creation of distinctions by which to observe organizations is related to the need for an enhanced capacity to design tools and mechanisms for managers to deal with the complex task of taking care of the organisation's viability.

The design and implementation of the capacity to modify the context in which people work in an organization is enhanced by a set of distinctions that are the tools for observation and reflection. This process will bring changes in the identity of the firm, in its vision of the future, and in its interpretation of performance and viability, generating new conversations for commitment and action.

Some of the basic distinctions to observe in organisations, are the following:

- **Identity**: the process of organizational self reflection allows for the rising of questions in which people can examine the meaning of their work as an enhancement of the organisation's viability. The understanding of work in the light of the whole allows for discussion about the balance between organizational policies and decision taking.

- **Distributed management**: as managers take care of multiple domains of action, networks of trust can be established to absorb the variety of contingent situations, the design of the networks involves the specific distribution of responsibilities to take care of complexity (Espejo and Garcia, 1984).

- **Complexity unfolding**: the understanding of viability allows for the proposition of a recursive structure of care that specifies domains of action that constitute the identity. This is the basic care structure.

- **Functional capacity unbalances**: the concern for the gap between what is being done and what is possible reveals functional capacity unbalances regarding structure, the conversational network and technological support.

- **Organizational Learning Inhibitors**, establishing conditions for organizational learning requires building up the organisation's self reference capacity which could be triggered by the adequate design of conversational support based on computers. The design should consider "cultural" as well as technological inhibitors.

- **A distinction as an observational device:** The design of DSS requires analysts who are capable of observing the human activity system from an organisational perspective, that is, starting from the concern for its viability (De Zeeuw, 1992; De Zeeuw and Schuurman, 1997).

3.2 Organizational Learning and Viability

Taking care of the organisation's viability under conditions of continuous change and increasing complexity requires the development of the organisation's learning capacity. It is not simple or easy to generate new behaviour. There is abundant evidence to quite the contrary, even in circumstances when viability has been at stake. Thus, in the present state of affairs, more that ever the organisation's viability is mediated by its learning capacity.

Our challenge is to increase the structure's plasticity, that is, to increase the possibility of new behaviour. We are not referring here to some abstract process: learning always implies a human involvement.

The organizational structure can be characterised from the perspective of its capacity to inhibit learning. The lack of conversations about what people do, the social impossibility for a beginner to ask for explanations, the understanding of the good professional as someone that does not commit mistakes, and excessive inbreeding are some of the organizational habits that we all notice.

The design of computer and communication support for management must include the concern for the learning process. This is a matter of organizational mechanisms capable of generating conditions for people to observe their own behaviour, as it relates to the system's viability and the emotional environment for changing it, accepting ignorance, blindness and mistakes.

3.3 Organisational Transformation

An organisational transformation is a managerial action to cope with the regulatory unbalances between his functional capacity and perceived complexity. To detect unbalances and to manage the required change process, the manager must characterize action and learning in the following domains:

- structural adjustment of the organization, which implies changes to the organisational identity, functional capacity, learning and adaptation mechanisms in order to absorb the complexity at different recursive levels within the contexts and domains to which an observer (the manager) is coupled.

- adjustment to the bodies, language, emotions, conversations that constitute the organisational network. This is the network of trust, collaboration, and solidarity. This domain shows up as the competence to listen, to speak, and to interpret.

These are the domains for action in which DSS must play a role.

3.4 The Metasystemic Perspective

The manager must not only observe the system under his care, he must also observe other Human Activity Systems in which it is embedded such as markets, government, industry, and technology. This is the metasystemic scenario.

To take care of the organisation, management must be aware and assesses the actions taken in the embedding systems (changes in the tax structure, new technologies, changes in the cost structure of the industry) or other systems that share its identity. and also generate interpretations about its future behaviour and its impact on viability (Garcia, 1989).

This capacity may be enhanced by technological support that combines the observation of domains related to the organisation's stability with the interpretation capacity of a network of experts. This network and the shifts it produces in the interpretation of what is relevant for the industry may also shift the stability criteria of managers.

New possibilities for action are made possible by the transformation of the interpretation that managers have about their environment. An opportunity for the redesign of the DSS framework also lies in the requirements for an effective navigation in the metasystemic spaces that are related to the taking care of organisational viability.

4 OUR PROPOSITIONS FOR DESIGNING AND USING DSS

To enhance the possibilities of the design of DSS it is necessary to shift the observer of computer and communication technology from its closure in the domain of signal and symbol manipulation to the domain of organisational transformation.

We propose that technology, in the context of organisational transformation, must be understood within the following context:

- As a functional capacity to regulate the balance between a human being and the Human Activity System under his care.
- To maintain the regulatory balance which implies the dynamic adjustment of the braiding of emotions and language that constitutes the Human Activity System.
- To design technology in the domain of organisational transformation is to create coupling conditions between the manager and the Human Activity Structure allowing for their mutual transformation

Mechanisms conceived from the perspective of an organisational transformation technology trigger conversations and emotions in the network of relations that constitute the organisation to take action in order to adjust the organisational structure, to modify the relational configuration and the use of technological support. Some of the contributions of devices of this sort could be:

- Enhancement of managerial capacity to observe the organisational activity and anticipate problem situations. In this framework the DSS should provide a capacity to measure activities that constitute the organisational identity according to the manager's concern for stability.

- Enhancement of the capacity to filter the variety that characterises organisational and environmental activity.

- Support to permanently assess the network of trust observing the state of mutual promises.

- Dynamic articulation of conversational networks of care according to problem situations.

- Triggering of conversations regarding the stability of the Human Activity System.

Amplification of the managerial capacity to reach out to different and distant networks that the manager relates to his own and organisational stability.

5 FINAL REMARKS

Managers need support to cope with the increasing rate of change of systemic and metasystemic conditions. Coping requires organisational transformations or adjustments. In order to enhance decision support systems, we think that research programs in the following areas may provide with a stronger language for design of DSS:

- The further development of distinctions and practices regarding the management of organisational transformation. The introduction of computer and communication technology changes the balances between people within the human activity system.

- The development of practices to enhance, trigger and regulate conversations associated to taking care of viability. Further work needs to be done regarding the conversations that constitute the observers of viability.

- The development of an educational capacity to show the impact of cognitive and cultural blindness regarding language, action and emotions would allow for the generation of new competencies in managers and analysts regarding the taking care of organisations and people.

- The inhibiting of learning in organisations. The role of technology in triggering learning situations and modifying structural inhibitions.

- The role of trust, and the generation of networks of trust, as enhancement of the manager's capacity to design organisational structures from the perspective of observing, learning and action.

- The conceptualisation of conversational filters and amplifiers to deal with complexity.

Research oriented towards these topics may help to deal with the dissatisfaction of different participants in the drama of organisational transformation. We are concerned with the dissatisfaction that we see in managers:

- There seems to be no adequate education for managers regarding design and management of organizational processes: managers must deal with organizational adjustments from their understanding of managing the business.

- There is an apparently low rate of success in organizational interventions that deal with what we may call the soft aspects of the organization such as learning, autonomy, identity, conversational networks and the emotional upheavals that are part of organizational adjustments.

We are concerned with the dissatisfaction that we see in consultants:

- Consultants have developed a strong understanding of specific, specialised and well defined interventions but this is no longer a strong base for business: today`s client's interest is not only technology or procedures but in a reinterpretation of their business that takes hold in their people.

- Normally consultants have no theory which allows them to be a strong partner of their client s, as they almost never work for the people who are actually in the jam of managing organizational viability and stability.

We are concerned with the dissatisfaction of professors and students:

- The present scientific approach to management appears to have failed: mathematical models operational research techniques have been recognised as able to deal with problem situations of very limited complexity and do not deal with human nature.

- Even though this has been recognised painfully by students who emerge into practical life, it is not fully recognised inside the ivory towers of institutional knowledge.

- Business schools that, theoretically, are preparing students to be managers have a technical, professional perspective that does not include an understanding of the human activity systems within which the professional activities take place.

- Organization is not understood as something that happens in the interpretation of people, and tends to be treated as an object which can be systematically analysed without reference to the different observers of activity (Habermas, 1992).

Our concern in writing this paper has been to make a contribution of use to the people concerned with effective organizational interventions and also to participate in the development of organizational theory, which we think is still in its early stages of development.

6 REFERENCES

Argyris, C. and Schon, D. (1978) Organizational Learning: A Theory of Action Perspective. Addison-Wesley.

Ashby, R. (1977) Introducción a la Cibernética". Nueva Visión, Buenos Aires.

Bateson, G. (1973) Steps to an Ecology of Mind. Paladin, St. Albans.

Beer, S. (1979) The Heart of Enterprise. John Wiley & Sons, New York..

Beer, S. (1985) Diagnosing the System for Organizations. John Wiley & Sons. Chichester.

Checkland, P. (1981) Systems Thinking, Systems Practice". Chichester, Wiley.

Checkland, Peter and Scholes, J. (1990) Soft Systems Methodology in Action Wiley, Chichester:

Davenport, T. (1992) Process Innovation. Reeingineering Work Through Information Technology. Harvard Business School Press, Cambridge, Mass.

Espejo, R. and García, O. (1984) A Tool for Distributed Planning. Baden Baden, Germany

Espejo, R. (1993) Strategy, Structure and Information Management. Aston Business School, Manchester, U.K.

Fick, G. & Sprague, R. (1980) Decision Support Systems: Issues and Challenges". Pergamon Press, Oxford.

García, O. (1989) Sobre el Diseño de Reingeniería Humana para la Acción". Documento de Trabajo del Proyecto de Investigación "CYBERCOM II: Rendimiento y Conversaciones en un Contexto de Efectividad Organizacional. Santiago, Chile

García, O. and Alvarez, J. (1991) Las Ontologías Cibernética y Conversacional: Un Examen Crítico. Instituto Andino de Sistemas, Lima, Perú.

Habermas, J. (1992) The Philosophical Discourse of Modernity". Cambridge, Polity Press.

Humphreys, P. and Berkeley, D, (1995) Organisational process modelling sensitive to local social and cultural conditions, *in Work and organisational psychology: European contributions of the nineties* (eds J. M. Piero, F. Prieto, J. L. Melia and O. Luque). Erlbaum/Taylor and Francis, Hove, U.K.

Humphreys, P.C., Berkeley, D. and Jovchelovitch, S. (1996) Organisational psychology and psychologists in organisations: Focus on organisational transformation. *Interamerican journal of psychology*, **30,** 27-42.

Keen, P. (1991) Shaping the Future: Business Design Through Information Technology". Harvard Business School Press, Cambridge, Mass.

Maturana, H. (1969) Cognition a Multiple View. Spartan Books, New York.

Maturana, H. (1978) Psychology and Biology on Language and Thought. Academic Press, New York.

Maturana, H. (1993) Desde la Biología a la Psicología. Editorial Synthesis, Santiago, Chile.

Maturana, H. (1994) Autopoiesis: la Organización de lo Vivo. Santiago, Chile.

Maturana, H. and Varela, F. (1984) El Arbol del Conocimiento. Editorial Universitaria, Santiago, Chile

Schlumberger, M. (1997) When wrong is right. *This volume*

Varela, F., Thompson, E. and Rosch, E. (1992) The Embodied Mind: Cognitive Science and Human Experience. Ed. Gedisa, Santiago, Chile

De Zeeuw, G. (1992) Competence and the Observational Language. Centre for Innovation and Cooperative Technology, University of Amsterdam, Netherlands .

De Zeeuw, G. 1993) Soft Knowledge Accumulation and the Rise of Competence". Systems Practice, **5**, 192-215.

De Zeeuw, G. and Schuurman, J. G. (1997) Support as intervention in decision processes. *This volume.*

7 BIOGRAPHIES

Osvaldo Garcia de la Cerda is a professor at the Industrial Engineering Department of the University of Santiago de Chile. His current research is on human re-engineering for action and on metasystemic design. He is the managing director of CIGAR Ltda., a management consultancy in the field of organization transformation.

Renato Orellana Muerman is civil engineer, graduate of the University of Chile. He has more than 20 years of experience in the field of organizational transformation and is a senior consultant with CIGAR Ltda.

3

Measures of Ethicality:- the Calibration of Corporate Moral Transformations

A. McCosh
The University of Edinburgh
Department of Business Studies, 50 George Square
Edinburgh EH8 9JY, Scotland UK
Tel: 0131 650 3801, Fax: 0131 668 3053
e-mail:A.mccosh@ed.ac.uk

Abstract

The paper notes the problems companies can have with ethical episodes, and suggests they sometimes need to transform their operations to cope with a new level of public perception of ethical behaviour. The paper makes a very preliminary attempt to derive a DSS which will predict the path of an ethical episode, for the guidance of corporate transforming agents.

Keywords

Ethics, Decision Support Systems, Measurement

1 INTRODUCTION

The literature on Decision Support Systems has been evolving in several directions since the first contributions in the 1960's. There has been a growth in the sophistication of the technical solutions, and a growth in the expectations of managerial users as to what the systems will be able to achieve. There has also been a move away from consideration of the systems which will help a single manager or employee to ones which will deal with the organisation as a totality. The work of IFIP Working Group 8.3 has been increasingly concerned with computer aided organisations, rather than computer aided managers. The 1988 Working Conference (Lee,McCosh, Migliarese,1988) was entitled "Organisational Decision Support Systems". The 1990 conference (Sol, Vecsenyi 1990) dealt with changes in the environment, and how these affected the DSS concept and its implementation.

The present paper addresses a particular kind of change in the environment. In this situation, the company or other organisation faces a major change in the way it is perceived by its public, in a situation where the change is in the company's stance on an ethical question. In this situation, the perception may change even if the company policy on the topic is unaltered, because the public becomes more conscious than before of the issue. The paper is designed to make a very tentative beginning to the formidable task of measuring the ethicality of a company policy.

2 PERIODS OF PROFOUND CHANGE

The task of transforming an organisation so that it can cope with a profound change in its environment is major, and there is a literature of change management as a separate subject within management (Mumford 1978, Cummings & Huse 1985). Some of these changes arise from a transformation in the market (e.g. the impact of xerography on carbon paper) or a transformation of the accessibility of the market (e.g. the granting of banking licences to UK building societies in 1986). They may arise through a technical product development, as in the invention of the long-lasting light bulb, and the steady improvement in the life expectancy of car tyres. They may arise from a technical process development, as in the case of computerised banking by telephone and direct selling of insurance by phone and computer link.

In each instance, the companies involved have been forced to effect a major change in their working practices. Generally, they have had to go out and buy the new technology and change their working practices to attempt to match the economic challenges posed by the innovating firms. Some firms have left the rectification very late, and are forced to make very sudden and drastic changes. Some leave the changes too late, and are either taken over (usually with large scale job losses) or closed down completely.

There is another kind of profound change, which can have just as severe an impact on a company or industry. These arise from a change in the public's opinion about a product or service or way of working. Cigarette makers have continued to grow on a global scale, but have had to move production and marketing efforts from the richer countries toward the poorer ones as demand has been squeezed out of the former by pressure groups. Public attitudes to pollution have also evolved, from a grim toleration at the time of cleaning up the mess in the heavily populated English Channel from Torrey Canyon, to a reaction which essentially demanded revenge when the Esso Valduz did much the same damage to a thinly populated Alaska.

In these and similar situations the industry involved, not just the single corporation, confronts a profound change in its public image, and would do well to have regard to this in its planning, as far in advance as can be arranged.

In the financial sector in the UK, the pension fund industry, and the pension fund management industry, are both subject to a significant public reappraisal at present. A report on what to do next has been produced by a law professor (Prof.

Goode). The main impetus for these change proposals was the eccentric investment behaviour of Maxwell Communications Company plc. The previous public image of pension funds had been safe, solid, boring, secure, and reliable. Indeed, some pension fund managers took pride in the fact that they hardly had any public image at all. Now there is a considerable level of public interest and concern that the fund managers and trustees behave in an accountable and observable way. This will probably mean the pension funds will have to produce accounts of their investment performance to the beneficiaries, with considerable cost implications. The fees payable to the fund managers and the pension fund consultants will also receive more attention than before, and this may lead to a perception change over time.

In the present paper the objective is to consider how public perceptions of products or services evolve, and the ways in which companies can react to, or anticipate, these evolving perceptions. The general area of study will be the judgements made about the ethical level of financial transactions. At this stage, the goal is to draw up a general model of the evolution of ethical perception. A future paper will be concerned with the tasks of calibration and quantification.

3 ETHICAL STANDARDS FOR CORPORATE BEHAVIOUR

It is clear that any attempt to create a model of ethical behaviour, which is to have the eventual attribute of being quantifiable, must include a definition or a series of definitions of what 'ethical' means in this context.

The obvious first place to look would be in the journals which take business ethics as their main theme. This has proved rather disappointingly unproductive. In a large number of cases the articles in these journals implicitly assumed that ethical was a word which meant 'conforming to the law of the United States'. Unethical, therefore, was defined either explicitly or implicitly as 'contrary to the law of the United States'. Vogel, for instance, having started from this implicit definition, manages to prove that US business had made more progress in ethics than business in other lands. This result is not surprising. If I were to define 'ethical' as being dressed in tartan, I am sure I could prove that the most ethical people were Scotsmen.

More generally, it is regrettable (from the viewpoint of the "consumer" of ethical guidance) that the work reported recently by philosophical and ethical writers seems to have concentrated on second order problems and third order problems, rather than first order problems. They have concerned themselves with the analysis of what a commentator meant, or on what a commentator about a commentator meant, rather than on whether a particular course of action was right or wrong. There is nothing wrong with making these second order analyses, of course, but they are of little help to people who have to decide on first order issues.

A search for an alternative anchor for ethical measurement led me at length to the point from which I ought to have started:- the ancient religious and quasi-religious philosophies. It is a fascinating and immense field, the study of which nobody can ever complete. Within the very narrow confines of my concern, however, my investigations seem to reveal an encouraging unanimity of view among the ancient writers. They give very little guidance on what actions people should engage in. What they all seem to consider important is that the reader should pay close attention to the impact of their actions on other people. Do not behave towards others in a fashion you would hate. Do unto others as you would have them do to you. There is very little discussion, that I have so far been able to locate, which seems to start from the view that there is a generally applicable basic ethical principle or set of principles. The idea that there is a "Form of the Good" which has some objective existence, even if no persons are around to observe it, does not seem to have many supporters in the older religious or quasi-religious works.

In the present paper, the goal is to produce a definition of ethical behaviour which has the potential to be quantified into an index of 'ethicality'. If this could be achieved, then one would be able to appraise two actions or courses of action which were being considered, and state, in advance of acting, that one of these actions was more ethical than the other. One would then be faced with the remaining decision, on whether one should choose the more ethical or the less ethical course of action. It will be presumed in the present paper that it is possible to behave too ethically, as well as it being possible to behave too unethically.

4 SOME COMMON GUIDANCE FROM THE RELIGIOUS SOURCES

At the time of writing, some progress has been made in reading the original source books of the various religions and quasi-religions, in translated form. The Bible, the Koran, the Analects of Confucius (as extended by Mencius and Chu Hsi), some of the Upanishads, and part of the Code of Maimonides have been consulted, as part of the search for corporate guidance along the lines of the previous paragraph. The Torah, some of the remaining Buddhist writings, and other sources remain to be consulted, and this may change the answer quite considerably. At the present stage, there is a degree of similarity among the sources, on this point, which was surprising. There were substantial differences also, of course. A large portion of each of the formally religious documents was concerned with market share matters, and with the issuance of assorted threats to those who failed to adhere to the "one true way". But on the specific point of issuing instructions concerning how people ought to behave toward one another, they said very nearly the same things, and sometimes in very similar wording. Generally, there were two parts to the instruction.

The first part was an instruction to behave in a charitable fashion towards one's fellow man. In the Koran, in Surah 110 (The Land) the companions of the right hand (= the ethical) are characterised by "the freeing of a slave, or giving food upon a day of hunger to an orphan near of kin or a needy man in misery" and by working with co-believers to "counsel each other in steadfastness and in mercy". In his interpretation and elucidation of the Jewish law, Maimonides sets out detailed rules for charitable giving, and how a man might be best able to work out whether he had done his share of the task of looking after the poor of the community and the poor who happened to be visiting the community at the time. These rules are written with exquisite clarity: one can only wish that our current tax codes (which are no more precise in what they say) had been drawn up by Maimonides. The Bible has several similar exhortations toward charitable behaviour, and the oldest source of all those considered so far, the Analects of Confucius, give pride of place to the attribute of "jen" or human-heartedness in describing the behaviour expected of a sage, the highest human rank of all.

The second part of the instruction was usually in the form of an explanation or clarification of just what the first part involved. A person who was predisposed to deal charitably with his fellow man might find it a bit difficult to tell whether he had actually done so to a sufficient degree. Most of the sources offer guidance on this topic. Some of them are rather hard to live up to. In the New Testament, we are instructed to be "perfect, even as your father in heaven is perfect", and when you fail to achieve this, to throw yourself on God's mercy and believe he will deal with the matter. In Surah 113, the reader is reminded that God has provided him with sufficient shelter, guidance, and material wealth, and instructs the reader to provide the same to others on a similar basis. Mencius, one of the two most prominent successors to Confucius, amplified the latter's concepts of Chung and Shu to enable people to understand the concepts better. We shall see below that shu is a viable business instruction. Chung, however, translated as "conscientiousness toward others", seems to mean that one should do to others as you would like them to behave towards you. This is often called the "golden rule" and appears in the Bible (Matthew 7:12) and several other authorities as well as in the Mencius. As will be established below, this is not a viable ethical instruction for issuance to a member of a group who is responsible for that group's relationships with other groups.

Some of the other instructions which calibrate one's charitableness are rather easier to cope with. In the Surah "Shrouded", number 74, it is made clear that the possession of wealth is not a bad thing; instead the continued piling up of more and more of it is condemned. Mencius' doctrine of shu is clearly dependent on earlier ideas of Confucius. In the Analects (12,2) Confucius identifies the concept of "shu" which is translated as altruism, but which is stated as the classical instruction of the silver rule. "Do not do things to other people that you would hate them to do to you". Similar words are used by Maimonides (book 13) in his discussion of judgements and of justice between debtor and creditor.

The very widespread support for the 'silver rule' and the narrower but still very extensive support for the 'golden rule' are both helpful. We shall see below that these two concepts are helpfully quantifiable. In the discussion to follow, we will adopt the apparently standard definitions, namely that the 'golden rule' is the injunction to behave towards other people as you would wish them to behave towards you, while the 'silver rule' is the injunction to refrain from taking an action toward another person if you would not wish them to take that same action towards you.

5 CHOOSING AMONG THE GUIDANCE RULES AVAILABLE

It has now been established that there is a substantial support from traditional sources of ethical guidance for the use of the silver and golden rules in selecting the behaviour one should adopt in dealing with others. It is now necessary to consider whether we can choose one of these rules in preference to the other one, in the context of a traditional business, and especially inter-corporate, negotiation process. The two rules were specified in the Analects of Confucius (12,2) as Chung and Shu. Confucius was anxious to promote humanness or human-heartedness, and therefore advocated 'loving others' as a general rule. To put this into effect, he advocated both 'shu' which means 'do not do things to others that you would not like to have done to you' and 'chung' which means 'the way to behave human-heartedly is to sustain and develop oneself by sustaining and developing other people'. Chung is therefore similar to the biblical golden rule, 'do unto others as you would have them do unto you', but is not quite so open-ended. The benefit to the other party is the same in both cases, but in the case of chung there is a prospect of benefit accruing (perhaps very indirectly) to the actor as well.

In negotiations between corporations, the concepts of chung and shu are widely adopted by sensible managers. You do not do things to the other party that you would dislike to have happen to you if you value the relationship at all. Deliberately to violate the rule of 'shu' is colloquially known as a rip-off in modern business situations:- such transactions are clearly unethical and will result in the termination of the relationship at the first chance the other party gets. An accidental violation of the rule of shu may be just as painful for the second party, and may result in just as large a lawsuit, but it is not unethical unless the first party promoted the transaction in a reckless and wanton manner.

When we come to consider the rule of chung the situation becomes less clear. Many senior executives engaging in negotiations with their counterparts in other firms would agree that is wise, profitable, productive, creative, and sensible to make sure that the other party to a deal is likely to come out of it with an enhanced position. In fact, it may be hard to arrive at an agreement if the second party does not perceive this result to be probable. However, most managers would feel it inappropriate to level a charge of ethical impropriety at the door of a fellow manager who takes no account of the counterparty's welfare. Such a manager would claim that this was the counterparty's own responsibility, and not his, unless the counterparty was disabled, blind, or otherwise disadvantaged.

Managers would resist even more vehemently any suggestion that they should 'do unto others as they would have others to unto them'. This Christian imperative is simply not a viable basis for conducting a business negotiation. Positively to defend and promote the interests of the counterparty constitutes, or is very likely to constitute, a treasonable failure to behave with 'uberrima fides' towards one's own company. This is a violation of every company director's 'oath of office'.

Perhaps this difficulty explains why there are so few philosophers running foundries or cement factories. Perhaps it explains why at least some of the writings of ethics are regarded as quite unhelpful and/or unrealistic by many business managers, even ones who are very positively inclined towards ethical behaviour. The golden rule conflicts directly with a company director's obligations of office.

It would seem, however, from the above discussion, that the silver rule, the rule of 'shu', does not so conflict. In devising a system for coping with organisational transformations, this paper will be based on the assumption that the boundary of business ethics is the rule of 'shu', or the silver rule.

It is important to note that both silver and gold rules of ethical behaviour are stated in terms which refer back to the original actor. Do not do things you would not like. Do things that you would like. This makes the creation of decision aide for ethical transformation considerably easier. The idea of founding an ethical decision on the collected views of a community, as that may evolve through time, clearly entails taking the risk that the whole community is wrong-headed. We currently believe that the cannibal communities were behaving unethically, though they may well have been unanimous about the practice. At the same time, the adoption of the silver and gold rules gives us a hook to hang the measurement process on, where none existed before.

If we are allowed to use the silver rule, we can then obtain the ethical opinion of the community by means of an opinion survey. Questions in such surveys must be devised by competent people who will avoid bias in the answers arising from the phrasing of the questions. In principle, it is an achievable task to carry out an investigation which will give collective measure of ethical opinion, at least with respect to those financial transactions in which the public has a reasonable level of involvement and at least a slight level of understanding. It would also be possible, of course, to carry out similar and perhaps more detailed surveys of more specialised groups. I do not for a moment question the difficulty of doing this survey as a practical matter. While obtaining opinions about ethical questions in finance is probably easier than obtaining valid ethical survey opinions in other areas, it still calls for very careful questionnaire design methods. In general, this entails asking questions in their full form. The respondent must be offered balanced questions. A high cost offering with a high and defined service element may be offered in contrast to a low cost offering with a low and defined service element.

If the attempt is to be made to study the cost or price of the financial service only, it will be essential to arrange for a series of values to be tested. It can safely be assumed that the reader will classify the highest cost item as unethical, not necessarily because he thinks it is unethical, but on the ground that he does not wish to look stupid. The interesting responses will be his choices among the various intermediate values. It will be proposed that the opinion surveys used to calibrate the evolution of the ethicality of a particular episode should be a series of small surveys at tightly packed intervals of time, as the episode evolves. This survey process, which may study the episode at monthly intervals or perhaps even faster, will enable the DSS for ethicality to be calibrated more quickly and to become more effective as a predictive device.

It has now been established that the silver rule is a more helpful guide than the golden rule in terms of ethical concerns for inter-corporate dealings. It has also been established that both rules can be calibrated by means of surveys, albeit with some practical difficulty. In the next section we will consider the mathematical formulation which will enable the evolution of this quantification to be studied formally. After that we will put the two together and consider the managerial consequences.

6 A BASIS FOR A MODEL

At this point it may be appropriate to move to a discussion of the mathematical approach which is proposed as a basis for describing the nature of an ethical question in quantitative terms. The Gompertz curve is proposed as a means of describing the level of 'ethicality' of a given business quantity or amount of money. The Gompertz has the property of possessing two asymptotes at points (-infinity, $y1$) and (+infinity, y_2). The general form of the equation is:-

$$y = c.\,a^{(b^x)} \qquad o< a< 1 \qquad (1)$$

and the abruptness of the move from $y1$ to y_2 is controlled by the value of b. When b = 1 the curve is a horizontal line. As b moves away from one, the curve tilts:- upwards for values of b below one, downwards (as x increases) for values of b above one. In addition, the further b is from unity, the more it takes on the 'S' shape which characterises the Gompertz family of equations. Figure 1 shows a relatively sharply defined Gompertz graph, with a b value of 1.1, while chart two has the less emphatic shape which arises when b = 1.01

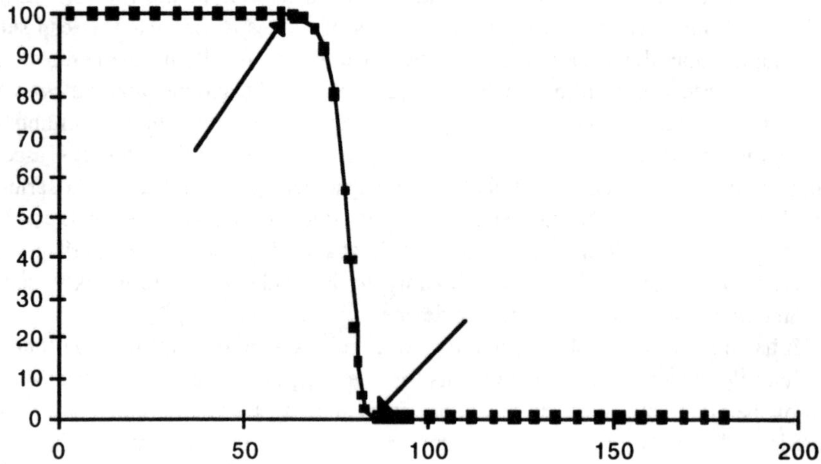

Figure 1 Opinion pattern late in an ethical episode. All those surveyed consider values up to about 65 to be ethical, while none consider values much over 80 to be.

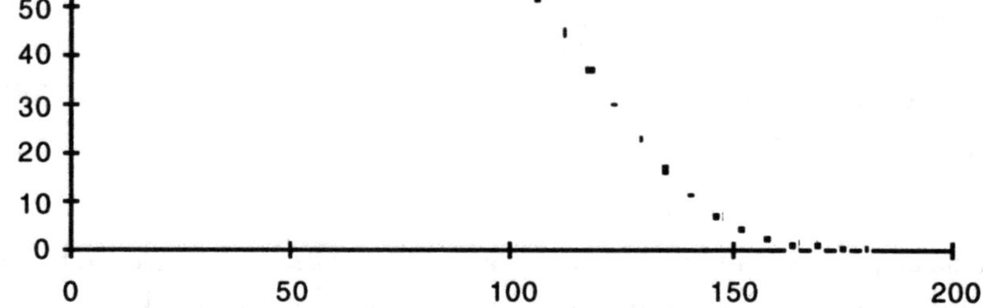

Figure 2 The acceptance pattern at an early stage in an ethical episode. More than 90% consider values of 40 ethical, while 10% consider values of 140 to be. This is a much wider range of opinion than is hypothesised to exist later in the episode, when opinion has "jelled".

6.1 The Modelling of A Business Ethics Problem

The Gompertz curve has been chosen to model an ethical question because it seems possible to describe the important aspects of an ethical problem, and especially its evolution over time, in terms of the Gompertz parameters. At the beginning of an ethical episode, it is hypothesised that the opinions of the populace on the ethical question are very diverse. There is a very wide range of opinions about whether the financial value of a transaction is or is not ethical, and little consensus. The populace differ widely on the level at which a price of an essential service becomes 'unethical' or an investment in protective equipment becomes 'too little'. This corresponds to the situation in chart 2, where b is close to unity and the curve slopes rather gently. The vertical dimension, y, is a measure of the proportion of the populace who consider the financial amount is ethical, while the horizontal axis, x, gives the values of the financial element which is under discussion.

Over time, as the ethical episode evolves, the opinion of the relevant populace on the topic changes. The populace become more aware of the existence of the question. Through wider coverage of the topic, in the media in some cases, there is a growing consensus about the range of values that seem ethically sound. The number who regard extremely low values of the financial variable as unethical will fall, while the number who regard extremely high values of the financial variable as unethical will rise. At some point, there evolves a rather narrow range of values of the financial variable within which the ethical boundary lies. This corresponds to chart 1, in which there is a small range of values of the financial variable which corresponds to a very large change in the proportion who regard the transaction as ethical. In chart one, approximately 90% are depicted as accepting a value of 65 for the financial item being measured to be ethical, while 10% are depicted as accepting a price of 80 as ethical. This narrow range (£15) of prices contrasts with the range of chart 2, where the same range of views (from 90% to 10% saying it was ethical) was depicted by a price gap from 40 to 140, a vastly greater range. It is hypothesised that the survey results will move from resembling chart two at the early stages, towards resembling chart one in the later stages of an ethical episode.

It is an empirical question as to how long it takes for the ethics of a particular issue to move from resembling chart two to resembling chart one. For the present, it is necessary to make an assumption. This might be that the ethicality changes with time, or that it changes with publicity, or that it changes abruptly a short time after a major but unpredictable incident. For the present paper it will be assumed that

$$\frac{db}{dt} = -k\,p \qquad (2)$$

where p is a measure of press coverage of the ethical topic, k is a scaling constant, and b is the Gompertz curve parameter. Preliminary simulation tests with artificial data suggest that the variable p has a relatively moderate impact on policy conclusions from the model. It affects the timing of the change from a "chart two" situation toward a "chart one" situation, which is important in determining how quickly the firm must respond.

From the viewpoint of a company, the very much more important questions relate to the point on the scale at which the major opinion change takes place. Consider the two arrows shown on each of the two charts. A company, represented by the two upward sloping arrows, which had been charging fifty, would find that its approval rating was increased as the episode progressed from chart two to chart one. The approval level moves up from about 88% to near unanimity in favour of their action. A company, represented by the two downward sloping arrows, would be severely hurt by the episode. Its price of a hundred was approved by slightly more than half of the population when chart two was in place, while nobody at all approves of the company's stance by the time the episode reaches the chart one state.

6.2 Horizontal Displacement

The standard Gompertz curve will always pass through the value (o, ac) using the terminology of equation one. This is not a realistic limitation of the model, but it can be rapidly rectified, at the cost of making the equation more complicated. First the range of the financial variable on the horizontal axis can be hypothesised, and mapped on a scale with the conventional range of x for a Gompertz curve. Almost always, $-100<X<300$ will be sufficient to allow the Gompertz to take on its characteristic S-shape. If the financial variable being studied, X, is believed to have a conceivable range from 0 to 40, the transformation

$$x = 10X - 100$$

can be applied. The transformation is a linear one, and requires two parameters. As a first approximation the scale parameter can be set at

$$\frac{400}{\text{Range of the financial variable}}$$

The other parameter will always be 100.

7 A DECISION AID ON ETHICALLY BASED CORPORATE TRANSFORMATIONS

Before any decision aid on this topic can become useful to the corporate sector, it must be shown that the aid is reasonably stable over time, and also that a model based on earlier ethical episodes can give guidance about future episodes. To establish this it will be necessary to follow a series of ethical episodes through on a "live" basis, so that the evolution of the opinion of the relevant public can be traced. The experiment now being reported is necessarily artificial, as the incident in question is now mature.

Insurance policies have been used for many years as savings vehicles. The amount of the commission payable to the salesman who persuades the insured to take out the contract is a very substantial portion of the first year's premium, sometimes (when other expenses are counted in) exceeding 150%. This is not too serious a matter for those who hold the policy until it matures. It can have a serious effect on those who have to cash the policy in early in its life, because they will get back much less than they put in. The newspapers decided to explore this topic, and a series of articles appeared, in several papers, most of them being highly critical of the insurers. Shortly, a series of response articles were published, basically on the theme that the insured should not have bought the policy if they had thought they were likely to need the money. A number of politicians published pronouncements which asked for the regulation of the industry, while others used the same evidence to ask for its deregulation.

For the present purpose, the amount of quantification in the newspapers articles was disappointingly slight. The first article in the series, which mentioned the 150% figure, was regularly quoted in the articles which followed. A detailed piece written three months later by an insurer, giving examples of much smaller numbers, was almost entirely ignored by other papers. Perhaps they could not understand the technical language, or perhaps the other editors did not want to admit that the insurers were not entirely in the wrong.

The procedure adopted was to examine each of the newspaper articles on this topic, and classify it as being at one of five points on a Likert scale. The scale points were labelled as being strongly pro-insurers, mildly pro-insurers, neutral, mildly anti-insurers, and strongly anti-insurers. The scores were weighted by the importance of the paper: 1 for a local paper, 5 for a regional, and 20 for a national. The resulting subjective scores were plotted over time, and the opinion showed a marked evolving trend. An initial heavy weighting towards the anti-insurer polarity was followed by a period of approximate equality across the option range. Then a second period of anti reporting, and a second equality period. This repeated twice more, and then the movements became unclear, partly because there was relatively little reporting after that. The whole episode took just over three years, ending in 1989. Clearly, it was not possible to measure the reaction of the public to these news article by means of surveys, as the incidents were already past.

It was, of course, a difficulty that the reporting was non-quantitative. To deal with this point, a group of 87 students (average age 27) was invited to assist. They were presented with a one page note which summarised the first twenty weeks of the press coverage, and asked to mark the ethically and commercially sound commission level on a scale, expressed as a percentage of the first year premium. They were next handed a second one page note, with the second twenty weeks of press coverage summarised, and asked to vote again. A third and last note gave them the chance to vote on the last twenty weeks of the ethical episode. While all the students responded to the first request, and seventy to the second, the third was answered by only forty students. No attempt was made to take a vote before the papers were handed out, because many of the students had already read about the topic.

The objective of this small experiment was to establish whether a full experiment should be carried out. Studies which depend on responses from students cannot be relied on, even if they are assured that it is not being graded. Students tend to be rather more idealistic than the population, and also tend to be rather dogmatic when they make judgements. As far as it went, the experiment gave some encouragement. The answers given by the students fitted the hypotheses to the following degree.

- The Gompertz fitted to the first response had a "b" value of 1.02, while that fitted to the second had a "b" value of 1.06. This transition is approximately equivalent to moving from chart two to chart one.
- The third, small sample did not seem to differ in any way from the views expressed in the second sample. The Gompertz seemed almost identical with the curve fitted to the second vote. It is possible that the students found no new information in the third information sheet, and therefore voted as before. It is important to note that the three votes all took place in the course of a single day. It is also possible, of course, that the students were simply bored with the project by this time.
- The mean value the students chose as being the boundary between ethical and unethical commission levels was the same at all three votes, being 80% of the first annual premium paid by the insured. The dispersion was much greater in the case of the first vote than for the other two. This unanimity of average score is potentially quite important, if it occurs often during later experimentation. It is obviously important to conduct a later experiment using a varying sample of interviewees.

8 THE PROBLEM OF QUANTIFICATION

The task of quantification has proved to be the hardest element of the experiments tried so far. The standardised Gompertz, if it proves possible to create one, will allow a company to predict the course of an ethical episode, and to identify the most appropriate action to take at each stage in the predictable pattern of the ethicality index. At the early stages, while the level of public agreement is low, the standardised model may enable a given firm to position itself on that part of the curve which will enjoy a positive boost as the ethical episode unfolds. It may also be possible to use the model to estimate the future consensus ethical value of the financial variable. This would avoid the problem of over-reacting to the furore, and the consequent difficulties of moving the price up again later. There may eventually be a science of ethicometry, though there is a very large amount of work to be done before we can define it.

It is clearly important, if the Gompertz is to be of any value as a predictive indicator of evolving future ethical pressure, to devise a procedure for calibrating it. When an ethical episode is at its early stages, it is quite difficult to recognise, and certainly to quantify. In the case of the commission on insurance investments, the issue has been known, to a large number of people, since the mid 1970s. It could hardly be described as an ethical episode until 1986, however, when public discussion of The Financial Services Act included extensive reviews of what the journalists sought to pretend were misdeeds of the financial services industry, after the two or three genuinely criminal cases had lost their news worthiness by repetition. The newshounds soon lost interest in the subject, but an ethical episode seems to have started. At that stage (1986) there was a noticeable increase in the amount of effort sophisticated consumers put into 'shopping around' for investment products, including insurance based ones, as the unsophisticated consumers piled into all kinds of conventional investment products and pushed their prices up. At the same time, the publicity on high commissions seems to have been noticed by potential competitors. A substantial number of newcomers entered the insurance industry, notably those using highest technology delivery systems to avoid brokerage charges. It is clear that an ethical episode has taken place, but it was not easy to recognise it at the start.

A series of other ethical episodes have been studied, and it has proved possible to apply a Gompertz to them on the basis of intuitive reasoning founded upon the documentation of the events as they took place. Validating these has, however, proved difficult, as will be discussed later. The procedure was to apply a very gently sloping Gompertz, similar to Chart 2, to the situation as at the date of start. This curve is represented by b = 0.99 (where low values are likely to be deemed unethical), or 1.01 (where high values are likely to be deemed unethical), and the other parameters were chosen to simulate the view that one third of the population consider it to be ethically unsatisfactory at the starting date. This assumption was totally arbitrary. The actual starting date is chosen to be the first occasion on which the computerised news service to which we have access starts to list articles on the ethical episode topic separately. The ending date of the investigation was taken at the date on which the additions to that service fell below one entry per week. It was obviously not possible to carry out opinion surveys in this preliminary trial. In addition, it has not been possible to establish what action the companies in the case episodes took in response to the public perception change.

The attempt to fit Gompertz curves judgementally to three ethical episodes were reasonably successful at first. These episodes dealt with the life assurance commission episode, the marketing of developing market unit trusts, and the commutation of pension payments to those who left a company before the normal retirement date. The parameters of the Gompertz curves in the three cases, as handled judgmentally, were as follows, using the terminology of the equations listed above.

		Project One	Project Two	Project Three
Parameter	a	0.9	0.9	0.9
	b (initial)	1.1	1.05	1.06
	c	to scale	to scale	to scale
	k	0.004	0.005	0.004

Severe difficulties were experienced when attempts were made to carry the three experiments forward to the next stage. The quantification of these initial Gompertz designs were intuitively pleasing, but could not be validated. There simply were not enough numbers in any of the reports to make it likely that two people would obtain the same answers for an episode that was already ended. It is a conclusion of this present study that the only way forward will be to build a series of investigatory surveys of ethical episodes as they take place. By this means, we will gradually become able to develop a valid library of cases and the Gompertz models that fit them, and to study the extent to which these models are stable across episodes, and stable over time. By similar means, we will be able to gradually work out what causes the shape of the curve to change. It may be simply the passage of time, it may be the amount of publicity, it may be something quite different.

9 THE DSS PROPOSED, AND ITS PROPOSED EMPLOYMENT

As will have become very clear by this time, the project is at an embryonic stage. The objective of the research is to depict an evolving ethical episode. A standardised Gompertz curve is being applied to the level of public coverage of the subject of the episode. From this, the level of ethicality of various prices of financial transactions is estimated, and the ways in which the ethicality of each price in the feasible range will change over time is also computed. It is clear that no company can obtain benefit from the research in its present state. It will be necessary to carry out a very large number of tests on a series of ethical episodes in order to calibrate the model properly. Studies have been performed by Reidenbach, Robin, and others concerning how to measure the level of ethicality at which a firm is operating. This is valuable, but it does not take account of the evolution of ethicality through time, which is an essential feature of ethics if the silver rule is to be employed as the standard.

It is clearly worthwhile to consider how to help companies to establish whether they are in good standing with respect to an ethical episode, or whether they are in difficulties. If the firm is in the range which seems likely to be subject to ethical criticism, the model in its more evolved form should permit the company to work out how long they have to fix the problem before the level of public criticism becomes too great to sustain.

10 REFERENCES

Al-Shamma, S.H. (1959) The Ethical System Underlying the Quran. Hopfer-Verlag Tubingen, Germany.

Arberry, A.J. (1983) Koran, translation by Arthur J. Arberry, Oxford World Classics.

Cummings, T.G. and Huse, E.F. (1985) *Organizational Development and Change*. West Publishing Company, St Paul, Minn USA, 4th edition.

Dawson, R.(1982) *Confucius*. Oxford University Press.

Fung, Yu Lan (1964) *A Short History of Chinese Philosophy*. Macmillan, New York.

Hopkins, E.W. (1924) *The Ethics of India*. Yale University Press, New Haven.

Lee, R.M. McCosh, A.M. and Migliarese, P. (1988) *Organisational Decision Support Systems*. Elsevier Publishing, North Holland.

Mackie, J.L. (1977) *Ethics:- Inventing Right and Wrong*. Penguin, London.

Peppercorne, J.W. (1840) *Mischna-Hathora*. 'The Laws of the Hebrews relating to the Poor and the Stranger' translation from the Code of Rabbi Maimonides, Pelham Richardson, London.

Rabinowitz, J.J. (1949) *The Book of Civil Laws*. Book Thirteen of the Code of Maimonides, translated by J J Rabinowitz, Yale University Press, New Haven.

Reidenbach, R.E. and Robin, D.P. (1988) "Some Initial Steps toward Improving the Measurement of Ethical Evaluations of Marketing Activities" *Journal of Business Ethics*. Vol. 7, pages 871-879.

Reidenbach, R.E. and Robin, D.P. (1990) "Toward the Development of a Multidimensional Scale for Improving Evaluations of Business Ethics" *Journal of Business Ethics*. Vol. 9, pages 639 - 653.

Sharma, A. (1982) *The Purusarthas:- A Study in Hindu Axiology*. East Lansing, Michigan, USA.

Sol, H.G. and Vecsenyi, J. (1990) *Environments for Supporting Decision Processes*. Elsevier, North Holland.

Vogel,D.(Fall, 1992) "The Globalization of Business Ethics: Why America Remains Distinctive" *California Management Review*.

Wing-tsit, Chan (1986) *Chu Hsi and Neo-Confucianism*. University of Hawaii Press

10 BIOGRAPHY

Andrew McCosh has been a member of IFIP since 1984. He was professor of management accounting at Manchester Business School from 1971-1985, and Dean of the Faculty for part of that time. He was professor of finance at Edinburgh University from 1986-1995, and head of Business Finance, Accountancy and Economics for part of that time. He has published forty papers and seven books on systems and on finance.

4

Structure and communications in the process of organisational change: Eastern European experience and its general relevance

P.C. Humphreys
London School of Economics & Political Science
Houghton Street, London WC2 2AE, UK
Tel +44 171 955 7711, Fax +44 171 955 7565
e-mail P.Humphreys@lse.ac.uk

E. L. Nappelbaum
Russian Institute for Systems Analysis
9 Pr 60 Let Octabryja, Moscow 117312, Russia
Tel/Fax +7 095 282 4275
e-mail ernapp@aha.ru

Abstract

Every organisational change creates some organisational stress and makes personnel both winners and losers within the organization. To a large degree this is a result of the inevitable change of the organization perspective as well as ensuing organisational restructuring. In this paper we investigate the organisational perspectives generally adopted by top management, and explore the consequential stresses generated in the attempt to implement the ensuing prescriptions for change.

We stipulate that middle management will feel themselves the most threatened by processes of organisational change instigated from above. We demonstrate how they transfer this feeling further down the hierarchical ladder. A major factor here is a virtual break in communication within the organization resulting from the radical change of the communication context. We illustrate how situation is further aggravated by middle management assuming the role of interpreters of top management's intentions and of the sole guardian of the power of the organisational unit they manage and hence of the protector of its personnel. In this way the previous organisational structure becomes an infrastructure for the pockets of tacit resistance to organisational change that may frustrate its purposes in the long run.

On the basis of the model for problem formulation and choice developed by Nappelbaum, this situation is examined and is related to the issue of implementation design for a strategic decision taken by the upper management. It is stipulated that team building is an inherent part of this process and should involve not only those who instigate the change and prepare corresponding decisions but also every echelon of the organisational management.

This understanding imparts a new flavour to the notion of participative management and imposes new requirements on organisational communications and on computer support for organisational change. In this respect the concept of variable precision modelling of knowledge about local enactment processes (developed within SASOS by Humphreys and Berkeley) becomes especially relevant. Within this framework, however, the notion of zooming is to be rethought from aggregation/disaggregation to reflection and analytic reinterpretation and creative synthesis.

Theoretical ideas to be presented here are illustrated by the recent experience of attempts at organisational transformation and business development within the Hungarian reform process and Russian *perestroika*. We consider that the experiences reported here are quite relevant to organisations in general, wherever in the world they are located.

Keywords

Organisational change, decision conferencing,participative management, Eastern Europe, business practice.

1 INTRODUCTION: THE CONTEXT OF ORGANISATIONAL TRANSITION IN EASTERN EUROPE

Today, after nearly a decade from the beginning of the new era in Eastern Europe which started in the mid 1980's at the time of perestroika in Russia, one may justifiably regard the processes that are taking place there as (among many other and probably much more significant things) a huge and most comprehensive study in social and organizational change. True, many people , both from the right and the left of the political spectrum, claim that many of the changes are very shallow and superficial in their nature. This, however, is simply a debate over the depth of the changes implemented and over their lasting values and desirability. The scope of the changes and especially of attempts to instigate some change is clearly evident.

These processes of change - how a change was conceived, planned, prepared for, implemented, fought against, perceived, and evaluated - if deeply, carefully, and objectively studied, might offer an incredible wealth of material for both theoretical and practical analysis. However, this is rarely properly done or properly documented and for several very good reasons. The most important of those is political sensitivity of the very issues involved as any statement about a change at any level and especially assessment of its desirability, planned nature etc. would be immediately exploited by one political side and as swiftly challenged by an opposite one. But, from a methodological viewpoint, it is probably even more important that any "objective" assessment should inevitably involve a common "frame of reference". Most of the material that follows argues implicitly that any change is first and foremost is a change in the frame of reference and hence should be judged on its own merits.

Nonetheless several illuminating conclusions can be made even at the level of pure "unequipped" observations, especially if they are made at "embedded observation" basis. These conclusions may be especially emblematic as they cover a wide spectrum of change stakeholders and their attitude towards this change. Indeed, it is equally interesting to observe what changes top management of various enterprises see fit to introduce in response to the ever-changing business environment and how it goes about it or how people at the grassroots level adapt to the changes and assess them.

One of our more interesting observations is that rarely does implemented change result in the state of affairs that was the objective of the change. Moreover in many cases the result of a change is totally counterproductive with respect to the underlying intentions. It would be easy and tempting to explain this discrepancy by either a deficient planning of the change or by hypocrisy of top managers who proclaim one thing but perform something totally different. The reality, however, is in many cases much more complicated. Time and again it became obvious that managers planning to enact a change failed to understand that each major change involves also a drastic change of perspective of all the actors involved, of their frame of reference, as well as of an infrastructure stability of which quite often is a major precondition of the success of the change instigated. Moreover, an obvious complexity of the social texture where the change is being enacted very often results in appearance of "emergent" effects that are very difficult to attribute to tangible causes and even more difficult to forecast and to allow for.

Not surprisingly, given the above observations, the reform processes in most countries in Eastern Europe have been accompanied by a decline in industrial production. Initially, the underlying severity of this process was masked by a low level of apparent profitability. This was sustained on what were increasingly loss making operations by using up assets and resources. As such accumulated resources become exhausted, the pressure for organisational transformation and new business successes comes ever more to the fore as an essential survival strategy. Now this in evinced even in the pressure from some quarters for a "re-transformation" to earlier organisational forms, remembered with nostalgia after the failure of interim attempts at transformation.

This apparent nostalgia stems from the way in which people at large assess the results of a change even when they shared the underlying values in terms of which the change was considered desirable. If the enacted change was successful these values become a stable feature of the everyday environment, and in human consciousness transfer themselves to the realm of the behaviour infrastructure which is generally taken for granted and does not enter in an assessment pattern. The change induces a totally different frame of references, in which comparison with the previous state of affairs plays a crucial role. This state is often assessed in a highly idealised way by disregarding the features that were the most distressing and hence led to the change and by overestimating the features that cause distress now.

The interim attempts at transformation have been generally characterised by the decomposition of inherited, overcentralised organization structures. However the idea of organisational *hierarchy,* with rigid distinctions between top management, middle management and workforce has, at the same time, been reinforced. Mirroring the contemporary political struggles founded on a competition to the death between stereotyped political forms, the appropriate design for an organization has usually been perceived as an outcome of a struggle between various organisational forms, in which the management-workforce control hierarchy, with strict accountability between levels (Jaques, 1989), has generally assumed hegemony.

Some interesting observations can be made, in this respect, concerning the attitudes and behaviour of top management of various enterprises. The most evident feature of those is a very strong resistance to changes in their own enterprises even if they are dictated by the changed business environment. In principle, old guard longs for the changes that are purely cosmetic and increases only their own freedom of manoeuvre and their benefits leaving the rest of the business environment intact and predictable. Surprisingly, such an attitude finds an unexpected support in the inner dynamics of change itself. Indeed, such changes create transient business environments in which it is exceedingly difficult to orient and to operate. In this kind of environment, perhaps the only factor of lasting value is the previously established personal relationships that allows the directors of the emergent enterprise to recreate, to a large extent, many salient features of the old distribution system. This serves to promote and maintain the myth that the old "directors' club" are the only people capable of managing large-scale industrial enterprises. This, in turn, has led to the temporary revival of seemingly rejected political doctrines, as can be publicly witnessed at election time in most Eastern European countries.

This process has also been accompanied by decentralisation of production and services, and the formation of new kinds of alliances and ventures under the rubric of "privatisation". For example, we frequently find short-sighted behaviour on the part the management of those plants that outsource an enterprise that acts as a main breadwinner. They may raise the prices for the outsourced material they supply in an attempt to benefit inordinately from their firm's monopoly position: dealing with the main enterprise very much in the same way as they were previously dealing with the state. Such practices have brought leading enterprises to the brink of uncompetitiveness, potentially distorting the very source of their own financing.

By the same token, in forming their partnership relations with Western companies, Russian large-scale enterprises prefer to establish them with very large-scale partners (sometimes clearly in disadvantage to their own good) which they try to deal with in much the same way they were accustomed to deal with the previous State owned enterprises.

Quite a different style of business behaviour is demonstrated by younger people in setting up their new and generally small businesses, especially if they build from scratch and build them up gradually, employing (especially in the beginning) people who are fully aware of what they are employed to build. These small businesses are usually intended, by those who set them up, to thrive on the rapidly changing, transient business environment. When they are formed as joint ventures, the local directors characteristically find fault and express disappointment with the behaviour of their Western partners, whose minds are tuned to a much more stable and less opportunistic economic climate.

The entire organisational structure emerging as a result of these attempts, however, has proved typically to be highly unstable and prone to serious calamities. The resulting very high degree of failure (both explicit and latent) among the newly created organisations is a good indicator that there is much which is fundamentally wrong with the current attitude to organisational transformation amongst managers operating in Eastern Europe, and probably elsewhere too.

1.1 The negative inheritance

To some extent, the roots of these failures can be traced to a heavy negative inheritance from past systems and in the lack of much attempt to understanding this inheritance (rather than trying to wipe it out of memory) and of its influences on the organisational future. Key issues from the past with negative carry-over to the present are:

- *Within the "first economy"* there were generally negative incentives for good, innovative management: Failures were attributed personally but success were attributed collectively; project management was limited to technical development rather than to managing all aspects of innovative projects, viewed as socio-technical and human activity systems. Risk analysis techniques were highly developed but only on an informal, not on a formal basis. Moreover the focus was on the analysis of political risk rather than business risk.

- *Within the "second economy"* there were, of course, economic rewards to be gained form the personal exercise of initiative and innovation, but such efforts were generally limited to commerce and were often clandestine. Within this sector, the mechanisms of production, where they were existed, were highly distorted and were generally parasitic on operations located within the first economy. Associated with the clandestine nature of these activities was the importance of *private* knowledge. Knowledge about "how to" was a commodity best kept in shortage, rather than to be shared publicly.

In general, very little pre-competitive infrastructure existed within the second economies flourishing in Eastern Europe, and that which existed within the first economy died with it. Its death throes were, for the reasons outlined above, accompanied by the subversion for the basis of trust within any organisational forms which would newly emerge, whatever their nature.

1.2 Importation of Western business practice ideas

The reasons for failures in organisational transformation and business development should not, however, be sought solely in the past. No less important reasons can be identified in shortcomings of the new ways of doing things in organisations, and of doing business in Eastern Europe. Prescriptions and the rationale of originating in Western business practice were, and continue to be, imported completely out of context. Scant attention is given to the differences in infrastructure on which business, private and even political life is based in the particular national context, compared with the context in which the imported prescriptions originated.

The pressure and the agency for this process of importation and re-implementation of perceived successful "Western" business techniques lies, increasingly, with those personnel who assume the "top management" of the emergent organisational units, even if they did not occupy such positions before. These are, typically, people having the agency and financial backing to perform "management buy-outs"; to liaise with venture capitalists and interpret their wishes; to form "joint ventures" with western partners, and so on. It is our experience (supported by Paprika and Zoltay, 1994) that, when help is sought by such people for professional experts, analysts and consultants in decision and management support, their first priorities are for support in regard of:

- Innovative marketing solutions, rather than market research;
- Brainstorming on new ventures;
- Negotiations with potential partners, banks, etc.;
- Techniques for increasing workforce efficiency while maintaining morale within a climate off staff cut backs.

The conjunction of these four priorities stems from a general belief that because the organization has, in the past, been successful in operational terms (provision of a specific type of product , service, etc.), the aim must now be to maintain and even enhance the success of the old, continuing, "operational core" in the newly emerging economic, social and political context.

What is not addressed in this view is the need for an understanding of why the organization was successful in the past, not just in operational terms, but considering all the kinds of resources in its constituent human activity system. Only then is it possible to understand how the resources currently surviving in the organization can, collectively, form the basis for its future success. Such an understanding involves a completely different conception of what is the "core" of an organization. This is something which we will explore further in section 3.

1.3 The split between organization and workforce

The priorities discussed in the previous section also reflect the concerns of top management within a perspective on their business which enshrines a fundamental split between organisational structures, which appear as autonomous with a life of their own, and human practices within organisations which appear as apart: thrown off centre from the decision making process. This perspective also promotes management-centrism: *Management* makes decisions; *Management* transforms the organization (Merkle, 1980). Attempts may be made to use participative techniques like *Kaizen* (Masaaki, 1989) among groups of workers and front line managers to boost morale, within a perspective which dissociates subjectivity from organisational tasks. Thus it seems to be a surprise to top management when such activities fall apart, in terms of their stated aims, when their own view that *"the bottom line is to reduce staff costs"* becomes common knowledge amongst the participants.

This is not to say that we are witnessing a return to "scientific management" according to the theories of F. W. Taylor (c.f. Taylor, 1947; Nelson, 1980). In the post-modern world, Taylorism is discredited in both Eastern and Western European management practices, being blamed for the development of distorted, fragmented and inhumane work methods of work practice during the period of modernist excesses in productive enterprises in both Western Europe (Morgan, 1986) and Eastern Europe (Beissinger, 1988), as well as in the United States (Wrege and Greenwood, 1991). Currently, in both West and East Europe, the impetus is on the replacement of the remains of Taylorism with the "Human Relations" approach which seeks to:

> " reshape the internal world of the organization so as to release the autonomous subjectivity of the worker in such a way that is aligned with the aspirations of the enterprise, now construed in terms of innovation, flexibility and competitiveness" (Rose, 1989).

We hear from top management, everywhere in Eastern Europe, a growing tendency to insist that development and transformation of their organisations should be made in the service of "increasing innovation and competitiveness," but the divorce of their workforce from the concept of their "organization" still remains in the discourse and practice of this level of management. Thus subjectivity is dissociated from organisational settings. The result is that the managers and their organisational analysts are located in professional roles, external to, and alienated from, the organisational process itself (Humphreys, Berkeley and Jovchelovitch, 1996).

2 TOP MANAGEMENT'S DESIRES FOR DECISION SUPPORT

A decade ago (Humphreys, 1984) we identified an almost complete absence in practical applications at top management level of interactive computer-based systems based on traditional DSS and IS design methodologies (Lederer and Sethi, 1988), a situation which continues today. We stated then that

> "the problem here is not simply a failure of decision support systems at higher levels. It may not be wise to attempt to formalise scenario generation techniques and problem structuring languages into automated decision support systems....Decision makers' scenarios need to be *explored* rather than be fitted into formal structures...It is better to develop techniques for the psychological validation of the decision makers' *own* problem structuring language than to try to invent a universal problem structuring language that will have to be taught from scratch to high level decision makers." (Humphreys, 1984, p. 20)

Phillips (1989) identified two approaches to GDSS for top management which were then beginning to emerge as a result of the failure of the traditional DSS/IS approach. The first followed from the view that "the most fundamental activity of group decision making is interpersonal communication and the primary purpose of a GDSS is to improve group communication activities" (DeSanctis and Dickson 1987), and sought to provide a computer-based workbench environment with the intention of facilitating group communication. Phillips claimed that this approach was inferior to the second approach which "provides a problem solving environment that is group centred and is primarily intended to help managers consider uncertainty, form preferences, make judgements and take decisions".

The latter approach, usually implemented at top management level in the form of "decision conferencing" (Phillips, 1992), has increasingly become the preferred approach to import from the West in the service of East European top management's desire for support in their efforts at organisational transformation (Fekete-Szucs, 1991; Vari, Rohrbaugh and Baaklini, 1992). Part of the reason for this preference is the recognition the particular validity in the context of the problems facing Eastern Europe of Phillips' (1989) claim that "concentrating only on the technology, computers, software and networks will not reveal the full potential of GDSS".

Phillips' criticism has generally been taken as a reason to dismiss the first approach on a wholesale basis but, in our opinion, this is unfair. The criticism only applies to a particular implementation strategy which is more appropriate in the cultural and economic context of Texas than of Hungary or Russia, and we will return, later in this paper, to the fundamental importance of improving group communication activities. First, though, we examine in more details the consequences of the hegemony of top management, following the second, approach for implementation of organisational transformation.

2.1 Consequences of planning organisational transformation through top management decision conferencing.

In decision conferences focused on organisational transformation, the participating top managers usually first plan the restructuring of the organization, reaching agreement on goals, strategies and future scenarios within which the chosen strategy appears to unfold successfully, and *then* calculate staff losses, redeployments, etc. (Bannon, 1997) Finally, agreement is reached on action. This usually means allocating and confirming responsibilities among the individuals present on the prescriptions each should issue to his or her subordinate managers in order to initiate the implementation process which, it is believed, will secure the desired changes (Fekete-Szucs, 1991; Phillips, 1992). The implementation process itself is usually not considered in any detail in the conference, as the necessary expertise is located at lower levels within the organisational process, split off from the experience and management concerns of the participants in the decision conference.

Our experience is that this agenda for decision conferencing tends to have the following unfortunate concomitants:

- Failure within the implementation scenarios to identify properly and provide for handling side effects of the main, intended, effect;
- "Throwing the baby out with the bath water" through focusing on the rolling back of initial scenarios without the opportunity to create innovative pathways to goals, as they lie off the roll-back route;
- Missing of opportunities and creation of problems for change implementation management;
- Underestimation of the value of (or even the existence of) local skilled knowledge in place within the organization.

These drawbacks are omnipresent not only in formal decision conferencing but also in the very formal and informal activities that enact a change and hence are very central in understanding some failures to implement a change and in improving the efficiency of the change management in general. They are as well as many other drawbacks are intimately related to a "linear mode of thinking about change" that remain prevailing in our theory and practice and in the final analysis of a linear model of choice and problem solving limitations of which were exposed in an old but still quite topical paper that is not very well known and which is published for the first time in this volume (Nappelbaum, 1997).

The main flaw of the linear way of thinking about change lays in its "measurement paradigm", a contention that the problem to be solved to enact a change and hence a change itself is some how "given", objectively present in the existing problem environment (or "problematique" to use a term popular in systems research) and that the problem of the management is to recognise it and to find the efficient way of its implementation.

This model of thinking does not recognise that the problem environment itself is nothing but a very subjective and very limited perception of a much more complex and much less manageable environment. Moreover this perception is not a mere partial mapping of this reality into a manageable representation but a result of a purposeful creative design effort involving complicated manipulation of the available data and establishment of powerful restrictions one of the major objectives of which is to make the representation manageable.

Nothing in this representation is "given": nor the way in which we describe the states we want to change as well as the state space boundaries, nor the frame of reference to be used in assessing whether a change is desirable or not, nor the scope and the content and efficiency of actions we are willing to allow in order to enact a change.

The mere fact that this representation exists and looks "natural" and unique is a good indication of its stability and previous success and there is a good chance that the desire for change is a manifestation of such a turn of the affairs that made this same representation suspect and not nearly as successful as it was in the past. Obviously any attempts to find the remedy within the framework of such a representation is doomed to failure and may eventually jeopardise the very idea of a change. It is in this sense we have alluded several times above that a real change (rather than a mere dynamics) involves always and foremost a change of the frame of references and even of a perception of the "objective" reality.

Another reason why the original representation appears to be an "obvious" one and a unique one is its holistic, robust nature. In (Nappelbaum, 1997) this is explained by an inner balance between its various components achieved during the original design of this representations, by its "cognitive closeness" requiring people who share this perception to reinforce in their thinking and their behaviour the validity of this perception very much in the same way in which "organizational closure", as described by Maturana and Varela (1979) is preserved. It is this inner holism and closeness of a perception that is responsible for a well-known effect of incomparability and irreconcilability of different personal attitudes with which every decision conferencing has to deal at some time.

Recognising a positive value of the difference in personal perceptions and at least on the face of it paying a special attention to a deviate opinion current conferencing techniques deal with the plurality of personal perceptions in a most negligent and cavalier manner. The only way in which the existing methodology knows how to enrich a perception consists of a mechanical merger of the attributes belonging to different cognitive closures and in looking for trade-offs between different assessments. In doings so, however, we destroy underlying tightly knitted structures of the merged perceptions and replace them with their flattened and hence placid projections, losing on the way some extremely rich semantic information.

Moreover, expanded perception cannot be balanced by definition and hence a superficial representation that we are trying to use for the search of a viable strategy lacks the very vitality, integrity and persuasive power so much needed if we want the designed strategy of change to be successful. We have argued (Humphreys and Nappelbaum, 1989, Nappelbaum, 1997) that a genuine approach to expansion of the perception of a problem environment can be only achieved through designing for the same objective reality as many competing and mutually incomparable representations as possible and to transfer a choice between various options to the choice between various perceptions each of which suggest an obvious solution of a problem it is expressing.

- In other words, a problem can be considered as "properly formulated" only if we know (or believe, probably erroneously) how to solve it and what is this solution.
- The issue, however, is to chose or more precisely to design, a problem we believe we need to solve.
- This choice, in its own turn, require involving perception of a higher level which may call for the rethinking of the very principles that the enterprise is built upon.

Thus, if we are to avoid the third and fourth "unfortunate concomitants of decision conferencing", described above (i.e., missing of opportunities and creation of problems for change implementation management; underestimation of the value of local skilled knowledge in place within the organization), this calls, first of all, for a profound analysis of the existing system of values constituting the very inter-organizational culture and checking its consistency with the value systems attached to every particular solution and its underlying perception.

This is a very important and an often neglected feature of organization of knowledge needed for planning and implementing a change. Each action which is going to be taken to implement a change, however small, brings with itself its own "native" perception involving its own frame of reference, its own system of values, its own set of instrumental intentions etc. And all this components belonging to perceptions of different levels should be innerly consistent. Their intrinsic inconsistency may result in emergent side effects that in the final analysis may jeopardise the very intentions for which the change was enacted.

That is why a detailed implementation plan - the *implementation definition cycle* - to add to the original *problem definition* and *situation definition cycles* - should be an indispensable part of any change management scenario. Such a cycle should not only to check whether we are dealing with a case of a "collective fantasy" (Humphreys and Berkeley, 1986, Humphreys, 1989) or the suggested solution is actually implementable but also to check the price of this implementation and not only in terms of the resources allocated but also in terms of the values compromised.

Consideration of the implementation definition cycle reveals also yet another extremely important dimension of the change management - an issue of *stakeholders* (Mitroff, 1983). Usually decision conferencing takes notice of the personal differences of a very limited circle of stakeholders - comprising mostly those who plan and manage the change process. In organizational setting, however, a real set of stakeholders are much larger and encompass both the *actors* and the "*consumers*" of the change and each of them brings into the process its own perception of that part of the overall reality that is relevant to them. Inconsistency of the "organizational" and individual perceptions and especially of its value components may destroy the manageability of the change process and compromise the entire endeavour.

Implementability of any change process and even its relevance is a very provisional thing strongly dependent on the existence and stability of the underlying infrastructure. In terms of the circular logic of choice (Nappelbaum, 1997) this infrastructure can be defined as those features of perception that are taken for granted and whose stability should not be affected by the planned change. It is precisely because of this uncontested nature of our beliefs about the existence and stability of the relevant infrastructure that makes its analysis so difficult and so rare. Design and analysis of alternative perceptions besides one that is used for the purpose of change management and planning can be instrumental in finding what is assumed to already exist or to happen by itself, what are the foundation for such believes and what external factor may affect the validity of such assumptions. In section In section 3, we will discuss how this may be done, taking into account the knowledge and subjectivities of all the participants involved in the transformation process.

2.2 Neglect by top management of situation and implementation definition cycles

We have shown above how unfortunate concomitants of decision conferencing follow from the usual practice of considering only the *problem definition cycle* within the three cycle scheme identified by Nappelbaum (1997) as essential for effective utilisation of the full range of relevant information and expertise existing in the organization in the planning, managing and implementation of the organisational transformation process. The neglect of the other two cycles in the scheme stems from the hegemony of top management's desires for change at the core of the planning for organisational transformation.

The *situation definition cycle* is neglected because handling information about the organization within this cycle means keeping aware of the recent history of processes and participants at all levels in the organization: something which senior management usually (and incorrectly) seek to identify as the core of the negative inheritance which is responsible for their current dis-ease.

The *implementation project definition cycle* is neglected as a consequence of splitting off the notion of the *organization* and its transformation from the subjectivity of those members of the organization who actually implement the transformation through the collective changes in their communications and work practice. Hence implementation project managers and their teams perceive the outputs of top management's decision making as *requirements for changes and deliverables:* They must analyse these requirements and implement the processes which will result in the deliverables within constraints set from above (Berkeley, De Hoog and Humphreys, 1990), but the possibility of generation of the requirements and possibilities for transformation is excluded at the levels in the organization where it should actually occur, rather than just be planned and prescribed.

In the following section, we examine the consequences of this neglect, focusing particularly on how it can destroy the participation of middle management in developing any kind of effective organic transformation process.

2.3 The problems of middle management

It is well known that adoption of a new policy generally entails structural changes; also the existing structure significantly constrains the type of strategy that an organization is willing and capable of adopting (Chandler, 1969). The latter is most heavily related to a mismatch between the top-level management of the organisational perspective and lower-level ones that may emerge at the stage of development and implementation of a new organisational strategy. We will refer to that issue as to the problem of vertical or structural implementability. The need to consider this implementability dimension stems from the fact that organization stakeholders and actors are by no means obliged to take new organisational objectives and policies, prescribed from above, in their stride. Rather, they tend to consider these as annoying constraints in their efforts to keep performing those activities which they know best how to perform and to change only the appearance rather than the gist of the change as conceived from above.

The vertical implementability issue can be further aggravated by structural stability which is built into every viable organization (Espejo, 1989). In principle, a change of the policy that inevitably involves a change of perspective and implies a change of the organization structure, unavoidably leaves some of the members of that organization worse off. More or less by definition, the most unfavourably affected and endangered strata of these members are middle management (Keen, 1986).

Indeed, top managers in an organization undergoing a change of structure, following the "preferred approach to decision making we identified in section 2.1, are likely to be more flexible in their capabilities, and better prepared for the changes which are planned to take place as they tend to be the owners of the transition problem. Similarly, the lower "technological" levels of the organization tend to be the "physical" incarnation of the organization competence. Hence the physical, technical, capabilities existing at these levels will be formulated in the course of the new policy development and, thus in principle, should be allowed for in the planned organisational transition.

Middle management, however, tends to represent the organization structure itself. Changes in organization strategies and the ensuing modifications in the organization structure inevitably imply redistribution of organisational power and, even more seriously, the *functionality* of various elements of organisational structure, to which middle management may be unwilling or even unable to find an easy answer, or any answer at all.

This situation is further aggravated by the fact that middle management traditionally constitutes the main network through which decision made by top management are transferred to the lower levels of the organization for implementation (Jaques, 1976). In making this transfer, middle managers do not merely pass the information along but also translate from the "strategic" (top management) language in which it is received into prescriptions and instructions in a language which they think will be understood by the "technical level" recipients of their communications lower down the organization (Jaques, 1989). In doing so, they must *interpret* this information (Cooper and Burrell, 1988; Checkland, 1994) and, through this traditional role middle managers obtain the possibility of distorting this information in the light that is beneficial to themselves.

In the cases of organisational transition we have studied in Hungary and Russia (and elsewhere, for that matter), top management usually turned out to be much more interested in finding an appropriate policy, and an appropriate set of objectives, and perspectives, rather than in team building and in propagation of their new vision through all the levels, right to the bottom of the organisational ladder. A perspective developed at the top level is generally very difficult to translate into the context that rules the behaviour of those who operate at much lower levels in the organization. They need time and effort in order to be able to develop an outlook that is well adjusted to the new top-level perspective (Yetton and Crawford, 1992). Moreover the amount of time and effort required to do this at the lower levels is usually much greater than that which was needed at the top level. The translation and implementation process is especially difficult at lower levels due to the lack of specialists in the highly creative business of planning organisational transformation. Most people employed at the technical level are much more accustomed to think in stereotypes which have been enforced by their entire previous life in the organization, and which are now being negated by the organization transition under way.

In such an environment of uncertainty and ensuing anxiety middle management get the chance to rally the support of the lower, largely disaffected strata in their organization in their efforts to resist those structural changes planned by top management that may remove them from the power or dilute their power. In calling for protection of the existing structural entities they lead, they portray their activity as a natural defence of previous "traditional" values as well as of the vested interests of the group they represent. In this way they hamper the very process of adaptation of the lower levels of organization to the new ideas born at the upper levels.

3. STAKEHOLDERS IN THE LIFEWORLD OF THE ORGANIZATION IN TRANSFORMATION

Considerations of the sort discussed above give a totally different meaning to the idea of participative management (Mumford, 1991). Now it becomes evident that, even at the stage of the development of the new policy, focusing on DSS to support the concerns and desires of top management is insufficient. One has to allow for the entire plethora of the new, more focused, perceptions and local policies that would inevitably emerge in the course of new policy implementation. These somehow have to be consistent with the "grand plan" of the organisational transition, conceived on the basis of larger strategic considerations applicable to the organization as a whole. It is no longer enough just to invite some representatives of the lower levels of management and of the workforce to take part in the development of this grand plan.

It is equally essential to give time and opportunity to all the stakeholders and actors to develop their own adjusted perceptions and policies and for checking the internal consistency of these perceptions and plans with the aggregated (rather than prescribed) one. These stakeholders and actors may occupy not only the roles of problem owner, decision maker, expert, i.e., those familiar to the participants in decision conferences on organisational change (Vari and Vecsenyi, 1984), but also a host of other roles in the organization lifeworld, reflecting the fact that they are, in various ways, the participants who are directly or indirectly affected by the global and local changes inherent in the transformation process.

This is a wider trawl of participants than the organisational stakeholders than commonly identified in "soft systems methodologies" for use by organisational analysts (e.g., Checkland and Scholes, 1990; Jackson, 1991) as it takes into account not only those considered to have a stake in the "transformation problem", as first identified, but also those who would experience the results of the actions taken in handling or "solving" the problem, and those involved in the results and side effects of the implementation of any "solution".

As a basis for communicative action (Habermas, 1990) all participants, thus defined, will, ideally, need to provide information about "what they know best". It is also necessary to organise, and feed back, on a distributed basis, an enhanced understanding of this collective knowledge, given that a suitable vehicle of communication could be found for this purpose. The major difficulty facing this enterprise is to elicit the knowledge participants possess in a way that understanding can be achieved, since disparate assumptions about possibly shared knowledge and interpretative frameworks (as commonly accepted within the organization) are likely to flavour individual participants' discourse.

Hence any effective vehicle of communication must orient the discourse within an interpretative framework where each participant's assumptions about what is (or assumed to be) commonly known within the organization can surface (McCaskey, 1988). The choice of the appropriate interpretative framework is a matter of sensitivity to local cultural and social conditions within the lifeworld of the organization (Habermas, 1989). It is not appropriate to presume the hegemony of the interpretations and assumptions of any particular group or stratum, such as top management, in this respect.

3.1 Sensitivity to local cultural and social conditions

In searching for the appropriate interpretative framework in any particular organisational context, the "organisational culture metaphor" is often invoked: i.e., the common notion that "culture is a determinant of social life in any particular context and that, by extension, organisational culture determines the interpretative patterning of organisational life (Handy, 1985). Essentially, "culture", itself a metaphor taken from agriculture, is a construct, controversial at base, under which a lot of different things may be glibly placed, explaining mainly *differences* between various groups. Emphasis on differences has obscured the realisation, fundamental to the agricultural use of the term, that culture is a *process* (originally of cultivating the land).

Individual organisations, which would seem to be situated within the same general cultural context, have their *own* cultures with a great deal of subcultural variation. Morgan (1986) identifies the fundamental criterion for the existence of an organization, in functional, process terms, to be the *enactment of a shared reality.* It is this enactment process which constitutes the "organisational culture" as a set of shared assumptions informing observation and action. It is maintained through formal and informal interactions between the participants in the organization processes and is expressed in human relations.

Nevertheless, organisations contain subcultures; thus enactment processes may be shared within particular groups or strata within an organization (c.f. Jaques, 1989), but not be homogeneous across them. Thus overall, organisational culture is patterned according to local conditions. Great differences may exist between different groups of people within the organization in terms of the expectations, assumptions, rules, etc. to which they ascribe. The resulting clashes and miscommunication can create problems for the organization as a whole. On the other hand, "cultural differences" may exist between groups of individuals which are external to the enactment process within the organisational context in which they work (e.g., age, sex, background, education, nationality, etc.). Although these differences can bring with them different expectations and assumptions, to the extent that these individuals can play their part in the enactment process, they may succeed in working together in an approximate equilibrium (Bateson, 1973).

Sensitivity to the existence of potential differences in organisational subcultures is often not sufficient if it is expressed only in terms of what can be observed and inferred: it must also address *local enactment processes.* Adopting this view means articulating the language of action as well as the language of observation in accessing this culture in enactment (de Zeeuw, 1993). The construction and maintenance of a shared reality allows this articulation to provide a vehicle of communication between participants who may yet have, and maintain, different perspectives and preferences during a successful process of organisational transformation.

3.2 Implementability and local enactment processes

According to our ideas, organisational transition (independently of the level in the organization at which this transition takes place) differs from mere organisational dynamics precisely through the need to design and use a new perspective, a new outlook (Humphreys and Nappelbaum, 1989, Humphreys and Berkeley, 1995). In respect of this outlook, some of the parameters of the organization activities that were previously largely irrelevant become crucially important and even central. In this sense, any movement within a pre-established state space corresponds to system dynamics, to quantitative, purely parametric changes while organisational transition is bound to involve changes of the state space itself which are not merely implicate changes in the transition function but rather presupposes some changes in the state variables themselves.

It has recently become fashionable when speaking about organisational transition and organisational change, to emphasise the role of implementability and of verifying implementability as one of the main prerequisites for a full-fledged systems analysis of the problem and its suggested solution.

In terms of the logic of problem formulation and choice (Nappelbaum, 1997) implementability, along with the higher principles of work design (Hackman and Oldman, 1980) is the main factor in reducing the versatility of problem perceptions to a sole choice to be realised in a subsequent course of actions. Curiously, however, in the analysis of organisational choice, both the implementability of the policy of organisational transition and the design of the problem perception itself remain on a purely personal basis. Indeed, in nearly every methodology has been proposed as suitable for importation to Eastern Europe to improve organisational transformation (e.g. organisational strategic planning and management systems, soft systems analysis methodology, decision conferencing, see section 2.0, above) only *one* overall problem formulation and hence only *one* systems perspective is sought for and the actions proposed to "solve" the problem are checked only for their horizontal implementability, i.e. for implementability within the context established through this perspective.

Meanwhile any organisational transition involves scores of individual and group perspectives to be developed and many individual and group problems to be formulated and acted upon in the process of individual and group adaptation to the new organisational policies and structures which have been adopted by top management, and to the new structures and styles that follow it. Implementation of organisational transformation is thus fundamentally located at the level of *local enactment processes,* and the resulting overall transformation is, for better or for worse, a synthesis of the outputs of these processes. Kieser (1997) identifies reasons why the authors of, and consultants on, such methodologies find this convenient for themselves.

3.3 Some consequences

The picture we have developed above of the preferred approach to organisational transformation in the emerging "Westernised" climate of Eastern Europe is not a happy one. Indeed it has engendered a very high failure rate in organisational transformation, resulting in many bankrupt organisations, and in some cases threatening to wipe out indigenous organisational activity in entire sectors. However, it is extremely essential, in this context, not to despair, not to consider that this prevalence of organisational failure should compromise the very idea of transformation and reform in Eastern Europe. Drawing such a conclusion, and acting accordingly, would be to undermine the trust between people - participants in organisations - that generated the hope and motivation for the overall transformation process in the first place.

If the general process of organisational, and societal, transformation is to build upon rather than subvert this trust, then, in our opinion a radical reconceptualisation of how this process is to be planned, analysed and implemented is required, quite different from the current "preferred approach" which we have reviewed above. In particular, as a result of this reconceptualisation:

- Participants in organisational processes are viewed as active change agents (valuable resources) rather than workforce (usable and disposable commodities). The focus is resource enhancement in cultural transformation, rather than resource utilisation in structural transformation.

- Discourse on organisational change will involve articulation of the language of action as well as the language of observation .

- Organisational personnel employed on productive tasks may also take up the role of the analyst, for a while: observing, communicating and acting with the aim of improving their own and the organization working conditions.

4.0 IMPLICATIONS FOR ORGANISATIONAL PROCESS MODELLING AND DECISION SUPPORT

It is not necessary that all assumptions be articulated concerning local enactment processes for a shared understanding, requisite in the context of organisational transformation, to be reached by participants in those processes. Neither is it possible, or desirable, to capture all relevant knowledge that exists within the organization. For successful organisational process model development, the fundamental issue is to discover, during moments of reflexivity, where one has reached a satisfactory understanding to be able to proceed further (on a conditional basis) with the analysis and synthesis of the material gained from organisational personnel that far during the process of the investigation.(Willis, 1980).

This (conditional) analysis should not aim to produce "complete" or "final" results. Rather, its aim is to increase the competence of the analyst to make accessible knowledge informing the actions of the participants in a way that it can be used as a creative resource by them in any synthesis. In order to come to understand the inherent processes, meanings and distortions, any methods used need to be flexible, sensitive and open, rather than prescriptive, at this level (Kersten, 1986).

4.1 Investigation, analysis and creative synthesis

The investigation process is typically considered the precursor of an analytic process whereby the organisational structure and procedures are investigated. However, an analytic activity which addresses all relevant aspects of an organization and which structures this information to represent *"what is"* in the realm of the participants' discourse still needs to be complemented by a synthetic activity: putting diverse parts of this information, which should be linked in reality, back together in various different configurations (checked for consistency and coherence) to find out *"what could be"* in actual, or potential (future) reality.

It is important that any actions and plans which emerge are based on investigation of the "real world" of the organization functioning (not on a world which simply structures participants' discourse). The basis for the preferred actions, the implementation route, and their potential side effects, need to be described and explored in a language to which stakeholders have access, and which extends their own discourse, thus offering them additional resources for communicative action (De Zeeuw, 1993, De Zeeuw and Schuurman, 1997).

This strengthens, in any local context, the possibility of taking informed action through Habermas' ideal process of "a forum of speakers exhibiting communicative competence (Jackson, 1991). It also obviates the need to reduce stakeholders from the role of active participants to that of merely "witnesses" (Ulrich, 1988) since the additional resources extend the language which they can use, within the context of the local conditions and culture to provide them, in practice, with the very competence which Ulrich (preferring to promote local cultural hegemony of the analyst's interpretation and language) rejected as “impractical", just as Eastern (and Western) European top management today often reject proposals for developing and exercising such competence within their organisations as “impractical”.

4.2 Support for the analysis and synthesis of organisational systems

Two major technological developments have made it possible for this idea to be implemented. The first one is the widespread dissemination of communications networking. The second must is a possibility of approximate modelling with variable degrees of precision in presentation, as well as, and independently from, traversing (for investigating horizontal implementability) and zooming and unzooming (for investigating vertical implementability). Few Decision Support Systems with this kind of capability have yet succeeded in practical application within implementation of organisational transformation according to this idea. One exception is SASOS (Support for the Analysis and Synthesis of Organisational Systems, *c.f.*, Humphreys and Berkeley, 1992) and so, in the following, we indicate some key design concepts which provided SASOS with this capability.

4.2.1 Views on organisational reality informing SASOS

Organisational reality is a complex entity, synthesised through the language and perspectives and shared assumptions of those who experience that reality. This "reality" is constantly transforming itself as people interact, activities are carried out, and change is affected by the mere passage of time. Any participant in this "reality", taking up the role of analyst for the first time, or any external, professional analyst, inevitably discovers, if he or she takes the effort, that it takes a considerable amount of time to come to learn about this reality and the rules under which it functions and the elements which constitute it.

The learning process involves not only the conventional focus of organisational analysis, i.e., observing the way that organisational activities transform resources. It also involves being told stories about the processes and actions which, by their very nature, are not accessible through observation (de Zeeuw, 1993) or being told about it:.

This kind of information needs to be initially collected and exchanged in the form of commentaries coming from different people, with different responsibilities, perceptions, and experiences within the organization. Such organisational discourse may include elements which contradict each other (even if only by virtue of the fact that they have been voiced by different persons) which the analyst has to make sense of. The commentaries address problems arising, the activities involved, the results (intended or otherwise) and side effects, the characteristics of the resources involved, or required, and so on. They often appear fragmented, difficult to integrate at once into a conceptual model (Checkland, 1981), and yet have the potential to provide the seeds for important lessons to be learned.

SASOS i.e. employed in organisational analysis to address the complexity of the myriad of local enactment processes which collectively constitute an organization in transition by encouraging its users to take partial views on this reality according to their own local knowledge, desires and experience, to describe their characteristics relationships and linkages. It offers support for synthesising what has been described to enable the tracing of how problem situations may arise, and the development of actions to transcend them.

Taking a partial view is a functional way of bringing to the fore certain aspects of this reality and considering them in detail while paying less attention to other aspects of it which, although important in understanding it, fall within another domain of concern. SASOS is organised around three different views that can be taken on organisational reality, determined by the three different types of information an analyst requires to carry out his or her work (Berkeley, Humphreys and Quek, 1992). Each view presents a different, although not independent, picture of this reality, provides different types of information, and provides opportunities for different types of usage of this information.

Each view is guided by a different motivation, it addresses a different analytic goal or creative desire and, thus, the exit point from model development within that view can be easily decided upon by the user himself or herself on the basis of whether, in his or her opinion, the particular goal or desire has been achieved (even if only tentatively), or is still to be achieved. Thus, SASOS can be experienced as flexible and responsive to the current needs of the individual in this work as it collectively progresses, rather than just being seen as a prescriptive device.

The three views are:

- A static entity-relationship view, which links and structures information from participants concerning "observable “entities and their relationships which define the organization and its function within the general environment;
- A process view, which links and structures information on the processes and actions that are carried out within the organization and the various functions of the organization
- A systemic view, which provides information on comments voiced and stories told by participants about existing and potential problems in the organisational lifeworld and about desirable future situations and potential pathways which could improve current conditions.

While it may be convenient to start the process of organising the information provided a participant within a particular view, care should be taken not to subsume the analysis, as it develops, under just one view. Any single view, naturally, presents only a fragmented picture of the organisational reality orienting itself under one particular concern. Moreover, all three views are different ways of taking a partial look at the same organisational reality. It is only through the combined results of the material elicited by taking all three views, that one can, potentially, discover all the relevant aspects of the organization which are important in the analysis and creative synthesis of the structures and processes which will emerge from the organisational transformation.

4.2.2 Representation means sensitive to local cultural and social conditions

SASOS's *representation means* provide a vehicle of communication for intuitive understandings about processes in the static entity-relationship view, where they can be only inferred intuitively, not observed. It enables them to be precised through employing the language of action (precising relations and rules of change) without needing to increase the formality of the (static) descriptions of the entities involved in these processes.

These descriptions remain in the form of the narrative text from accounts given by organisational participants, and articulates their own language. There is no need for an analyst to interpret this text according to his or her own (local culture and motivation bound) assumptions in translating the language of the participants into some kind of formal extension of his or her own observational language[1]. All that changes is how the narrative hypertext structure is cross-referenced to elements and regions of the process model as it is generated through the actions of an analyst interacting with SASOS.

While SASOS offers support for process model generation at all levels of precision from exploration of hypertext at one extreme to simulation of predicate-transition nets (Genrich, 1987) at the other, this is not the only kind of support which is requisite to improve the communicative competence of the analyst and the other organisational participants involved. It is also necessary to support the *visualisation of what is being modelled,* in a way that is sensitive both (i) to what the user's (viewer's) visualisation problem is, and (ii) to the kind of visualisation language which will promote an efficient and appropriate interpretation of what is "seen" through its use. The latter, of course, will be highly dependent on the local culture, the social conditions determining the use of the "views" thus provided, and the (un)familiarity of the participants with representation techniques which employ particular kinds of visualisation
language.

Hence, SASOS provides for the particular visualisation language and techniques employed in any context when working on, or viewing a process model both (i) to match the user's visualisation problem and (ii) to be customised to employ a visualisation language which appears "natural" to the participants who view what SASOS can show them. It is these customisation facilities, offered by SASOS, which ensure its ability to support and guide the user in a modelling enterprise that will effectively increase participants' communicative competence in discourse on organisational transformation.

---

[1]Thus, within the scheme described by de Zeeuw, 1993, this enables the synthesis of extensions to participants' own language(s), l.'s, rather than utilizing some extended language L' which may work against any such synthesis.

4.2.3. Zooming and unzooming within variable precision modelling

As well as variable precision modelling, SASOS's representation means offer zooming (refinement) and unzooming (coarsening) facilities over the whole range of information to which it has access, regardless of the level of precision at which this information is represented (from hypertext to exact nets).[2] The need for these facilities is more or less obvious. Participants in different levels of the organisational structure use different, though "nested" contexts to develop their perceptions of the small world they have to operate within[3], and of the local enactment processes within that world.

Exercise in the concurrent development of the entire set of these perceptions supported by SASOS' machinery of variable precision modelling and zooming and unzooming facilities can be instrumental in:

- facilitating the development of local perceptions on different levels of organisational structure and hence checking the vertical implementability of any policy developed at the top, and contributing, bottom-up, to its construction and refinement;
- helping lower levels of the organisational structures to dispel their fears and phobias about impeding changes and in shortening the adaptation period;
- unclogging the middle management bottleneck mentioned in section 2.2, above;
- opening the possibility of top level policy adjustment that will allow for the special interests of lower level stakeholders and actors and hence removing unnecessary barriers on the implementation path for the top level policy.

---

[2] See Richter *et.al.,* 1987 for a detailed discussion, with examples, of the distinction refinement and precision in organizational conceptual model development and exploration.

[3]The idea of "nested perceptions", however, is by no means clear. The rules that govern nestedness or internal compatibility of differing scale perceptions is not only central in providing the kind of support but also for the whole concept of cognitive closure. It is clear that approximation mentioned above in this case does not amount solely to shedding certain details or to disaggregation of certain aggregated variables used in a higher level perception. In supplementing these with some other components (that may be totally foreign to the higher level perceptions) it creates its own concepts in which "borrowed" components may be differently interpreted and evaluated.

There are at least two distinct cases of incompatibility that may hamper vertical implementability of the transition policy referred to earlier:

- it may involve opposite value judgements of the same cognitive component interpreted differently on different levels; or
- it may involve emergence of a neglected feature in a higher level perspective as a result of aggregation of representations developed below.

It is essential also to understand that the vertical compatibility mentioned above does not possess any monotonicity or transitivity in a sense that some lower level perception that is perfectly compatible with its immediate predecessor may prove to be incompatible with some higher perception even if it is fully compatible with its immediate predecessor[4]

At the same time, within the organisational framework, these issues deserve special attention and should allow also for the specific social climate of a particular organization, its scale, its built-in culture and cultural differences between various levels and communication problems that exist and can be both alleviated and aggravated by the emergence of the instrument of a kind we have just suggested. Decision support systems that would develop (among others) the capabilities we have been trying to focus upon may deserve the name of organization transition support systems.

5 CONCLUSION

In this paper we have traced the high failure rate of attempts at organisational transformation in Eastern Europe, in part at least, to the desire of top management to import, and employ, techniques for analysing the conditions of their organization and formulating prescriptions for change in which subjectivity, while recognised, is divorced from organisational setting. This serves to reinforce the domestication of the productive participants in their organization and to undervalue to the knowledge they possess about local enactment processes, and how they might be improved.

We have proposed an alternative approach in which the process of creative transformation of organisations can be brought to centre field, and have shown how

---

[4].The issue of vertical compatibility and implementability outlined earlier may appear to relate only to decision making of strategic purport within an organisational framework. However, we believe that it is equally important for purely personal decisions, because thinking about implementation of personal decisions also involves focusing and defocusing, framing and reframing and zooming and unzooming.

support may be provided to organisational personnel at all levels (not just top management) in this process of creative transformation, promoting, rather than restricting, analysts' and management's abilities to be sensitive to local cultural and social conditions.

We have explored the implications of this understanding for organisational process modelling, starting from the need to *discover,* not to assume, what to observe and to articulate the language of action as well as the language of observation in accessing the culture in enactment. The aim is to support not only organisational analysis but also creative synthesis
of possibilities for organisational change and transformation. We believe that the need to defocus on this aim is an urgent priority in order to arrest and reverse the general process of organisational decline which we are currently witnessing not only in Eastern Europe, but also in many other parts of the industrialised world.

6 REFERENCES

Bannon, L. (1997) CSCW - A challenge to certain (G)DSS perspectives on the role of decisions, information, and technology in organizations? *This volume.*

Bateson, G. (1973) Steps to an ecology of mind. Paladin, St. Albans:.

Beisinger, M. R. (1988) Scientific management, socialist discipline and Soviet power. Tauris, London:

Berkeley, D. de Hoog, R. and Humphreys, P.C. (1990) Software development project management: process and support. Ellis Horwood/Simon and Schuster, Chichester.

Berkeley, D. Humphreys, P.C. and Quek, F. (1992) Dynamic process modelling for organisational systems supported by SASOS, in *Dynmod 3: proceedings of the third international conference on dynamic modelling of information systems.* (eds. H. G. Sol and A. Verbraek), Technical University Press, Delft.

Chandler, A. D., Jr. (1969) Strategy and Structure. Cambridge, MIT Press, Cambridge, Mass.

Checkland, P. (1981) Systems Thinking, Systems Practice. Wiley, Chichester.

Checkland, P. (1994) Conventional wisdom and conventional ignorance: the revolution organization theory missed. *Organization*, **1,** 29-34.

Checkland, P. and Scholes, J. (1990) Soft systems methodology in action. Wiley, Chichester.

DeSanctis, G. and Dickson, G. W. (1987) GDSS software as "shell" system in support of a programme of research, in *Proceedings of 20th annual Hawaii conference on systems sciences.*

Cooper, R. and Burrell, G. (1988) Modernism, postmodernism and organizational analysis: an introduction. *Organization Studies,* **9,** 91-112.

Espejo, R., 1989. A method to study organisations, in *The viable system model.* (eds. R. Espejo and R. Harnden) Wiley, Chichester.

Fekete-Szucs, L. (1991) Decision conference for strategic issues: theory in practice, in *Environments for supporting decision processes* (eds. H. G. Sol and J. Vecsenyi) Elsevier, Amsterdam.

Genrich, H. J. (1987) Predicate/Transition nets, in *Petri Nets: Central Models and their properties* (eds. W. Brauer, W. Reisig and G. Rozenberg) Springer-Verlag, Berlin.

Habermas, J. (1989) The Tasks of a Critical Theory of Society in *Critical theory and Society: a reader* (eds. S. E. Bronner & D. M. Kellner) Routledge, London.

Habermas, J. (1990) The theory of communicative action. Volume 1: Reason and the rationalisation of society. Polity press, London.

Hackman, J. R. and Oldham, G. R. (1980) Work redesign. Addison Wesley Reading, Mass.

Handy, C. (1985). Understanding organisations. Penguin, London. (3rd ed.)

Humphreys, P.C. (1984) Levels of representation in structuring decision problems. *Journal of applied systems analysis,* **11,** 3-22.

Humphreys, P. C. (1989) Intelligence in decision support: a process model, in *Knowledge based management support systems* (eds. G. Doukidis, F. Land and G. Miller) Wiley, Chichester.

Humphreys, P.C. and Berkeley, D. (1992) Support for the synthesis and analysis of organisational systems in deciding on change, in *Decision support systems: Experiences and expectations* (eds. T. Jelassi and W. Mayon-White) Elsevier, Amsterdam.

Humphreys, P.C. and Berkeley, D. (1986). Organisational knowledge for supporting decisions, in *Decision support systems: a decade in perspective* (eds. E. R. McLean and H. G. Sol) North Holland, Amsterdam.

Humphreys, P.C. and Berkeley, D. (1995) Organisational process modelling sensitive to local cultural and social conditions, in *Work and organizational psychology: European contributions of the nineties* (eds. J. M. Piero, F. Prieto, J. L. Melia and O. Luque) Erlbaum (UK) Taylor and Francis, Hove.

Humphreys, P.C., Berkeley, D. and Jovchelovitch, S. (1996) Organisational psychology and psychologists in organisations: Focus on organisational transformation. *Interamerican journal of psychology*, **30,** 27-42.

Humphreys, P.C. and Nappelbaum, E. L. (1989) Strategic Analysis of organisations in transition: knowledge structuring, conceptual modelling and implementation of changes. Organisational Research Group, LSE, London.

Jackson, M. C. (1991) Systems methodology for the Management Sciences. Plenum, New York.

Jaques, E. (1976) A general theory of Bureaucracy. Heinemann, London.

Jaques, E. (1989) Requisite organization: the CEO's guide. Casson Hall, Arlington, Virginia,

Keen, P. G. W. (1986) Decision support systems: the next decade, in *Decision support systems: a decade in perspective* (eds. E. R. McLean and H. G. Sol) North Holland, Amsterdam.

Kersten, A. (1986) A critical-interpretative approach to the study of organizational communication: bringing communication back into the field, *Organization <-> Communication: Emerging perspectives* in (ed. L. Thayer) Ablex Norwood, New York.

Kieser, A. (1997) Rhetoric and myth in management fashion. *Organization,* **4**, 49-74.

Lederer A. L., and Sethi, V. (1988) The implementation of strategic information system planning methodologies. *MIS Quarterly*, **12,** 445-461.

McCaskey, M. B. (1988) The challenge of managing ambiguity and change, in Managing ambiguity and change, (eds. L. R. Pondy, R. L. Boland, Jr and H. Thomas) Wiley, Chichester.

Masaaki, I. (1989) Kaizen: the key to Japanese competitive success. Random House, New York.

Maturana, H. and Varela, F. (1979) Autopoesis and Cognition. Reidel, Boston.

Merkle, J. A. (1980) Management and ideology: the legacy of the international scientific management movement. University of California Press, Berkeley:

Mitroff, I. I. (1983) Stakeholders of the organisational mind. Jossey-Bass, San Francisco.

Morgan, G. (1986) Images of Organization. Sage, London.

Mumford, E. (1991) Decision making and the organisational environment: today's problems and tomorrow's needs, in *Environments for supporting decision processes* (eds. H. G. Sol and J. Vecsenyi) Elsevier, Amsterdam.

Nappelbaum, E. (1997) Systems logic for problem formulation and choice. *This volume.*

Nelson, D. (1980) Frederick W. Taylor and the rise of scientific management. University of Wisconsin Press, Madison.

Paprika, Z. and Zoltay, A. (1994) The Current Hungarian Business Climate. BEAMS Doc. UR-RR-006, Department of Business Economics, Budapest University of Economic Sciences, Budapest.

Phillips, L. D. (1989) People-centred group decision support, in *Knowledge based management support systems* (eds. G. Doukidis, F. Land and G. Miller) Wiley, Chichester.

Phillips, L. D., 1992. Gaining corporate commitment to change, in *Executive information systems and decision support* (ed. C. Holtham) Chapman and Hall, London.

Richter, G., Humphreys, P.C., Voss, K., Berkeley, D., Genrich, H., Domke, M., Griebler, H. and Wisudha, A. (1987) GOFOR: Generic Office Frame of Reference. Annex to Final report, ESPRIT project 56. CEC, Brussels. (Abbreviated version published as Chapter 4 in G. Schafer (ed),*op. cit)*

Rose, N. (1989) Governing the soul: The shaping of the private self. Routledge, London:

Schafer, G. (1988). Functional Analysis of Office Requirements: A multiperspective approach. Wiley, Chichester.

Taylor, F. W. (1947) Scientific Management. Harper and Row, New York.

Ulrich, W. (1988) Systems thinking, systems practice and practical philosophy: A programme of research. *Systems Practice,* **1,** 137-163.

Vari, A., Rohrbaugh, J. and Baaklini, A. I. (1992) Decision conferencing GDSS in the Hungarian Parliament: A case of systems planning, In *Decision Support systems: Experiences and expectations* (eds. T. Jelassi, M. R. Klein and W. M. Mayon-White) Elsevier, Amsterdam.

Vari, A, and Vecsenyi, J. (1984) Selecting decision support methods in organisations. *Journal of applied systems analysis,* **11,** 25-36.

Willis, P. (1980) Notes on method, in *Culture, media, language* (eds. Hall, S., D. Hobson, A. Lowe and P. Willis) Hutchinson, London.

Wrege, C. D. and Greenwood, R. G. (1991) Frederick W. Taylor, the father of scientific management: Myth and reality. University of Illinois press, Homewood, Illinois.

Yetton, P. and Crawford, M.· (1992) Reassessment of participative decision making: a case of too much participation, in *Decision making and Leadership* (ed. F. Heller) Cambridge university press, Cambridge.

de Zeeuw, G. (1993) Soft knowledge accumulation and the rise of competence. *Systems Practice,* **5,** 192-215.

de Zeeuw, G. and Schuurman, J. G. (1997) Support as intervention in decision processes. *This volume.*

7 BIOGRAPHY

Patrick Humphreys is a founding member of IFIP working group 8.3. He is Professor of Social Psychology at the London School of Economics and Political Science, where he convenes graduate courses on Organisational Social Psychology, Decision Making and Decision Support Systems and the Social Psychology of the Media. He led the LSE teams on CEC ESPRIT projects on *Functional Analysis of Organisational Requirements* and on *Project Integrated Management Systems* and directed the CEC TEMPUS project *BEAMS - Business Economics and Management Support* and many other projects on decision making, organisational process modelling, networking and communication support. His books include *How Voters Decide*, *Analysing and Aiding Decision Processes*, *Effective Decision Support Systems*, *Exploring Human Decision Making* and *Software Development Project Management: Process and Support.*

Eric L. Nappelbaum is Vice Chancellor at the Moscow School for Business of Political Science and Law and Research Director at the Moscow Institute of System Analysis, faculty of Operational Research. He studied Physics and Computer Sciences at the Moscow State University and did his PhD on Control

Problems at the Moscow Physical Technical Institute. Dr Eric L. Nappelbaum is member of All Russian Academy of Science , Department of Operational Research and IT Strategy. Dr Eric Nappelbaum has published more than 40 international papers. He is Visiting Professor at the London School of Economics and Political Science and at the International Management Centre in Budapest. The research interests of Dr Nappelbaum include Organisational Transformation, System Analysis and System Logic.

5
How right is wrong

M. Schlumberger
Cap Gemini Innovation
Les Jardins de Maupertuis
Bat. Karelian - 7 Chemin de la Dhuy
38240 Meylan, France
Tel +33 76 76 47 77 Fax +33 76 76 47 48
e-mail mschlumb%cgsmail@capgemini.fr

Abstract

Experience shows that in many cases it is better to reach the « *wrong* » decision rather than wait for the « right » one, specially when there exist mechanisms to monitor the outcome of the decision and support the improvement of both this outcome and the decision making process itself. This paper shows practical examples from various sources to develop this theme.

Keywords

East Europe, decision making, reporting and monitoring, process improvement, changing short term mentalities.

1 INTRODUCTION

This paper is based on experiences both personal and reported. It came to being written after the "collapse" of the so-called socialist systems in Eastern Europe. Having had the opportunity to work there with decision making experts, it became evident that only some parts of the system needed improvement, in my mind mostly because the system insisted on reaching the right decision only. Many similar situations that could greatly benefit from allowing for errors can be found elsewhere, including of course in Western Europe.

- In the first section this paper surveys some of the advantages of reaching the "right" decision in a given situation, as well as gives a few caveats to many reward systems that are associated with this approach.
- The second section develops the reporting and monitoring issues, showing that these have in fact a profound pavlovian impact on how people behave in day to day situations.

- The third section builds the central idea of the paper, that nothing is ever always right, and that it generally is better to be able to cope with wrong decisions than to impose to (and bear with) be always right.
- The next section focuses on the improvement issues, of the decisions themselves, but also of the processes used to reach those decisions.
- This is followed by a conclusion summing up the main points and messages, as well as indicating points of further interest.

A decision here is considered as more than just having an idea. A decision has some visible (big or small) effects on the world at large.

2 MAKING THE RIGHT DECISION

Many, if not most cultures take pride in insisting that it is essential to do one's utmost to reach the "right" decision. Hence possibly the flourish of the so-called "Decision Support Systems", be they anywhere from simple Information Systems, to fancy Organization Transformation Support Systems (Humphreys, 1989).

Reaching this "right" decision can be a matter of life and death in many cases, such as driving one's car or reaching a medical diagnosis. Many school tests are examples where the difference between right and wrong can be quite expensive, in time, in money, in opportunities. Hence we are expected to take to heart finding this "right decision". Yet costs associated with achieving this proper choice may be out of balance in view of the expected results, and there are cases, at least in the Western culture, where short-cuts can be accepted and are at times encouraged.

For instance, a well known (to students) statistical fluke in a many multiple-choice tests, is that one is often better off to randomly answer questions, hence get an average score, rather than not answer them, or, of course, always answering wrong.

Absolutely right or right now

Another example is deeply linked to the culture, where one is - or isn't - expected to answer a question quickly rather than accurately. This difference is specially visible when an American is faced with an Arab, East Asian or a Soviet environment where reaching the right decision is more important (for various reasons, such as not loosing face) than reaching any decision fast.

Western Culture, such as the "typical" American one, strongly pushes people to reach a decision quickly, and accepts in many cases that this decision may be flawed in the middle to long term (Phillips, 1992; Humphreys and Nappelbaum, 1997). It is considered normal in this sense for laws (and even "constitutions") to change, and for politicians to modify their position on issues. It is accepted that other professions can also make "mistakes", and there are many instances and methods to correct these.

> Driving is a case we all know, where when you reach a fork in the road, you must choose a turn. If you keep the course, while deciding on the best option, you crash.

This paper tries to explain the consequences of this difference in attitude towards reaching a decision on organisations. Most of this difference does not seem to be ingrained, but rather probably comes from the global organisational attitudes towards failure, imposed, or reinforced within organisations, by the reporting and monitoring schemes. A similar attitude can be observed in organisations undergoing change, as shown elsewhere (Schlumberger, 1994).

3 REPORTING AND MONITORING

A previous paper (Schlumberger 1994) has shown that reporting and monitoring within an organisation reinforce specific attitudes in people reporting their results and being monitored. The Hawthorne experiments already showed this in the late 1920s (Roethlisberger and Dickson, 1939), with the often told conclusion:

you improve what you measure (or at least pay attention to)

When setting up reporting schemes, organisations should decide whether they want their stake-holders to reach the *right* decision, or simply to reach a *reasonable* one, the difference having far-reaching consequences both on the behaviour of the people concerned and on that of the organisation, internally and externally. Most organisations rarely if ever make this choice consciously, and obviously they do not realise the full consequences of such a choice.

In many cases, we are faced with the « street light syndrome[1] » where reporting focuses on easy to obtain figures rather than on relevant ones. Reporting sales is relatively easy, but a company lives on margins not on sales. Determination of real margins is more difficult, and less often reported!

This occurs much more frequently than one would expect, with as a consequence that people focus on getting good figures for reporting rather than on getting the deed done as well as possible. One old but still valid example is that of the « Great

---

[1] So, late one evening you meet this drunkard kneeling in the gutter, under a street lamp, obviously looking for something:
- What are you doing there?
- Oh I'm looking for my car key, I lost it when I locked my car.
- But where is your car? I don't see it, why don't you look next to your car?
- My car is down there, but there is no bloody light nest to the car!

leap forward » in China, where one of the success measure was the gross production of pig iron, which did, in deed boost, but that came to nothing, in part because of the very low quality of the results.

Another example is linked to the measure of « productivity » most often used for software: KLODC (line of code delivered per day per person), which pleads for the insertion of neutral lines, safe, won't do any harm, but will boost the « productivity » figure.

Pavlov conducted his most famous experiments on dogs, but his conclusions apply to people in organisations, in ways that both the organisation and the concerned individuals are usually unaware of (Homans, 1961). The measurements used in organisations push people to do what is needed in order to improve the readings, pretty much independently of the ultimate benefits incurred.

The next section shows the importance of focusing on the ultimate goals of the organisation, hence on accepting that issues may be at a given time monitored negatively, yet keeping an environment where some mistakes can be accepted socially!

4 MAKING A WRONG DECISION

In all cases, a "wrong" decision is not as "good" as a "right" one, so why argue about this? The answer is quite simple and lies both in the time it takes to reach a decision and on the real consequences of not having any decision, or worse, any one willing to make a decision, and to take responsibility.

> The example of reaching a fork in the road is a simple one that reinforces the message. The faster you drive, the faster you have to decide, in order to survive. A « bad » decision (taking the wrong turn) is much better than no decision (crashing the car).

Giving someone responsibility for something implies allowing, accepting that this person makes mistakes on the issue. This is in fact much more than a jest. It really should mean (although we shall soon see it does not always) what it says, i.e. when someone is responsible, this person can also make mistakes, this is part of the assignment!

Most organisations, be they social or business oriented, recognise that people "naturally" make mistakes. Suffice it to see the importance given to atoning for one's sins in most if not all religions, i.e. these religions have placed a process whereby they accept the mistakes (in their definition) made by people and give a way to recover from these. Religions that do not forgive or allow people somehow to recover from their sins have few followers.

Reaching the "wrong" decision is a common occurrence while the consequences of this decision depend in part on the immediate environment where this decision was reached, and in part on the way its consequences are treated later on. A decision that is deemed « wrong » at a given time can turn into the right one later!

Before going any further in this discussion, one should be fully aware that "no decision" is, in all cases, a decision, i.e. keeping the current orientations has its own set of consequences. For many people not rocking the boat is no decision, and is easier than any kind of decision.

> Sailing is another example, where when a craft is going towards some danger, no decision is in practice a very dangerous course to follow!

A common misconception is that you can delay making a decision. In fact, in most cases, this simply prolongs the *status quo*, which, in itself, already is a decision, with its usual set of consequences. *Not making a decision is making one!* One way around this issue is to have a regular change of direction by default, which forces the issue of keeping the current track.

> This is for instance what is done in modern freeway design, where there are no long straight lines, but regular wide curves, that force the driver to stay alert and in active control of her car.

Yet many environments, not least the educational one, strongly push for only reaching the « right » decision, and avoiding an answer to a question rather than giving the "wrong" one, which does not prepare for real life situations.

Time is more and more « of the essence », both because there is less time available to reach a decision (think of the driving or sailing analogies above), but also because, as the environment evolves faster and faster, the right decision under today's conditions has a good chance of being the wrong one for tomorrow.

A simple consequence of this continuous change is that the longer you ponder your decision, the more chances there are that it will **not** be right when you reach it, as external circumstances will have changed by then. Many decision making and decision analysis practitioners have had to come to terms with this!

In a fast changing environment, you do much better with a reasonable decision taken for the short term (which could known to be bad in the long term), along with some monitoring system in order to make sure that whatever needs to be done to keep up with the environmental modifications, is done, rather than sticking with some long term choice that will most presumably start and stay bad.

This pushes for a reinforced dichotomy between the means and the end, whereby the immediate decisions reflect on the means to be taken now , that must change in time, and corrected when necessary, while the end, the purpose, the objective stays constant over a longer period.

Responsibility for achieving a specific end must be given relatively independently of the means used to reach this end (within ethical and resource bounds of course). Overall responsibility for reaching a goal implies acceptance and support from the hierarchy of the (possibly) « wrong » decisions taken to reach it. People are to be judged on results before being judged on means, even if it is much easier to evaluate the current means spent than the end to come. Responsibility is also a matter of trust.

handing over responsibility implies acceptance of mistakes

5 IMPROVEMENT OF THE RESULTS AND THE PROCESS

"Wrong" decisions are common. If people are restricted to "right" decisions, they naturally avoid taking decisions and responsibilities as much as possible, as this avoidance entails fewer personal risks, and personal consequences than taking a "wrong" decision.

Rather than limiting people to reaching the "right" decision, hence leading to decision avoidance, with all of its consequences (driving has been used as an example, but politics is another well described one), it is better to accept the fact that « wrong » decisions are made, and to have the organisation cope with this.

The two main aspects of coping can be described as:

- Improvement by eventual change of the decisions, in view of its results, and
- Definition and improvement of a full decision making process that monitors decisions and their results, in order to allow for the improvement of the results.

These two aspects are further described below.

Improvement of results

The issue here is to accept decisiòns, whatever they are, and to focus on improving their results.

"You improve what you measure" could be a conclusion of the Hawthorne set of experiments, or a re-wording of a famous quote from Lord Rutherford.

This is so true that, for instance in software development, measuring the results in terms of lines of code produces... mostly lines of code, that as often as not have little relevance to the problem to be solved (Jeffery and Lawrence, 1979)!

Organizations that want to improve the results of decisions must monitor these results. The earlier the consequences of a « bad » decision are found, the more one can do about it. Yet some of the reluctance shown towards accepting bad decisions, may be linked to the reluctance of some organisations to monitor their own effectiveness in an objective way.

> A classical case has been that of governments trying to lower unemployment rates (instead of unemployment). When unemployment stays at high levels, two common solutions are first to change the definition of unemployment, generally lowering the "official" rate, or second, to ignore the results, describing these as irrelevant to the current economic or whatever situation.

Once results are properly monitored, and only very few organisations actually seem do so in serious terms (there is a legal obligation to monitor the financial results, mostly for tax purposes though, which is not always the best incentive), can these organisations start to monitor the influence of decisions and work on improvements.

Despite the trend to play ostrich, most organisations have found that monitoring improves results, and insist on reporting schemes that could allow them to find, fast and effectively, what is actually going on. Yet, given the flood of data streaming in, there is a chance that most of it is simply ignored, unless some automatic monitoring system is there that at least reports grossly out of line results.

In all cases, improving the result implies that challenging the current course followed (after a decision) is an accepted fact of the social life of the organisation. Most organisations do not accept such challenges, as they can wreak havoc with their internal workings. Yet consensus-based organisations have a much easier time to challenge continually the course followed than do authoritarian organisations. Without accepting this continuous challenge, any improvement is very difficult.

Improving the result normally implies, beyond measuring the actual result you want to improve, improving the process that reaches this result. Indeed, as mentioned above, in most cases, current processes do not condone, or even accept "bad" results, hence must be improved before this can be done. This process improvement is the topic of the next section.

Improvement of process

In order to allow for "bad" decisions, and to be able to improve on them, most organisations must improve their current decision making and evaluating process, and all must continually improve this process. Yet, the current process typically the result of such a "bad" set of decisions! This section elaborates on this process improvement issue, by giving the general guidelines of such an improvement and the sort of process resulting from such an effort.

The Software Engineering Institute (SEI) in Pittsburgh at the instigation of the US Department of Defence, which wanted to improve the quality of the software it outsourced, has formalised five levels of Software Development Process in an organisation, that can pretty much be applied to any decision making process (Humphrey, 1988). Reworded, these are:

- Nothing: there is no such process known
- Aware: There is a process, somewhere,
- Repeatable: a process can be done a second time around
- Defined: a process is known and explainable
- Optimised: the process is continuously measured and improved upon.

Practical experience has shown that you can go from your current level up one at a time, no more. Experience also has led SEI to refine its definitions and assessment methods, as well as focal points that help an organisation going from one stage to the next.

This change in the SEI model reinforces the point of the paper: the issue is not to have the right answer, but an answer that is confronted to reality and improved accordingly. Improving an organisational process thus requires first the awareness that such a process exists, and then at least an attempt at the understanding and formalisation of the process. Once this is formalised (and the use of computer based process management tools is pushing a number of organisations in this direction), improvements can be thought and tried out.

In the same line of improvement, one must recognise that the current situation depends on past decisions (both active and passive), and that, in order to judge the validity of these previous decisions, one must know which ones are currently at stake. *Keep a log of decisions (active and passive ones) and reasons for those.*

Then, if the judgement to be applied is a commercial (or say a political) one, decisions should be judged on this measure, and no other. There are no "good" or "bad" decisions, in commercial terms (or political) there are "beneficial" or "expensive" ones, and each can be measured. In order to improve the decision process, one should at least try to find the "objective" causes for costly decisions, these are usually linked to the environment, not to the people who "decide".

Organizations, as well as people within them have to accept socially and psychologically that decisions often are flawed, and that this should not systematically bear on decision makers. The process improvement is concerned with improving the chances of reaching good decisions (as compared to always reaching the right decisions), as well as minimising the consequences of a bad one in the short and long term.

The decision « log » will help in many ways: it will explain why a given decision was reached, and will force the next decision makers to consciously choose to approve or disapprove it on valid grounds. It will also serve as a basis for formulating the decision process and eventually improving it, again on a sound basis.

6 CONCLUSION

This paper has shown how the organisational pressure to always be right is both unrealistic in its expectations and in it consequences: people do and will continue to make mistakes, and when pushed not to make them, they will abstain from any initiative. Organisations should focus instead on accepting this foible and improving both the decision making process and the uptake of decision. A few salient points have been made, to be used by organisations that are intent on improving their attitude towards decision making:

- Accept "wrong decisions", and work with, instead of against them: monitor them and improve (if given a chance), not changing the current course **is** such a decision.
- Improve process to accept these, evaluate results, and make certain things improve
- Focus on difficulties in changing the short term mentalities in evaluation of results, this will make it easier to progress towards set goals that reinforce the strength/purposes of the organisation.

7 ACKNOWLEDGEMENTS

Acknowledgements are due to Patrick, Zita and Feco.

8 REFERENCES

Homans, G. (1961) Social behaviour: Its elementary forms. Harcourt Brace, New York.

Humphrey, W. S. (1988) Characterising the software process: A maturity framework. *IEEE Software*, **5**, 73-79

Humphreys, P. C. (1989) Intelligence in decision support, *in Knowledge based management support systems* (eds. G. Doukidis, F. Land and G. Miller), Ellis Horwood, Chichester.

Humphreys, P. C. and Nappelbaum, E. L. (1997) Structure and communications in the process of organisational change: Eastern European experience and its general relevance. *This volume*

Jeffery, D. R. and Lawrence, M. J. (1979) An inter-organisational comparison of programming productivity, in Proceedings of the 4th ICSE, Munich, pp. 369-377, IEEE Catalogue No. 79CH1479-5C

Phillips, L. D. (1992) Gaining corporate commitment to change, *in Executive information systems and decision support* (ed. C. Holtham) Chapman and Hall, London.

Roethlisberger F. J. and Dickson, W. J. (1939) Management and the worker. Harvard University Press, Cambridge, Mass.

Schlumberger, M (1994). Project Management considered as an impediment to change. Proceedings of the IFIP WG8.3 conference on Decision Support and Organizational Transformation, San Sebastian, Spain.

9 BIOGRAPHY

Maurice Schlumberger is Scientific Director of Cap Gemini Innovation, scientific research centre of Cap Gemini. He has directed many projects on software development, and information systems and project management systems development..

6

Support as intervention in decision processes

G. de Zeeuw
Centre for Innovation and Cooperative Technology
University of Amsterdam
Valckenierstraat 65, 1018 XE Amsterdam
The Netherlands
Tel: +31 20 5256338, Fax: +31 20 5255778,
e-mail: zeeuw@phys.uva.nl

J. G. Schuurman
Technical University of Twente
Faculty of Instructional Technology
P.O.Box 217, 7500 AE Enschede
The Netherlands
Tel: + 31 53 4894201, Fax: +31 53 4892895
e-mail: schuurman@edte.utwente.nl

Abstract

People's activities tend to deviate in many ways from what are considered 'rational' theories of decision making. In trying to interpret these deviations increasingly complex theories have been formulated. The deviations may also be interpreted, more simply, as a falsification of the method used for their study. This paper suggests a different approach to the study of decision making: decision theory should be considered as an element of the class of action languages, that is of languages that support the improvement of individual and collective actions.

Keywords

Decision, support, research, language, qualification, skill, collective, actorship

1 INTRODUCTION

Decision theory aims to help people improve on their action, by adding the possibility of a choice. The theory formalises the option of comparing actions and choosing or selecting what in some way is 'best'. This option may be implemented in different ways: with the help of a decision analyst, or through organisations that help clients access the resources needed to make a choice. Machines that are programmed to do the same are among such organisations: they can help to retain the observations and produce the events that people need to make decisions.

It is in the sense of adding a choice that one can say that decision theory was developed to support people. It was intended as a theory for improving on actions. It aims to help explore available resources and to formulate recommendations for their use. To accept such support will require some guarantee that an improvement can be realised. A guarantee implies the notion of quality. Two forms may be distinguished. One is based on the notion of qualification. The other on the notion of skill. Both types are needed–together and interactively.

Qualification refers to the insight that adding a choice is an act of choice itself: it may detract as well as add to one's actions*. One may come to regret–post-decisionally–the choice made, in the same sense that one may come to regret the use of the wrong medicine. There are other reasons for lack of quality: one may not be sufficiently skilled, and unable to capture exhaustively the resources to use, or to select what is 'best'. Lack of skill usually implies that learning to use decision theory did require too much effort, so one may become too hasty in making choices.

The literature on decisions seems mainly concerned with increases in skill, and not with qualification. People are assumed to be qualified under any circumstance. This suggests that decision theory is not used as a theory for people to add choices to their actions, but as a theory of individuals who make decisions. This suggestion is in line with the questions that researchers have tried to answer: how well do people do in comparison to the theory, when do people deviate from the theory (Klein et al, 1992, Beach and Lipshitz, 1992; Tversky and Kahnemann, 1981)?

Lack of attention to qualification may explain the ambiguity that often appears to creep into the interpretation of results. What if decision makers do not automatically structure improvement in terms of decision theory (Watson, 1992)? What if people deviate from what the theory prescribes? Without knowledge of qualifications no judgement of skill is possible. Without it one can detect deviations, but not explain them–except through vague notions like personal experience or context. And also, if one can not predict deviations, one will be prone to find additional ones.

The issue of qualification is not restricted to the notion and techniques of decision making. Doubts have been expressed regarding the possibility of qualification in

---

* The so-called 'frame-problem' is well-known in the field of artificial intelligence (Boden, 1979). An early statement of the issue of qualification appears in De Zeeuw and W).

operational research and in cybernetics (Taket and White, 1993; Rosenhead, 1989), as well in problem solving (De Zeeuw, 1993*). Each discipline appears able to boast examples where users appear qualified without apparent effort. Each also has to admit to cases where becoming qualified seems to be rather an arbitrary, high-handed affair, requiring one to impose or 'force' people to qualify.

Organisations provide many examples of 'forcing' people into pre-defined qualifications. Given their prevailing division of labour they assign the task of making decisions. In this case, if employees become skilled in the techniques of decision making (such as estimating probabilities, assessing values and computing recommendations), they must be high quality decision makers–as they then combine both qualification and skill. The organisation that originally bestowed the qualification may go broke, of course, having divided its labour ineffectively.

In recent years the possibility of turning the results of decision research into support has developed into an industry. However, preferring the search for theories of, over theories for, does not seem to have been a detour only. It still is part of the present academic interest, as opposed to a sole interest in support as theories for (although there is attention to friendly computer interfaces: Larichev, et al., 1990). This has important implications, including the possibility that the industry is one which aims first to 'program' people to qualify as decision makers, second to provide the tools they then need**.

In this paper we will consider how to avoid this form of imposition as well as judge the quality of what is offered. This implies having to explore approaches to research which take the notion of qualification as central. Such research obviously will not be classical, as the latter assumes that qualifications are 'given' (by nature). It also may not be research, in the sense that it may prove impossible to suggest qualifications that are not in some way preferred by the researcher, identifying the latter as a politician rather than a researcher. Fortunately as it turns out, there is an in between.

The paper is set up as follows. First, we will introduce two examples to clarify the role of qualification (section 2). Secondly, we will re-interpret the examples in terms of classical science, and present a re-formulation of the re-interpretation to facilitate thinking about it (section 3). Thirdly, we will indicate some consequences: what the reformulating implies in terms of the process of research (section 4), and in terms of the characteristics of its results (section 5). Finally, and by way of a conclusion, the argument of the paper is summarised (section 6).

---

* The issue of qualification as regards problem solving has been dismissed by Newell (1990).

** The analogy with the tobacco industry seems unavoidable.

2 EXAMPLES

In this section we present two examples that appear extreme relative to the notion of research. The first example derives from the work of Fischhoff (1992). It is intended to show that research that interprets decision theory as a theory *of* individual behaviour fails in the sense that support in terms of a theory *for* would have been more appropriate. The second example deals with an area similar to that explored by Fischhoff. The example does not make use of decision theory, although the results of the study also were intended to support improvement of action.

Fischhoff (1992) is interested in supporting women to prevent or evade rape. He proceeds by assuming that women are to be seen as instances of some 'hypothetical individual', acting as a decision maker. The instances will differ among themselves of course but will have some common characteristics: by increasing their decision making skills they will be able to improve their actions and prevent being harmed. Fischhoff intends to provide recommendations concerning what alternatives to choose, what probabilities to estimate, what values to assess.

The first step involved collecting possible options–from which to develop advice–from the literature as well as from various groups of people: (female) 'students at the University of Oregon; alumnae of the University (all over 40 years of age); and mothers belonging to a parenting program, largely from low-income homes. We also had samples from male students, paralleling the female ones, and samples of sexual assault experts, drawn nationally from private consultants, criminal justice personnel, counsellors, and researchers' (p. 579).

The resulting set of 'options for reducing the chance of being raped' totalled more than 1,100. Next it was attempted to reduce this set in terms of 'good' decision making, by re-writing each option as advice to "Doing action X in order to achieve intended effect Y". It was tried to identify consequences Y, and to estimate their probabilities, for example on the basis of reports from women in 'rape crisis centres, self-defence instructors, hospital emergency room personnel, crime reporters, sex offender therapists, and national victimisation surveys'.

It proved impossible to perform a 'comprehensive analysis', and 'infeasible' to find one advice or strategy (or a small set) which could be 'believed to reduce the risk of rape', and nothing else. There was no 'best possible strategy for a particular individual in a particular situation', in the form of 'simple rules, capturing some of the wisdom of decision theory, which they [the women] might apply to their personal situations'. The material collected did not show how becoming more skilled as a decision maker might help to prevent or evade rape.

This failure is especially striking as there was no warning. Proper research procedures were followed. The number of observations was sufficient to apply the usual methods of analyses, without the need for further observations. The study even can be seen as more extensive than standard studies in the area. A reason for the failure is suggested however. Each woman herself might have to '[c]onsider where [she] might fit in' the material collected, rather than accept classification by the researcher as an instance of the 'hypothetical' decision maker.

This suggestion appears to indicate that Fischhoff in the end changed his mind. Women came to be seen as *users* rather than instances. They are not the *object* of study, nor their actions. They become the *addressees*: their understanding and subsequent action depends on whether they feel addressed by some advice (counsellors and others might feel addressed as well). Recommendations thus should now serve mainly as an 'aid in coping with [a stressful topic]', and as injunctions to 'keep thinking', or organise 'one's thinking'–in a process of awareness raising.

The difficulties Fischhoff encountered appear to be due to the use of decision theory as a theory *of*. He recognises that his users reject this and take his results as a context to express themselves, that is as a theory *for*, or a suggested qualification. His recommendations thus became a *system*, an entity that survives only given that it is used by users. Survival therefore is not guaranteed. It is in the interest of the system to make *access free* (users do not 'pay'), and to honour use–by helping to structure 'one's thinking' (the system 'pays'). This becomes explicit in the following example.

Van den Berge et al (1980) consider the plight of homosexual men who run the risk of being beaten up by 'potenrammers', people who gang up with the explicit purpose of harming them. Their plight is somewhat similar to that of the women in Fischhoff's study. They do not want to be beaten up, but also do not want to prepare themselves by becoming experts in karate, or by not making use of streets and parks. The cost of the latter type of preparation is seen as too high–as would be the cost of 'reduc[ing] men's propensity to rape', and of 'creat[ing] full employment', suggested in the Fischhoff study.

Van den Berge et al (1980) do not assume homosexuals to be decision makers. They rather become 'qualified' as 'victims'–by the hunter-like behaviour of the 'potenrammers'. As victims they appear unable to think of anything but being beaten. It seemed necessary to change this 'qualification', rather then to make the homosexuals more skilled–in running, or in fighting, or in getting protection. It turned out that there were anecdotes about this change. These were collected, as many as possible, and rewritten while being tested on 'ease of understanding', 'grippingness', etc.

One of the anecdotes is about someone who is walking alone in the park. When noticing that he attracts the attention of some 'potenrammers', he starts to dance and flap his arms and yell 'Pewit, I am a bird'. His assailants walk away in disgust. He is mad, and no longer of interest. The change implies a change in qualification: from homosexual 'victim' to 'mad person'. This change requires little training and physical investment, but has large (and desirable) effects. A selection from the anecdotes was published. Some 1500 copies were sold in Amsterdam.

Interviews with some of those who had bought a copy indicated that the effect was as intended. The anecdotes were not interpreted as (repeatable) solutions to a problem or as general strategies. Rather, they introduced a 'way of thinking'. This was facilitated by their form or structure: a situation was described, then a danger, then a change in the interpretation, then the surprising consequences of the change.

Anecdotes are, of course, quite near to the 'moral tales' that help people use to 'extract lessons' (as Fischhoff mentions). Most cultures cherish them.

After some years the anecdotes no longer were talked about in Amsterdam. Also, if there was any lasting reduction in the number of beatings, this effect may have been due to more general social changes or become embedded in them. The study is summarised here only as it shows an approach opposite to Fischhoff's study: the authors aimed to address people so they might adapt their qualifications to become 'instantly' skilled using their experience. The authors did not intend to train people in skills they might lack assuming a *fixed* social 'qualification' (such as a lack of strong friends).

3 RESEARCH AND QUALIFICATION

The paper by Fischhoff has been published in a high status journal (the American Psychologist). It is set well within the academic tradition. Adherence to that tradition is confirmed when Fischhoff claims that 'one should no more expose people to untested advice than to untested medicine' (p. 583). But in the end his work seems to burst out of that tradition. His concluding statements rather apologetically claim results to be but an 'aid to coping', 'lessons', something to be 'considered'–statements one would not expect in connection to *tested* medicine.

Van den Berge et al clearly start where Fischhoff ends. The authors aim to provide lessons, and to reduce the effort people must invest in learning skills. They end by realising something at least very akin to their aim. Still, they did not achieve high academic status (although there have been related studies: Vahl, 1992; Van Haaster, 1991; Guinée, 1994; Kline, 1979). One reason may be that they did not 'burst out' of anything. From the start they intended to order their observations (responses in the form of stories) on the basis of a pre-selected and pre-conceived form, that of the anecdote.

Their approach clearly differs from the traditional one, although there are similarities: it does emphasise the need to order observations, to find out which observations belong together and can be combined into higher quality observations (e.g. averages, and theories). However, it does not stress the need to observe what makes observations belong together itself, as one would need to observe a 'scientific object'. It does not require that the ordering (as anecdotes) be chosen by 'nature', or reality*. This leaves the choice of an ordering more or less open.

One might conclude therefore that the work of Van den Berge et al is not scientific, or at least that it does not obviously fit the traditional mode. The authors chose the form of what makes observations (answers from respondents) belong together (the anecdote). This form is not an observable object itself therefore. The

---

* The notion of reality should not be taken as indicating some epistemological position. Wagenaar (1974

study thus does not satisfy the criteria of what is 'demarcated' as science and is not within the 'agreement or convention' proposed by Popper and others (for example Popper, 1959). Still, its results do not appear to be entirely useless.

It is possible to interpret the approach differently therefore. Anecdotes do transfer something when used as an 'aid in coping', as a 'lesson', etc. They even do two things: they *address* users, thereby orienting and *qualifying* them to *express* themselves in certain ways and not in others; they also indicate in what way the addressees can become *skilled* in expressing themselves. In this interpretation it is not the anecdote which is to be made visible. It is the way anecdotes make it possible for users to find coherence in new experiences, and to show and express what they can do.

At the basis of this type of expression is a linguistic structure or *language*, therefore: the double form of the anecdotes. Sentences in this language suggest qualifications as well as how to become skilful. Advice (as implied in the anecdotes) is thus not the same as a medicine and can not be tested as a medicine. It is not a particular effect one is after, but rather a change in a development, with a variety of effects. Or in other words: one does not test the consistency of the way the body's mechanism reacts to an input, as in the case of medicine, but rather its flexibility.

The notion of a language is not entirely strange to traditional science (Kuhn, 1962). Its results address users–who are thereby shown how to identify some object (become qualified to do so), and to observe variation in the properties of the objects' instances (become skilled to do so). To describe results in this way the language of *variables* is used. In terms of its purpose this language is effective and efficient. There are some dangers as well. Its use can impose 'objectness' as an inflexible qualification, in particular when it proves impossible to identify objects in a more traditional sense.

To deal with this type of situation other languages developed. They do not impose objectness, but rather allow their users to express themselves *as if* they are objects. Users thus have to maintain their 'objectness' themselves, but also may choose a language that helps to realise objects with preferred properties. This suggests the possibility of a test as in traditional science: whether for example the form of an anecdote (and its instances) can help addressees to 'express' themselves and not get beaten up. If anecdotes fail this test one should look for other forms.

Awareness of the importance of 'addressing' seems to be relatively general. For example, it often happens that the results of a commissioned study are not used–which can be explained through the notion of 'addressing' (Vahl, 1992). Usually commissioners are familiar only with the language of variables. Results thus may become based on an imposition of objectness. When they are made available, employees may disagree, and start to modify what 'belonged together'. The more they achieve their own preferred expression, the more they reduce the validity of the commissioned results.

The dangers involved in un-informed 'addressing' seem especially clear in the case of organisations 'undergoing profound change', and having to re-structure in the 'transition'. Members may feel addressed both by proposed structures and by the 'theory for' needed to realise those structures. They may resist or comply with the qualifications involved. A series of interactions between individuals thus may ensue in which none of the earlier qualifications remains, so all previous skills become useless. The organisation may be worse off than before.

Humphreys and Kirtsoglou (1997) note the ubiquity of 'addressing' in all social spheres. They describe for example how a drug peddler is outfaced by a client in daily life. Two types of languages appear involved. One is the language of *scarcity*: the drug peddler not only manipulates prices but also the expectations of those he will sell to. The client uses the language of *access*: she indicates that she is used to better quality than is being sold. When she succeeds in having the peddler accept her 'qualification', he loses the one in which he was skilled, and has to lower his prices.

The use of a language implies a collective in which the language is used. Members of this collective can be addressed and will respond. They can not be taken for 'objects' of traditional science, but the collective can. The more observations on the collective begin to belong together, the more stable the members of the collective respond to each other. This implies that the collective can be studied in the way of traditional science. Results will include what language is used to establish the collective, and how this language relates to other, desired properties of the collective*.

Although it could be argued that the study by Van den Berge et al is not inside science, the above seems to show that this is predicated mainly on the anecdotes themselves being seen as scientific 'object'. Another interpretation takes the collective of the addressees of the anecdotes as the object. Each addressee will be qualified in terms of the collective. If the distribution of qualifications stabilises, the collective stabilises. The anecdote quoted above describes for example how to become qualified as 'mad': by creating and stabilising a collective mainly through the use of body language.

Decision theory has been argued to fail when studied as a theory *of* decisions concerning rape (section 2). It can be re-interpreted as a theory *for* in the sense of Van den Berge et al's anecdotes. This would lead to studies of the properties of the collective that results when its members address and qualify each other as decision makers. It is the *form* of decision theory that matters here, not the content. The 'aid in coping' should thus be tested in terms of its ability to influence the attacker's 'thinking', to change and add a choice to the attacker's actions (Beach, 1993; Steier, 1991).

---

* As is to be expected a number of such languages has developed, in daily life and elsewhere, without explicit testing in research. An interesting example is the language using the notion of system: it is used in research, as well as in the development of collectives that seem to have little connection with research, for example based on the use of certain techniques (Checkland and Scholes, 1990, and others).

4 FORMS OF RESEARCH

The re-interpretation in the previous section suggests that one see the results of the study by Van den Berge et al (1980) as 'scientific', and those from the Fischhoff (1992) study as 'failed scientific', or possibly as non-scientific, in contrast to what appeared to be the case at first sight. The results of the latter study seem to be due to a too uncritical use of decision theory as a theory *of*. This kind of use warranted various apologies, the gist of which was that the results should function only as stimulants, to highlight what is useful in the experience of their users.

The re-interpretation makes use of the notion of a collective. Although this could be interpreted as a 'scientific' object, it clearly does not refer to such an object in the traditional sense. It becomes such an object only if it certain events take place. Members have to address each other and to be addressed. This process is expected to result in two types of observable effects: the development of the collective, and of some stabilising form of exchange. It is the latter which now can be described as a theory *for*. It refers to what happens *inside* the collective.

A number of consequences may be noted, for example a partial reversal of the roles of observation and action in research. Traditional research is interested only in what can be described by a theory *of*. It is not interested in the use of such a theory, that is in theories *for* action which are based on theories *of*. In the re-interpreted approach there is such an interest: to create a collective one has to find a suitable theory *for*, suitable in the sense that it allows for the development of a theory *of* the resulting collective*. This theory may then be used in any action, that is become part of any theory *for*.

One may also consider the following. A basic element in traditional research is the search for high quality observations X, Y, Z, etc. Results take the form of statements in the language of variables: 'if observation X, then observation Y', given some object. Note that nothing is said about the improvement of action, only of observation. This is different in the re-interpreted form. Members of a collective aim to change their actions and observations and improve on them in the sense of achieving a preferred expression. Results take the form: 'if observation X, do action A'.

There is a big difference between the two types of statement. The first relates only to improved observations. These may support action, for example by making better visible when to do something. They can not say anything about action itself however, that is about its goals. The second relates to observations as well as actions. The former can be made 'better' if they 'belong together' given a particular action. The latter can also become 'better': if they contribute to establishing the collective. In this approach increasing quality is not restricted to observation.

We may re-consider decision theory in terms of the two types of statements. It takes as its output an action, that one that is selected from a set of actions. It takes

* This relation may be used as a criterion as well. The notion of orthogonality has been introduced (Higo, 1996; De Zeeuw, 1997).

as its input a series of estimates, that is of observations that may influence the choice of the action. These observations are taken to belong together in terms of the action to be taken. Statements in decision theory thus have the form: if observation X, do action A–precisely the form of what should help establish a collective. What does not seem to be clear yet is what properties this collective will have (Klein, 1992).

This formulation can be related to the way Fischhoff formulates advice: 'doing action [A] in order to achieve intended effect Y'. This form emphasises the effects of action A, made visible as high quality observations Y. In contrast the form 'if X, do A' specifies resources inside the collective, but does not indicate any immediate effects of A, as these may differ substantially from the effects of all A together*, that is from what is expressed through the collective. The link between the two types of effect is indirect** , rather than direct as Fischhoff seems to assume.

This separation of the immediate and mediate effects of actions by the members of a collective has an interesting consequence. The immediate effects should be usable only inside the collective. The mediate in any action, by anybody, including the members of the collective. If the latter are to profit from the mediate effects these should be full expressions of what the members can do, and should not be manipulated by them to be useful only for their actions inside the collections. In other words, being member of a collective should help avoid being corrupt*** .

Not becoming corrupt is not guaranteed, of course. Members may decide to defect from the collective, for example when they find the effort to maintain the collective too heavy. It will be the task of research to discover what language will minimise defection, and thus will be 'best' to prevent corruption. In an important series of experiments Axelrod (1984) seems to have demonstrated that defection is minimal when the language does not imply some stop or end to the collective. If the end would be known, members might prefer to defect before others do.

Although the differences between the traditional and the re-interpreted form of science are extensive, there also are similarities. Notions like objects and qualifications clearly are of a comparable nature, as are properties and skills. Both have similar roles. The first two notions relate to what can be generalised; the second two to what summarises the particular. A division of qualifications in a collective bestows *actorship* on its inside, given the constraints imposed by the collective, and also allows *objectship* to be achieved on the outside.

---

* This is the case especially when the number of participants is large.

** This difference is related to the notion of 'pluralism', as defined but not studied by Jackson (1990).

*** Although not explicitly developed to be used in this context, the notion of 'closure' may be mentioned here: it is used to indicate for example that what makes observations belong together should be observable itself.

5 JUDGING QUALITY

Even after noting that Fischhoff's (1992) work failed, and that his recommendations seem but apologies for this failure, it still may be rated highly, for two reasons. Firstly, the observations he collected are thought provoking. Secondly, he did create a story, or a series of lessons that people might do well to take to heart–notwithstanding the cost of implementing advice such as 'never drive alone'. This raises the question how to judge good advice. The most obvious source is to look at advice from the point of view of the re-interpreted approach to research.

Although there is no precise and generally accepted 'demarcation' to research, there is some consensus as to what it aims for. Results should not be characterised in terms of who is going to, or is allowed to use them. Later results should improve on earlier ones, that is it should be possible to accumulate results. Use should be inexpensive in the sense that further testing can be reduced (Rosen, 1993). It is on these criteria that Fischhoff's results seem to score relatively low, and those of Van den Berge et al relatively high (see previous section).

This raises the question how to achieve results that realise these aims–in all cases where one has to cope with disruptions, or breakdowns, such as being attacked or molested, having to face the competition, etc. Some suggestions seem in place. We will summarise them in terms of four puzzles (De Zeeuw, 1995): what observations to start from, how to operate on them to achieve high quality observations, how to justify them, and how to combine high quality observations so they satisfy the above criteria, e.g. not to exclude pre-specified groups of users.

The first suggestion is to interpret the notion of observation quite broadly. It may refer to any statement by those who are to participate in the research. Their quality should be increased in the process. This implies finding rules of the form 'if observation X, do A', for each participant. They may be found by introducing some language having this form, in the way of hypotheses, or by allowing participants to discover their own preferred language. When a collective develops, one should note its properties: what languages go together with what other characteristics.

The next step in the research process is of course to test whether rules that developed in one collective can be used to develop collectives elsewhere. Note that it may be possible that collectives develop that are not considered supportive in the sense used here: they do not necessarily lead to improvements of action that do not require effort, and are 'free' to all participants. Testing will be extremely important therefore: there may be a difference between what helps in the case of 'breakdowns', or to express new and culturally useful abilities.

This approach to research has a distinct Darwinian flavour. Results may increase in quality: languages may be found with growing 'carrying power', where what is 'carried' is a–speedy, effortless–recognition of what others in the collective do. Collectives based on such languages should be stable in many circumstances. This is not to say of course that progress will only go in the direction of generality: there may be languages that turn out to be 'best' in some circumstances, next to languages that have a wide range of applicability (as has the language of variables).

Returning again to the decision language, Watson (1992) has noted, for example, that in practice it often is replaced by other languages ('theories') that are characterised by the fact that they help to decrease the information processing load for users, or distribute memory requirements among those involved. The same type of development can be found in Fischhoff's work (Fischhoff, 1992; appendix B). General forms of advice such as 'question universal recommendations', or 'recognise lay expertise' no longer take the form of the language of decisions.

6 CONCLUSION

The starting point of this paper was the observation that although the origin of decision theory is supportive (a theory *for* rational action), the notion of support seemed to have been lost relatively early. Efforts to develop decision support still seem to be based on the interpretation of decision theory as a theory *of* rational action. An example was presented: the work of Fischhoff (1992). This interpretation seems to lead to failure, to ever larger numbers of variables (Beach, 1993). It was noted that there is a need for a return to the original notion of support to improve action.

To exemplify ways of satisfying this need another example was considered: the development of anecdotes as support systems. It was argued that the use of anecdotes may be considered 'non-scientific', but also that it can be seen as scientific. This re-interpretation makes heavy use of the notion of a collective, the inner structure of which is regulated by a language, and the outer structure of which is observable and can be used as a resource. These notions were developed in some detail, including the form which the languages may take.

In this way an answer was found to a dilemma: that Fischhoff's results have a high academic status but also seem to represent a failure of accepted research practice. The answer clarifies the characteristics of support systems, as well as how such systems may be implemented. The major shift it introduces concerns the transfer of observations: one should distinguish between transfer inside and outside a collective. Suggestions were made on how to stabilise this distinction: languages with high 'carrying power' can help to create new collectives out of those that face some breakdown.

7. REFERENCES

Axelrod, R. (1984) The evolution of co-operation. Basic Books, New York.

Beach, L. R. (1993) Four revolutions in behavioural decision theory, in *Leadership theory and research: perspectives and directions* (eds. M. M. Chemers and R. Ayman) Academic Press, San Diego.

Beach, L. R. and Lipshitz, R. (1992), Why classical decision theory is an inappropriate standard for evaluating and aiding most human decision making, in *Decision making in action: models and methods*. (eds. G. A. Klein, J. Orasanu, R. Calderwood, and C. E. Zsambok) Ablex, Norwood.

Berge, F. van den, Bossewinkel, W., Groeneveld, S., Muis, M. and Wildschut, H. (1980) Flikkers en agressie. Universiteit van Amsterdam, Amsterdam.

Boden, M. (1979) Artificial Intelligence and Natural Man. Basic Books, New York.

Checkland, P. and Scholes, J. (1990) Soft systems methodology in action. Wiley, Chichester.

Fischhoff, B. (1992) Giving advice: decision theory perspectives on sexual assault. *American Psychologist*, **47**, 577-588.

Guinée, I. (1994) Leiding nemen als optie. Thesis Publishers, Amsterdam.

Haaster, H. van (1991) Wartaal. Een onderzoek naar methoden van competentiev-erhoging in de geestelijke gezondheidszorg. Thesis, Amsterdam.

Higo, H. A.-W. (1996) *Research-based action in the process of socio-economic development in Sudan.* Unpublished Ph.D. University of Lincolnshire and Humberside, Lincoln.

Humphreys, P. and Kirtsoglou, E. (1997) Violence within the post-structural economy of shortage. Unpublished manuscript, London School of Economics, Department of Social Psychology.

Jackson, M. C. (1990) Beyond a system of systems methodologies. *Journal of the Operational Research Society*, **41**, 657-668.

Klein, G. A, Orasanu, J. , Calderwood, R. and Zsambok, C. E. eds. (1992) *Decision making in action: models and methods*. Ablex, Norwood.

Klein, G. A. (1992) Twenty questions-suggestions for research in naturalistic decision making, in *Decision making in action: models and methods*. (eds. G. A. Klein, J. Orasanu, R. Calderwood, and C. E. Zsambok), Ablex, Norwood.

Kline, E. (1979) Planning side-effects, in *Problems of context,* (eds. G. de Zeeuw and P. van den Eeden), Free University Press, Amsterdam.

Kuhn, T. S. (1962) The structure of scientific revolutions. University of Chicago Press, Chicago.

Larichev, O. I., Mechitov, A. I., Morgoev, V. K., Moshkovich, H. M. and Furems, E. M. (1990) .Exact duplicates of human judgements, in *Contemporary issues in decision making*. (eds. K. Borcherding, O. I. Larichev and D. M. Messick), North Holland, Amsterdam.

Newell, A. (1990) Unified theories of cognition. Harvard University Press, Cambridge, MA.

Popper, K. R. (1959) The logic of scientific discovery. Harper & Row, New York.

Rosen, R. (1993) Some random thoughts about chaos and some chaotic thoughts about randomness. *Journal of Biological Systems,* **1**, 19-27.

Rosenhead, J. (ed.) (1989) Rational Analysis for a problematic world. Wiley, Chichester.

Steier, F. (ed.) (1991) Research and Reflectivity. Sage, London.

Taket, A., and White, L. (1993) After OR; an agenda for postmodernism and poststructuralism in OR. *Journal of the Operational Research Society* **44,** 867-883.

Tversky, A. and Kahnemann D. (1981) The framing of decision and the psychology of choice. *Science* **211,** 453-458.

Vahl, M. (1992) Stories and scientific enquiry, in *Cybernetics and systems research '92*. (ed. R. Trappl), World Scientific, Singapore.

Watson, S. R. (1992) The presumptions of prescription. *Acta Psychologica*, **80,** 7-31.

Zeeuw, G. de and Wagenaar, W. A. (1974) Are subjective probabilities probabilities?, in *The concept of probability in psychological experiments.* (ed C.A. Stael von Holstein), Reidel, Dordrecht.

Zeeuw, G. de (1993) Increase of competence via shared workspaces. *Systems Practice*, **6,** 155-173.

Zeeuw, G. de and Vahl, M. (1994) Intervention and Research. Technical Report CICT, Amsterdam, TR/94-46.

Zeeuw, G. de (1995) Values, Science and the Quest for Demarcation. *Systems Research* , **12,** 15-25.

Zeeuw, G. de (1997) Knowledge acquisition in changing realities (accepted for publication in *Kybernetes* , October 1997).

8 BIOGRAPHIES

Gerard de Zeeuw is Professor of Complex Social Systems at the University of Amsterdam, Faculty of Mathematics, Computer Science, Physics and Astronomy. He studied at the Universities of Leyden, Rotterdam, and Stanford and did his Ph.D. at the University of Amsterdam. Twice he was a fellow of the Netherlands Institute for Advanced Studies. He is Visiting Professor at the London School of Economics and at the University of Lincolnshire and Humberside. He has published extensively, for example Model denken in de Psychologie.

Jan Gerrit Schuurman studied Experimental Psychology at the University of Groningen, and will finish his Ph.D. in 1998 at the University of Enschede, Faculty of Educational Science and Technology. He is interested in transfer: of skills, of knowledge, of ways of thinking. He has developed TILT, a computer game to study the development of co-operation.

7

CSCW - A challenge to certain (G)DSS perspectives on the role of decisions, information, and technology in organizations? *

L. J. Bannon
Interaction Design Centre
Department of Computer Science and Information Systems
University of Limerick,
Limerick, Ireland
Tel:+353-61-202632, Fax: +353-61-202572
e-mail: liam.bannon@ul.ie

Abstract

This paper initiates a dialogue between two related, yet distinct research communities investigating the use of information technology to support work activities - GDSS and CSCW. The paper discusses a number of issues concerning the conceptual framework underpinning work in the area of Group Decision Support Systems (GDSS). It then examines a particular body of work within GDSS, namely that of the Arizona MIS group, who have developed one of the most well-known GDSS environments - Group Systems. This approach is then critiqued, in the light of concerns within the CSCW field. The intent of the paper is not simply to critique certain approaches but to re-frame certain key concerns in the field of decision support, and more specifically, group decision support. In conclusion, the paper suggests several topics that both the GDSS and CSCW community might usefully study.

Keywords

Group decision support systems, computer supported co-operative work, electronic meetings, decision-making, talk, groups, anonymity

---

* An initial version of this invited paper was presented at the IFIP WG 8.3 Working Conference on Decision Support in Organizational Transformation in San Sebastian, Spain, Sept, 4-9th 1994 and appears in the Proceedings of that Conference. Portions of the paper subsequently appeared at the 5th European Conference on Information Systems (Bannon,1997). This is an updated version of the 1994 paper.

"Decisions in organisations involve an ecology of actors trying to act rationally with limited knowledge and preference coherence; trying to discover and execute proper behaviour in ambiguous situations; and trying to discover, construct, and communicate interpretations of a confusing world."

James March, 1991

1 INTRODUCTION

The intent of this paper is to initiate a dialogue between two research communities that appear at times to be oblivious to each other, namely the decision-support system (DSS) community, more especially that subset concerned with group DSS (GDSS), and the computer supported co-operative work (CSCW) community. I realise that any attempt such as this is fraught with difficulties, as one is liable to be criticised by members of both communities for not arguing their respective cases properly. Indeed, the whole topic of my presentation may seem premature or ill-judged, as both the "fields" of CSCW and GDSS are poorly defined and the terms as we shall see are often used quite loosely, so attempting to set them up as distinct approaches may seem ill-advised. While I recognise that there are many differing perspectives[1] on the object of research and appropriate conceptualisations *within* the two communities, for the purposes of my arguments here I will at times characterise work in CSCW and GDSS in somewhat simplified ways. I have attempted to initiate the dialogue in a somewhat controversial fashion, namely by critiquing a single body of influential GDSS work from a CSCW perspective, thus inevitably ignoring other, sometimes radically different, GDSS approaches. My rationale is simply that the GDSS work cited is known to me, and to many in the CSCW community, whilst other GDSS approaches are, perhaps unfortunately, not so familiar. This obviously results in a biased view of the range of approaches extant in GDSS, and the lessons that the CSCW community in turn could learn from such GDSS approaches. I am quite aware that there are many important aspects of DSS and GDSS research from which the CSCW community could and should learn, but as I am not an expert in their field, I have not been able to present the complementary arguments in this paper. So what is presented here is only really half the story, but perhaps it can serve as a spur to efforts to initiate further discussion among GDSS and CSCW researchers, so that we can both learn from each other. Failure to engage in such a dialogue may result in both "fields" atrophying, due to their "closed" community walls.

For many in the CSCW community, (G)DSS - as exemplified by the papers that occasionally appear in CSCW conferences - is still seen as a field of study that relies too heavily on a set of overly rationalistic assumptions about human

---

[1] For example, I have discussed some of the different perspectives on CSCW that co-exist within that community in Bannon (1993).

behaviour in organisations, focusing on economic and psychological models, whose experimental studies are conducted in laboratory settings involving too much reliance on artificial tasks and student subjects. In contrast, I would hazard a guess that from the perspective of (G)DSS, the CSCW field is seen as relying too much on either political - sociological or ethnomethodological approaches to the study of phenomena, over-emphasising ecological validity relative to experimental rigour in its social science studies, or alternatively having an overly technocentric focus, lacking in theoretical sophistication.

The intent of this paper is to present my view on work in (G)DSS and its attendant problems, then show how some work within CSCW might usefully provide alternative perspectives for viewing some of these problems, and conclude with a set of research topics that might engage both communities. The argument here is not to argue for the primacy of any particular perspective, although as researchers, we each have our preferred viewpoint, but to enlarge the universe of discourse about the observable behaviours of people in organisations and our understanding of them. For instance, it is my belief that one area where CSCW can contribute is in the discovery and description of the different ontologies and epistemologies of participants in organisations. Perhaps in our uncovering of such differences, we can contribute to a better understanding of how organisations function, and thus contribute to the theme of how to bring about organisational transformation.

The structure of this paper is as follows. In order to put my remarks in context, I provide a personal and necessarily biased outline and critique on some of the work in the (G)DSS field, focusing on some of the underlying assumptions that appear to be built into the set of tools, techniques, and methodologies of the area. This is followed by a short outline of some key features of the CSCW field, again from a personal perspective, showing what is possibly new about the idea of computer "support" for co-operative activities, and its potential relevance for (G)DSS. Finally, I outline some topics for a programme of research that could provide a basis for useful (G)DSS - CSCW interaction.

2 THE CONCEPTS OF DECISION-MAKING AND DECISION SUPPORT

Models from mainstream economics, decision theory and "cognitive sciences" are not - and must not - be the only kinds of intellectual approaches which can help to grapple with the problems of the (re-) organisation of work and the (re-)allocation of resources. (Kjærgaard, 1989)

The purpose of this section is to make explicit some of my assumptions about work in the fields of decision-making and decision support, as a frame for my forthcoming critique of certain (G)DSSs later in the paper. What seems to be covered under the umbrella term of "decision support systems" (DSS) includes information technology applications that "support" people in making choices about what actions to take in organisations. Thus the area subsumes much of what is often termed management information systems (MIS) and executive information systems (EIS). In some cases, there is an interest in having the systems operate as "decision systems" rather than "decision support systems", as witnessed by some strands of work in the area of expert systems or what is called, more neutral, knowledge-based systems (KBS) where artificial intelligence is used to augment decision making. The basic constituents of these systems are a model base that provides some form of representation for a particular domain, and an interface that allows the user to interact with the system. Concerns centre around the veracity of information in the model, and the quality of the human-computer interface. In many cases, these systems serve as a top-layer of a larger information systems infrastructure containing databases of information about a domain, and the system provides support for the manager to "drill down" into the data and examine relationships between aspects of the data in interesting ways.

Much of the work in the DSS area that I have encountered has tended to rely on a conception of individual problem-solving and decision making heavily influenced by ideas from cognitive psychology, especially the work of Herb Simon, who in his own work, and subsequent collaborations with people such as James March and Allen Newell, developed a comprehensive framework for understanding problem-solving activity - involving notions of representations of problem spaces, and search strategies through these problem spaces. In this approach, people are viewed as information processing mechanisms, and decisions are made by people making rational choices between differently weighted alternatives. While subsequent work, by Simon himself, developed the concept of "bounded rationality" so as to account for the fact that human decision makers could not always be modelled as having perfect information, or utilising optimal strategies, this particular view of decision making as an aspect of problem-solving, of problem-solving as consisting of search through state spaces, of humans as information processors, etc., coupled with a number of conceptions about Homo economicus concerning maximisation of expected utility, preference functions, etc. has held sway for almost half a century in the cognitive science field. The upshot of this work has been a generally accepted set of conventions about how people make decisions, and about the way in which information systems might "support" this process through providing access to the appropriate kinds and levels of information and problem representations that decision-makers require in order to be able to make good decisions. The research work undertaken by this programme has covered such areas as studies of behavioural decision making, the development of appropriate models, and the improvement of the quality of the interaction between the user and the information systems artefact. While accepting the important contribution of this grand programme to our collective understanding of how people think and act in the world, it is important to note that this perspective, like any, is open to criticism, and has its blindness.

There are a number of grounds for being concerned with this grand vision. One line of argument focuses on the groundedness of certain of the concepts that seem to form the very stuff of these accounts. The "cognitive representationalist" conceptualisation of the human has begun to be queried, both for its adequacy and completeness (Winograd and Flores, 1986, Suchman, 1987, Bannon, 1990). Other sets of concepts have been suggested that might provide a better coupling between human action and the experienced world. These accounts problematise such basic notions as "problem", "information", "decision", "plan", "representation", "goal", etc. and argue that such concepts may not bear much relation to the everyday mundane realities of how people think and act in the world. As a powerful example of an alternative approach, Winograd and Flores (1986) provide a radical critique of the Western intellectual tradition, which they claim is based on a limited concept of rationality that underlies the majority of the work undertaken in management information systems. The certainties of basic concepts in the field are problematised and re-interpreted by others, relying on a hermeneutic and phenomenological position (e.g. Boland, 1985, 1987, Preston, 1991). The emphasis on quantitative models gives way to an examination of the qualities of accounts, description gives way to interpretation. Such approaches argue for a radical overhaul of our accepted ideas on the appropriate ontologies and epistemologies for studying the computer support of human and organisational action.

At another level, the accepted framework has been criticised on pragmatic grounds, in that practitioners claim that their experience does not fit with the models and expectations of the researchers. Many empirical studies have shown that people make decisions in organisations - or perhaps it might be more correct to say that decisions simply get made in organisations - due to a variety of reasons that are poorly accommodated within the standard model of ratiocinative behaviour. The accepted view that managers constantly seek additional information in order to improve the quality of their decisions has been discounted by empirical evidence. Indeed it appears that often the reverse is the case, they try to reduce the amount of information that is to be considered. Whether or not the view of managers as "decision-makers" is even appropriate is targeted by some: for example, Mintzberg has noted how people do many things besides making decisions in their work, and March (1991) notes: "Decision makers often operate in a surveillance mode rather than a problem-solving mode...they characteristically do not "solve" problems; they apply rules and copy solutions from others." Perhaps "decision" is not the most appropriate concept upon which to develop a theory of support. The awareness of motives and politics in the construction and use of "information" is also neglected in this perspective on DSS, and in MIS more generally. As Keen (1981) noted, some time ago: "Information is only a small component of organisational decision processes; human information-processing is experiential and relies on simplification, organisations are complex ..... Data is not merely an intellectual commodity but a political resource, whose redistribution through new information systems affects the interests of particular members. " It should be noted that such challenges to the accepted position have been proffered over the years by a variety of scholars, including from certain quarters within the MIS/DSS area itself . For example, from an early stage, Huber (1980) has noted the limited applicability of the standard model and pointed to the need for alternative decision models. The later work of March himself adds to the critique. Member of the Irvine group - Rob Kling, John King, Ken Kraemer and others - have contributed both conceptually and empirically to a somewhat different account of how people act in organisations, and the way computer-based systems can be appropriated for a variety of ends. Also, in a paper only recently brought to my attention, Jones (1994) notes similar critiques of the rationalist position in the context of GDSSs.

In sum, in recent years we have seen an attack on the accepted position of managers as primarily decision makers, based on both conceptual and empirical grounds. The studies paradigmatic of the decision making genre, involving experimental laboratory studies, using students as subjects, has been exposed as of little relevance to what happens when decisions occur in organisations. The neutral conception of topics such as "information" has been demolished. There is a concern about the social and organisational aspects of decision making and technology support, which go beyond sterile conceptions of "context" as an additional variable that needs to be added to our existing models. The limitations of the models we build and use need to be recognised. There is an interest in allowing for richer forms of interpretation of how people function in organisations, and of how actions are taken. The information processing view of how people function is being enriched, if not replaced, by a range of perspectives such as symbolic interactionism, ethnomethodology, cultural-historical theory, phenomenology, which require us to re-examine the ontologies and epistemologies espoused in traditional material. However, this paper is not so much a simple critique of DSS as it is a view on certain group decision support systems (GDSSs) and the assumptions they embody, to which we now turn.

3 INVESTIGATING GDSS

"The field of GDSSs is as yet not well developed, even as a concept. There are divergent and conflicting definitions of what the term means....moreover, even the simple technologies of GDSSs have had only limited adoption and use in organisations."

Kraemer and King (1988)

Group decision support systems (GDSSs) can be seen as DSSs that have been augmented by the fact that there is more than one decision maker involved, and so some computer support for communication and the integration of multiple inputs is provided. The interest in GDSS stems in part from the rise of interest in the area of technological support for groups, which can be seen in a variety of other research areas - for example human-computer interaction and organisational design - in recent years. While there are a variety of different kinds of GDSS systems around, both experimental and commercial, our focus here will be on a class of systems generically referred to as Electronic Meeting Systems (EMSs) or computer-augmented meeting rooms. Such systems have received a lot of attention of late, in both the information systems and the organisational literature. They can be characterised as comprising three components - a physical setting, a set of computer-based tools, and a meeting facilitator who moderates the meeting, and supports the group in their use of the tools. The settings can range from the very specialised - such as the early rooms configured for the University of Arizona work, and the original POD (marketed by ICL, Lucas Interiors, and AudioVisual Material Ltd.) - which can cost many thousands of pounds to equip with special workstations, computers and group displays, configured work surfaces, modifiable lighting, etc. through to ordinary meeting rooms, where portable PCs can be set-up on a local area network in minutes and be ready for use. The tools usually include some support for different phases of group activity, such as idea generation and selection, and various decision models. While some GDSSs can be used by the group on a "stand-alone" basis, in a number of cases they require a meeting facilitator who acts as a chauffeur for the group, helping the group in the development of the meeting agenda, and in the use of appropriate tools for the groups activities. Some well known systems include the University of Minnesota SAMM system, the Capture Lab in Michigan, the University of Arizona spin-offs GroupSystems marketed by Ventana, as well as the version called TeamFocus by IBM, and VisionQuest marketed by Collaborative Technologies Corporation.

Much published GDSS work that I have come across perseveres with the accepted rational cognitive model of decision making activity previously described in this paper, with a concern for understanding the decision making process, basically still individual cognition, but with the proviso that now there are multiple people - a group - that is involved in the decision, so there must be some attention to "group process". As an exemplar of this approach, for further discussion, I will refer to the work of Jay Nunamaker and his colleagues at the University of Arizona, who have been involved in the development of GDSSs for a number of years. Out of this work initially came the software tool PLEXSYS, then the commercial system GroupSystems V, sold by Ventana Corp., and a related system marketed by IBM known as TeamFocus. The system consists of a number of different tools that are intended to assist in aspects of the group decision-making process. These tools have evolved over the years as a result of experiences of use. There is support for brainstorming activity, for ranking alternative choices and voting on them, for preserving anonymity, etc. Focus has been on the support of co-located real-time teams, but the technology can be adapted for use in remote situations or for non-real-time use. There have been numerous studies conducted on the system, both in the laboratory and, more recently, field settings. The work of this group has been documented extensively in a plethora of reports, theses, and conferences and journals in the areas of MIS, DSS, and CSCW. For an overview of this work, see Nunamaker, Dennis, Valacich, Vogel, and George (1991). Indeed part of the reason why this work will form the basis for discussion is precisely because it is so well-known and available[2]. First let us note some of the claims made for the system, and the framework within which is was developed and analysed. Some of the major advantages of the system claimed by the developers are the following:

- people work on the system in parallel, so it is possible to get a lot more ideas into circulation and captured quickly using the system during brainstorming
- since the input is anonymous, there is equal opportunity for participation by all at the meeting, unencumbered with power or status differentials
- the system purportedly enables larger group meetings to be effective through control of the process
- the system permits the group to choose between a variety of techniques
- the system offers access to external information sources so that can be utilised in the group decision process more easily and effectively
- the system supports development of an organisational memory, by keeping a record of the inputs of the participants during the meeting, and of the choices made.
- use of the system in a number of organisations have lead to significant productivity gains based on much shorter lead times for getting decisions made in large groups through use of the system.

We will examine some of these claims later in the paper. The conceptual framework which is used by the University of Arizona research group to support their claims is based on a model that comprises four major factors that are seen as contingently involved in the use of EMSs - these are labelled group, task, context and technology factors. Thus group factors include such issues as size, proximity, composition, cohesiveness etc. Task factors involve the nature of the particular task - brainstorming, decision making, complexity etc. Context factors include such things as - organisational culture, time pressures, evaluative tone of meeting, and the reward structure. Obviously different kinds of technology, and the quality of the interfaces, the familiarity of the technology to the meeting participants, etc., will also have some effect on the meeting process and outcomes. Also, the research framework identifies a set of four conceptual mechanisms by which one can analyse meetings. These are, briefly:

---

2 My own direct experience with the system involves demonstrations and trials. I have experienced a number of the tools available, and have had discussions with a number of people who have used the system, including, importantly, one of the facilitators for meetings using this system.

- *Process Support* - focusing on the communication infrastructure and its support for such features as parallel communication, group memory, anonymity;
- *Process Structure* - focusing on the rules that direct patterns of activity, e.g. by providing agendas for meetings, or implementing specific forms of turn taking protocols;
- *Task support* - refers to the information and computational infrastructure that supports the accomplishment of the actual task, e.g. - external databases, spreadsheets, organisational memory elements.
- *Task structure* - refers to the techniques, rules, and models available to the group for analysing task-related information, akin to the DSS models used by individual decision makers.

It is within this espoused framework that Nunamaker and his research group discuss EMSs, and perform experiments to tease out the contributions of certain identified factors to the overall effectiveness of the group decision making process. Since this approach and exemplars of studies that utilise it, and summaries of the body of work completed to date are widely available, I will not take the time here to describe in further detail this rationale or the empirical studies, but will instead move directly on to a critique of some of the underlying assumptions of this approach, of its methodology, and of its interpretation of the results of its empirical studies. Once again, I accept that there are other approaches to (G)DSS that differ from this paradigm, but I wish to critique it here due to its visibility within the MIS and CSCW communities, where it is viewed, rightly or wrongly, as prototypical of GDSS. This is then followed by a Section that outlines how current work discussed within the CSCW community, while not answering these criticisms, might provide researchers in GDSS with other lenses with which to view the work.

4 A CRITIQUE OF CERTAIN GDSS ASSUMPTIONS

First of all, it is important to note that, even within the GDSS field, there is no uniformity of opinion as to what is the best approach to the development and use of GDSSs[3] - for some discussion, see the articles in Stohr and Konsynski (1992). What has been described above is however a prototypical example of work in the field that has received widespread exposure and so is a legitimate target for critique. The critique focuses on several distinct aspects of the approach, but emphasises the

---

3 For example, the work of John King and his colleagues at UC Irvine embodies a perspective on issues in GDSS distinct from much of the prototypical MIS work, and indeed more akin to CSCW work discussed later in the paper.

over-reliance on the rational model of decision making that has been critiqued earlier and on the nature and use of the group concept in GDSS. Since some of the general critique of this model as being the only or the most appropriate model by which to understand human decision making behaviour has already been presented, comments here will emphasise additional concerns when discussing "group" decisions.

As Whitaker (1992, 1994) has cogently argued, much of the work in GDSS has focused on "collecting unit elements, organising and arranging these units, and voting or ranking them"[4]. Such activities do not circumscribe the range of activities that are important at meetings. Specifically, they ignore or relegate to minor importance such crucial aspects of the meeting process as the initial environmental collation of information, generation of options and concurrent initial interpretation phase, which serves as the very basis or context for all subsequent activities. There is a large body of work from a number of systems perspectives that would consider GDSS as consisting of four major stages, viz. 1) Recognition of a need or problem; 2) Generation of evaluative context; 3) Evaluation of actions and consequences; 4) Selection of action. Whitaker and many others (e.g. Jones, 1994, Humphreys and Nappelbaum, 1997) point out that many current GDSSs ignore stage 1, and much of stage 2, focusing on stages 3 and 4. There is too much focus on the selection stage, and insufficient time given to understanding the context of the different options. The consequences of this approach are serious. Since there is no room for discussion amongst the participants of the grounds on which information is deemed relevant to the task at hand, this model implicitly imposes a set of normative assumptions on the nature of the meeting process. Again, if I may refer directly to Whitaker, who has I believe presented this argument most starkly, the implications of this approach are the following:

- all parties to the decision process are operating with respect to a presumably common ontological foundation
- all parties are capable of submitting ontologically comparable unit options for consideration
- all parties are capable of manipulating these ontologically comparable unit options under conditions of epistemological equivalence during consideration.
- all parties are capable of conducting their epistemological equivalent data manipulations under conditions of uniform rationality."(Whitaker,1992:36).

Both Whitaker and I would dispute the veracity of these assumptions for the majority of meetings. A simple aggregation and selection of options may be defensible where collaborators are uniformly knowledgeable on the background to the problem, issues, etc. at hand, but is unlikely to be sufficient in cases where we are dealing with actors having differential knowledge, for example, in dealing with

---

[4] I make extensive use of the thesis work of Randall Whitaker in this paper because I believe that it provides a sustained and effective critique of such GDSS systems.

multidisciplinary teams or indeed, the majority of situations, where a crucial component of the meeting should involve dialogue and discussion about the nature of the events to be debated and decided on, what counts as evidence, etc.. In these cases, formulating the very task itself may form an essential aspect of the meeting. It is in the "support" of such aspects of meetings that many current GDSSs fall down. At the same time, I am aware that there is a body of work on problem structuring methods which do attempt to support these early stages of group activities, e.g. Eden's (1989) SODA methodology concerning cognitive mapping, the work of Dick Boland and his colleagues (1992) on systems to represent different participant's perspectives, even Checkland's Soft Systems Methodology (1984), but these do not appear to have been taken up by many in the GDSS field. In the remaining part of this section, I investigate a number of problems thus encountered by current GDSSs, including the problem of disparate and discrete ontologies among meeting participants, the politics of decision making and meetings, the importance of talk, dialogue, or conversation in the meeting process, followed by a number of other criticisms that have been voiced about these systems.

a) the problem of different ontologies

As noted by a number of commentators, the work of meetings is often not simply about making decisions about items on the agenda, but ascertaining whether the language used to describe topics is held in common among the members of the group at the meeting. What one person means by a term of phrase is commonly found not to be the same as what others might mean by the same term or phrase.

The problem is often either pushed under the carpet by the assumption of shared views on the part of the meeting convenor, or else an attempt is made to reconcile possible differences through the establishment of some form of prescribed common dictionary of concepts that all must follow. This latter approach has its difficulties, as has been enumerated in a number of papers (Robinson and Bannon, 1991, Schmidt,1991, Davenport, 1994). While Robinson and Bannon were looking at the problems of "ontological drift" as designs move between groups during the systems development process, the underlying issues we raise in that paper are fundamental to the point under discussion here, as already noted by Whitaker in his GDSS critique. In our paper, we comment that :

"Different groups, professions, and subcultures embody different perspectives. They communicate in different "jargon". Much of this cannot be translated in a satisfactory way into terms used by other groups, since it reflects a different way of acting in the world (a different ontology and epistemology). Distinct groups of this sort will be referred to as semantic communities. The problem is not resolved by promoting the necessity of open communication -- since this assumes the different groups can be framed in a single semantic world. The meaning of terms is not transparent across groups.. (Robinson and Bannon, 1991)

Schmidt (1991) cites Savage (1987) on a similar point: "...each functional department has its own set of meanings for key terms....Key terms such as part, project, subassembly, tolerance are understood differently in different parts of the company" (Savage, 1987). Likewise, Davenport (1994) notes: "No matter how simple or basic a unit of information may seem, there can be valid disagreements about its meaning" and provides several examples from the business world. In such a situation the task of the group in a decision process is not simply "getting it right", as there may be no clear "right" answer. Rather the group must come to some accommodation about the differing world views of the participants, and about the adequacy of the models they employ in their decision process. As Gerson and Star (1986) note: "No representation ..... is either complete or permanent. Rather any description is a snapshot of historical processes in which differing viewpoints, local contingencies and multiple interests have been temporarily reconciled." Many current GDSS systems do not address this fundamental issue, or else handle it in a rather superficial way. Yet there is increasing evidence that the handling of this issue is crucial in terms of meeting outcomes (cf. Jones, 1994).

b) incorporating a political perspective

The MIS and DSS literature is replete with discussions of conceptual frameworks and resulting software applications that fail in use due to the lack of attention paid to "political" aspects of the problem under study. Too often, the assumption is made that information is a neutral concept. As March (1991) notes: "Most information is subject to strategic misrepresentation or unconscious bias". Such observations assume special importance when we come to discuss the "sharing" of information for the purpose of discussion and decision-making. Apart from the difficulties adumbrated above concerning the potentially different and divisive ontologies of the actors who produce and use the information, information is a strategic resource that will be jealously guarded by owner-actors and used in carefully circumscribed ways at meetings. The failure to take into account the political perspective creates many problems for the utilisation of information and information technology among certain groups.[5] In the area of EMSs, Grudin (1989) describes how a particular GDSS - gIBIS - which was being used by a group to provide a group memory representing arguments for and against certain design decisions was thrown out by the manager of the group, who was afraid that such an instantiation and reification of the disagreements within his group might be used inappropriately by others in the organisation! Similarly, Lyytinen et al. (1994) in their analysis of diplomatic meeting protocols, note how at many junctures in this complex process the archival properties of a GDSS would preclude its actual use!

As Jones (1994) notes:" it may be argued that conflict is endemic to organisations and that such 'political' use of IT is therefore likely to be more widespread than is often assumed, as Langley (1989) describes."

---

[5] See Kling (1980) for a classic account of different perspectives. Kjaergaard (1988) argues for a political perspective to be added to the preferred cognitive approach, based on her field experiences involving the deployment and use of a DSS.

c) the importance of talk

One of the surprising features of a number of the available GDSSs is their lack of support for conversations among the group[6]. Whereas certain views on what meetings are about would give primacy to such discussions among participants, this does not seem to be the case from the (G)DSS perspective. In some cases, group discussion tends to be tightly controlled and orchestrated by the facilitator, who tries to re-focus attention on individual member's tasks at their workstation. In such cases, participants at the meeting report a feeling of dissociation from others, due to the lack of interaction allowed at the meeting. As Whitaker notes, the group are "co-located, yet remote"(Whitaker, 1994). A recent report (Docherty, 1992) documents these concerns. Members of the group experienced their use of the system as constraining: they felt that the system had too heavy an emphasis on hierarchically-organised meetings with the facilitator in control, where there were constraints on interpersonal communication caused by the temptation to focus on the individual workstation, thus leading to a rather impersonal setting where people felt they were acting individually. They also felt that the exclusion of non-symbolic aspects of communication reduced the effectiveness of the meeting.

Alternatively, the group discussion that does take place happens completely outside the information technology. GDSSs neither support the discussions about the topics entered into the system, nor do they provide any record of any such discussions that may have gone on around the material on the screens. For instance, in an interesting analysis of meeting support system failures in real-world contexts, De Vreede and Muller (1997) note that one of their groups felt that "the group support system (GSS) [GroupSystems] did not enable them to *discuss* issues, only to put them on the table."(p.1281). They also note how some groups felt uncomfortable communicating via GroupSystems, to such an extent that the group regularly "pushed the keyboards aside and started discussing issues orally"(p.1278) In another example, (Whitaker, 1992) recounts how when the members of the group "broke ranks" and spoke to each other about how to co-ordinate their activities though the system only the results of the decision went into the group memory - the argumentation and discussion about the topic was not captured or marked in any way in the GDSS. This resulted in the situation that much in the way of background context for the decisions taken by the group, the efforts at sense making and attempts to come to a common understanding of the items depicted in the system, were not preserved in the system, and thus not available to others who might wish to review this meeting process at a later date. This poses the question of exactly to what extent do these supposed group support systems actually support the work of the group.

Reflecting on the situation, there appears to be an assumption that too much time at meetings is taken up by "idle talk", and that the preparation of an agenda

---

6 Indeed at least one early version of the University of Minnesota SAMM GDSS was so constructed that participants at the same co-located meeting using computers were actually seated back-to-back!

and the pacing of the meeting via the facilitator and software tools will improve effectiveness. I will come back to this issue of efficiency and effectiveness of meetings qua meetings below, but would like to dwell briefly on this apparent disregard for conversation or talk in meetings. If we believe that meetings are a place where different social worlds interact and attempt to understand each others' perspectives on problems, then it would appear that more rather than less emphasis should be given to supporting conversation between members of the group. To reduce oral communication to textual messages on screens does not on the face of it appear to be a way of enhancing group process. As Whitaker (1991) notes: "...the very sort of dialogue current GDSS overlook or relegate to external channels is the very element introduced in shifting information technology support from individual decision makers(DSS) to groups (GDSS)". There appears to be an assumption that what conversation -talk - consists of is simply a series of messages by one person followed by responses from another. Such a view of conversation is known to be far from accurate[7]. Due to the work of conversation analysts and others, we have become aware of the richly nuanced ways in which speaker and hearer "co-produce" their utterances. Making sense of each other is not given a priori. This is admirably described in the following quote from McDermott, Gospodinoff, and Aron (1978).
"In addition to sharing knowledge about each other, and whatever it is they are doing together, actors .... struggle to make sense of each other and do work to help generate the kinds of recognisable contexts for common sense to be achieved from one moment to the next. As Garfinkel has pointed out often, the problem facing people in interaction is never simply one of shared knowledge or overlapping interpretive grids. No matter how much people know in common, they must still work at constructing the environments that their mutual knowledge leads them to expect, and any relaxation of this effort can have disastrous consequences. People never know exactly how to make sense of each other.

Recent empirical studies confirm the importance of conversation and communication in the group meeting and decision-making process (Jones, 1994, De Vreede and Muller, 1997).

d) examine the nature of "groups"

The 'group' concept in GDSS is problematic on a number of grounds. Firstly, there is little consistency in the meaning of the term among research groups and practitioners. In some cases, it would appear that groups are characterised by a number of specific properties, for example, that all members are homogeneous, of equal status, engage in frequent face-to-face contact, share a common goal, etc. Yet others seem to use the term for any agglomeration of people - for example, in his book on Groupware, Johansen (1988) mentions "teams, projects, meetings,

---

7 Indeed, failure to take this into account was shown to be a prime cause of problems for one group support system - Xerox PARC's CoLab(Tatar et al, 1991).

committees, task forces" etc. as examples of "groups" and even includes interaction among workers, supervisors and management in manufacturing operations, "often across both distances and work shifts", under the same notion. Secondly, even on the rare occasions when real world groups are investigated, there is an emphasis on studying small, integrated, focused teams, with a well specified shared goal, which again is hardly representative of the way people work collectively in many settings. As Lyytinen et al. (1994) note:

"---the conception of a small cohesive team with fixed participants, a clear task, and shared goals is not necessarily appropriate in informing the design and examination of all EMS systems. Groups are not always small, their participants come and go, their goals are neither shared nor existing, and their tasks can be ambiguous, and under constant shift and drift."

Investigating actual work situations, we discover that there are a variety of ways in which people work together, but that many of them do not conform to any of the images of "group" work. We certainly do not want to restrict the scope of GDSSs to those cases where the responsibility of performing a task has been allocated to or assumed by a relatively closed and fixed collective. This would lead us to ignore or even dismiss the major challenges posed by the design of systems that support co-operative work arrangements that are characterised by a large and maybe indeterminate number of participants, differing conceptualisations, incompatible strategies, conflicting goals and motives, etc.

e) critiquing GDSS empirical research methodologies

While a large number of empirical studies are cited by GDSS researchers in support of their claims, many of them need to be treated with caution, due to a number of limitations of the published studies. Much of this research is overly technology-oriented and exhibits a relatively narrow conception of 'meetings'. Critiques of the studies come from those within the DSS community as well as outside. For example, a recent (G)DSS review book accepts that the majority of published DSS studies have been laboratory bound often with students as subjects and argue that: "We must begin to study real people in real settings working on real tasks"(Elam et al., 1992:69). In sum, they comment, and I would agree strongly:

"Specific laboratory studies have been criticised because they use student groups and artificial tasks rather than ongoing groups that have decisions to make that are of importance to the group; they usually involve only a single meeting; they assume that the particular GDSS and experimental situation are representative and can be used to draw conclusions about all GDSS; they focus on changes in outcomes and individual satisfaction, but not on changes in group process or group dynamics, and they differ only slightly, typically in one or two variables being set at different levels, from previous experiments." (Gray et al., 1992:83)

While some of these problems are being tackled in more recent GDSS work, much of this criticism remains valid.

f) a critique of efficiency/effectiveness claims

As noted earlier, some of the claimed benefits of GDSSs are that they decrease the time spent on meetings significantly, and lead to greater satisfaction on the part of the group members. It can be difficult to assess the validity of these claims, as often the comparison is made between "time taken to reach a decision with the system" versus "people's estimate of how long it would take to make the decision without the specific technology". Such estimations are difficult to validate. Also there are questions about how to measure the quality of a meeting, from whose perspective, and to the commitment of the participants to the decisions reached in the meeting, as the meeting is but part of an organisational process to implement the decisions reached. Measuring such aspects is a difficult process.

Much has been made of the increased efficiency of groups using meeting systems through the ability to each group member to input ideas in parallel via the computer system, rather than turn-taking in a face-to-face meting situation. There area number of issues that are need to be mentioned here. Firstly, the very idea that this sort of parallel brainstorming is effective, in the sense that it produces (collectively) better ideas is dubious (Cf. Hoffman, 1978, cited in Whitaker, 1992). Secondly, the focus of these measures is in terms of quantitative units of ideas produced, with little focus on the qualitative dimensions of the concepts. A number of empirical studies have noted this problem. De Vreede and Muller (1994) note that the participants themselves focused on the number of ideas that served the meeting goals, not simply the number of ideas generated. Thirdly, the dialogue directed toward analysing or critiquing the atomic "ideas" themselves remains outside the shared information space that is produced: “In GroupSystems, brainstorming is performed by a group but not as a group” (Whitaker, 1992). Granted, this method does produce a lot of material, but then again, there is a trade-off between the individual production of text and the time taken to read and evaluate it all by the whole group, as described in Docherty (1992).

More generally, there is the question of what kinds of meeting are such systems appropriate for? In situations where the group agrees on the general framework of important factors in the decision-making process, then the system may speed up the process, but in situations where the major topic of the meeting is arguing about the very grounds for making the decision, it does not seem that the rather simple model of decision-making embodied in these systems would be appropriate. While not denying that the use of GDSSs can have positive outcomes, I believe that there is a need to examine some of the claims carefully, in order to understand what exactly is going on. Once again, there does seem to be an emphasis on certain quantitative measures, without sufficient explication of what exactly such measures might mean. As noted by Lyytinen et al. (1994), reduction in meeting time is often too simplistic an output measure. Indeed, depending on the kind of meeting, they comment how it may be the way in which the “idle time” between meetings is managed by the meeting organisers that can significantly affect the final meeting outcome, rather than what happens in the meeting per se.

g) the relevance of anonymity

Again, the claims made for the benefits of anonymity with electronic meeting systems need qualification, especially as this feature is so often highlighted as a key feature of certain GDSSs. While undoubtedly there are cases where there are benefits, it is also the case that there are many exceptions. Reduced user identity can be dysfunctional in certain settings, as noted in a number of empirical studies. For example, De Vreede and Muller (1997) note: "Participants appeared to find anonymous discussing to be too impersonal, too sterile....anonymity was sometimes considered to harm the quality of information exchange" (p.1276). Lyytinen et al. (1994) also raise this concern. In many situations, it is crucial to know who says what, as not all members at the meeting are perceived as equally competent. Anonymity is also counterproductive in situations where specific individuals are necessarily linked to given positions or where the goal is "sharing personal perspectives" between the group members. Much closer scrutiny needs to be paid to this whole issue, as certainly general statements as to the benefits of anonymity seem increasingly dubious in the light of recent studies.

5 WHAT'S NEW IN CSCW?

Having now explored some of the claims of certain work in the (G)DSS area, and noted some problems with the work to date, I wish to turn my attention to CSCW and see to what extent this field may be of interest to GDSS, and why. My purpose is not to give an overview of the field here, as I have done this elsewhere (Bannon, 1993), but to focus on issues and aspects of CSCW that are relevant to the concerns expressed already in this paper. After a short introduction, I focus on a few key features of work in CSCW that may be of interest to the GDSS area, before discussing some possible lines of co-operation between the communities in the concluding section.

The term "Computer Supported Cooperative Work" (CSCW) has come to embrace a variety of research in such overlapping areas as workgroup computing, collaborative computing, groupware, co-ordination technology, augmented business teams, group decision support systems, and co-operative work support. Some of the key features of this agglomeration of terms, as distinct say from more general fields such as management information systems, or human - computer interaction, is an interest in supporting groups or ensembles, rather than individuals or whole organisations, with information technology. CSCW entails both a wider remit than traditional information systems as regards the different settings in which it is appropriate to study co-operative work arrangements, as well as a more explicit focus on the "support requirements" of co-operative work and the way people create, manage, disable, modify, etc. computer-based mechanisms of interaction than is seen in the other fields. Studies in such diverse areas as computer-aided design (CAD), computer-integrated manufacturing (CIM), computer-aided software engineering (CASE), group decision support systems (GDSS) etc., are all relevant to the CSCW field to the extent that they study the use of computers to support cooperative work in different domains. A focus on the multiplicity and complexity of co-operative work arrangements and problems and prospects for their computer augmentation is what some would regard as what is "new" in the field. For others, CSCW is more a paradigm shift in the way we perceive how work is accomplished, one that focuses on the sociality of work and the consequences of taking this notion seriously in designing computer support.

So, how does this relate to the (G)DSS field described above? In a recent (G)DSS book, the authors note: "Obviously, CSCW intersects with GDSS. CSCW focuses on the use of computer-based connectivity to support co-ordination and collaboration of knowledge workers and to enhance efficiency and effectiveness of knowledge work processes in general. On the other hand, GDSS tends to focus on processes that lead to management decisions. " (Stohr, Konsynski, and McGee, 1992:20). So, on this view, GDSS is a subset of the more embracing CSCW field. The fact that papers on (G)DSS have appeared in CSCW conferences supports the notion that the two fields are closely interlinked. Despite this apparent overlap of fields however, I would urge some caution, as I do not believe that the GDSS studies and systems that I have described above share the same set of concerns evident among many in the CSCW community concerning the nature of work in organisations. The point here is not that one perspective is necessarily more "correct", but rather to point out that much of the literature that appears under the rubric of GDSS stems from a different tradition and different practices to the work in CSCW. In this section I will outline some features of the "new" field that I believe are distinct.

First of all it is important to note that, just like in (G)DSS, there is no single view of the nature of the CSCW field. I have elsewhere described a number of different viewpoints that can be found in the literature, from simply viewing CSCW as "software for groups", to seeing it as a new paradigm for the building of information systems in general that pays attention to the socially organised character of work activities (see Bannon, 1993). Another view focuses more specifically on co-operative work as a distinct category of work, and investigates the features of co-operative work forms, focusing on the ways in which people cooperate, and the mechanisms of interaction that have evolved (Schmidt, 1990, Bannon and Schmidt, 1991, Schmidt and Bannon, 1992). It is an interdisciplinary community, embracing the software and social sciences. One of the important contributions of CSCW work has been the detailed investigation of exactly how work gets done in organisations, with a particular focus on co-operation, co-ordination and communication in work. An influential voice in this community is that of ethnographers, who have raised the awareness of systems designers to the problems caused by information systems constructed according to simplified models of work activities. These researchers have pointed to the need for detailed studies of the circumstances in which work is conducted, at all levels in the organisation, from the factory floor to the executive boardroom. Office room talk is subject to the same scrutiny as management "decision-making" activities. This is one area where I believe the work in CSCW may be of interest to (G)DSS. The CSCW work highlights a number of important features of real world co-operative work, including the following (Bannon and Schmidt, 1991, Schmidt and Bannon, 1992):

- co-operative work involves far more than what is commonly seen as group work
- co-operative work requires articulation work as well as task-oriented work
- co-operative work may occur even in the absence of explicit communication between parties
- decision making is often distributed and discretionary, requiring mechanisms to handle the reconciliation of different conceptualisations and heuristics used by the ensemble of co-ordinating actors.

In the material following, I have highlighted some of the areas where I feel the approaches and insights expressed in the CSCW arena may be of particular interest to the GDSS community.

a) The role of models: from depicting to reframing

While early CSCW work focused on the modelling of human roles and activities, and human communication patterns, there has been a growing realisation that the standard ways of viewing such activities and behaviours has suffered from too narrow a view of how people act in the world. There has developed a new awareness of the role of models in systems development, away from a prescriptive stance. A view of modelling that sees it merely as a description of an accepted reality, or an abstraction of it, can lead to serious difficulties. Accepting that there is a sense in which all description is really interpretation (Geertz, 1973) causes us to be more careful in ascribing veridicality to our models. In an earlier paper by Mike Robinson and myself, we have described some of the problems found when people model:

- There is a constant temptation for designers to confuse the models with an underlying reality.
- The models impose an ordering on people and or events, often unilaterally.
- The models are difficult for "users" to understand and thus
- preclude people from appropriating and re-working the model in situations of use.
- The models do not define their basic concepts adequately.
- Emphasis appears to be on model form and elegance over actual coverage and practicality or usefulness.
- Emphasis is on "determinism" at the expense of "interpretation" in work processes.

- The models embody an inappropriate correspondence theory of truth, and thus make the untenable assumption of a specifiable, one-to-one, decontextualized relationship between an instruction and the action that satisfies it. (Robinson and Bannon, 1991).

Much work in CSCW has come to re-appraise the role of models, and has begun to pay attention to ways in which people use these models as guides for behaviour, rather than as prescriptions. "Models are then seen as interpretations, as constructions, which for some purposes, under certain conditions, used by certain people, in certain situations may be found useful, not true or false. We thus see the modelling process as one of reframing rather than describing or abstracting". (Robinson and Bannon, 1991). While the thrust of our remarks were oriented to people doing office or work modelling, the implications of such views for work in (G)DSS - and indeed, CSCW itself - need to be examined in greater detail.

b) more distributed, less group, decision-making

As we noted earlier, it has - implicitly or explicitly - been the underlying assumption in most of the (G)DSS and CSCW-oriented research thus far that the cooperative work arrangement to be supported by a computer artefact is a small, stable, egalitarian, homogeneous, and harmonious ensemble of people, - a 'group'. But if we investigate actual work situations, the privileged status of the "group" concept quickly dissolves. Other factors come into play, if we are to understand how work gets accomplished, and what kind of computer support is required. As Schmidt and Bannon (1991: 15) note:

- Cooperative ensembles are either large, or they are embedded within larger ensembles.
- Cooperative ensembles are often transient formations, emerging to handle a particular situation after which they dissolve again.
- Membership of cooperative ensembles is not stable and often even non-determinable. Cooperative ensembles typically intersect.
- The pattern of interaction in cooperative work changes dynamically with the requirements and constraints of the situation.
- Cooperative work is distributed physically, in time and space.
- Cooperative work is distributed logically, in terms of control, in the sense that agents are semi-autonomous in their partial work. Cooperative work involves incommensurate perspectives (professions, specialities, work functions, responsibilities) as well as incongruent strategies and discordant motives.
- There are no omniscient agents in cooperative work in natural settings.

Since there is no omniscient agent in many of these situations, decision making is inevitably distributed among the decision making agents, who have unique situations to face, and their own sets of perspectives, goals, interests to take into account. As Boland et al. (1992) describe it: "Distributed decision making involves a set of actors who are autonomous within their sphere of concern, and who act independently based upon their own understanding of the situation they confront, but who recognise that they have interdependencies among themselves." The cooperative process of decision making in such situations is a very differentiated process involving the interaction of multiple goals of different scope and nature as well as different heuristics, conceptual frameworks, etc. (see Schmidt, 1990). Much GDSS work pays relatively scant attention to handling such issues, and the broadening of the scope of classic GDSSs to handle them might be informative.

c) Aspects of Information

Within CSCW, there has developed an awareness of the *nuances* of the concept of "information" in organizational life. Information is not seen as some neutral concept, but as one with political and contextual connotations. Indeed, Kjeld Schmidt and I have outlined how it is important to understand the source of information, the context in which information is produced and the politics of information production and use in some detail elsewhere (Schmidt and Bannon, 1992). Suffice it to say here that the consequences of such a perspective for information system development are serious, and raise a lot of questions as to the generally accepted view of information as discrete, factual and non-negotiable. On this latter point, especially in the context of distributed decision-making, it is imperative that the origins of the information are known to all concerned, in order to allow the exercise of mutual critique of the decisions arrived at by colleagues, in that different people may use different problem-solving strategies. Others involved in the distributed decision-making may wish to ascertain this background information, in order to balance individual biases. Cicourel (1990) illustrates this need powerfully in the context of medical decision-making, noting that "the source of a medical opinion remains a powerful determinant of its influence." That is, "physicians typically assess the adequacy of medical information on the basis of the perceived credibility of the source, whether the source is the patient or another physician." Thus "advice from physicians who are perceived as 'good doctors' is highly valued, whereas advice from sources perceived as less credible may be discounted."(Cicourel, 1990). Relatively little attention to such differences appears to have been paid in the GDSS literature on groups and decision-making that I am familiar with.

In CSCW, attention has shifted away from questions of support for face-to-face meetings and group decision-making towards the development of an understanding of how to support distributed decision-making and cooperative work activities where people are working at "arm's length", without much direct communication and without necessarily even knowing each other or knowing of each other. In such cases, people must cooperate via a more or less *shared or common information space*, that is, "a 'space' comprising data, personal beliefs, shared concepts, professional heuristics etc."(Bannon and Schmidt, 1991). By ignoring the diversity and discord of the 'goals' of the participants involved, the differentiation of strategies, and the incongruence of the conceptual frames of reference within a co-operating ensemble, much of the current GDSS (and indeed CSCW) research evades the problem of how to provide computer support for people co-operating through the establishment of a common information space (Schmidt and Bannon, 1992). In this perspective, shared databases do not guarantee shared interpretations of the data, but actors must locally and severally jointly construct shared meanings for this data, and even when such shared meanings are arrived at, they are still seen as contingent, local, and temporal (cf. Bannon and Bødker, 1997).

d) Work requires articulation

The importance of articulation work (Strauss, 1985) - the work that is required to be done in order for any division of labour to function smoothly - in understanding how people manage to co-operatively accomplish their work is another insight that has been investigated in some detail in CSCW work (Schmidt and Bannon, 1992). This is of some relevance in the context of our discussion of GDSSs as it points once again to the work that has to be done in order to allow "work" to be done, something that is ignored in many functionalist information systems models.

Building computer systems where the work is seen as simply being concerned with 'information flow,' and neglecting the articulation work needed to make the 'flow' possible, can lead to serious problems. The organisational models embedded in CSCW applications should be treated as *resources* for competent and capable workers rather than as executable code. That is, the system should make the underlying model accessible to users and, indeed, support users in interpreting the procedure, to evaluate its rationale and implications. It should support users in applying and adapting the model to the situation at hand. The system should even support users in modifying the underlying model and creating new models where appropriate in accordance with the changing organisational realities and needs. The system should also support the documentation and communication of decisions to adapt, circumvent, execute, modify etc. the underlying model.

e) Understanding practices

There is a body of work in CSCW that pays particular attention to the nature and organisation of everyday work practices and their centrality in the accomplishment of work activities. This increasingly prominent view re-conceptualises the nature of work and organisational life, and the role of information technology support. It emphasises work practices, and the way learning is accomplished within communities of practice. It argues that learning and action are 'situated' (Suchman, 1987), and that work is a complexly social affair, mediated by other people and artefacts. Such a view contrast strongly with a number of common assumptions about work, found in areas such as human engineering, scientific management, and cognitive science, and still underlying many aspects of GDSS. Sachs (1995) argues passionately and cogently for this need to re-conceptualise the nature of work, away from what she terms an "organisational" view, to one she labels "activity - oriented". To synopşize these perspectives the organisational view is still the predominant one in organizations today, grounded in scientific management ideas, focusing on training, tasks, procedures, workflow and teams, in contrast to the activity-oriented view focusing on learning, know-how, networks, conceptual understanding, work practices, judgement, and communities (of practice).

The relevance of this perspective to our present discussion is twofold. Firstly, it is yet another voice that is arguing for the need to understand the details of work *in situ* in order to provide appropriate technology to support it. This has implications for GDSSs, in that the tools they provide need to be developed and tested within ongoing work situations in order to truly assess them, rather than in the lab. Secondly, it suggests the idea of learning over time, in communities. Recently, much attention has been paid to how technologies evolve in use. This concern with the evolution of skills with artefacts focuses our attention on the need to study how people appropriate technology over time, through use, and even creative misuse. As Mackay notes, more generally:" Software does not remain static when it is introduced into an organisation. People in the organisation evolve their individual patterns of use, share them with each other, react to external changes, both technical and non-technical, and sometimes pro-actively modify the system to produce significant innovations." (Mackay, 1990). Thus not only must we embed our systems, of whatever form - including GDSSs - into particular situations, but we should observe how these systems are used by people over time, and how use changes. In my reading of GDSS literature, such issues are rarely to the fore, and yet, while preparing this paper I came across a paper which presented a very similar argument (Poole and DeSanctis, 1989). Briefly, while they frame their remarks within adaptive structuration theory, some of their observations are identical. They note, for instance, "it is use that makes GDSSs what they are in a given context and gives them reality...It is not sufficient to treat the GDSS as a given technology and assume it has determining effects on users. Nor is it sufficient simply to study user attitudes toward and acceptance of the system. The GDSS and users are bound up in an encompassing process that shapes and mediates the GDSS impacts." I would certainly agree with this, and my next question would be to what extent have such ideas influenced GDSS work?

6 CONCLUDING REMARKS: OPENING UP CONVERSATION BETWEEN GDSS AND CSCW

The intention of this paper has been to open up a dialogue between two communities which up until now have not cross-fertilised each other to the extent possible, given their stated concerns. I have tried to provide an account, from my own personal perspective, of where I see problems with a certain body of literature and systems which I have encountered to date in the field of (G)DSS, fully acknowledging that this view is certainly selective in scope and that my arguments do not apply to all work in the field. I have shown briefly where I feel that some of the concerns of the CSCW community might be of interest and raise debate and discussion on these issues in the (G)DSS community. To my mind, much turns on how one approaches such concepts as "decision-making" in organizations, i.e. whether one narrowly delimits the field of enquiry to a particular category of actions and settings, or whether one accepts that in the end, most work activities, throughout an organization involve sense-making, interpretation, and, yes, on occasions, decision-making. It should be obvious from the foregoing that I am of the latter persuasion, which is why I have included so much material about work activities more generally, because from my perspective, they too are relevant to the discussion at hand.

Clearly, this is only half of the story. I would encourage members of the (G)DSS community to compose the other half of the story, by investigating work in the CSCW field and providing a complementary critique of CSCW in the context of (G)DSS perspectives. In the meantime, let me conclude this paper with a brief list of some themes or topics that it might be fruitful for the CSCW and GDSS communities to jointly explore and debate:

- *Pluralism in conceptual frameworks*

The rational actor model of decision-making is a powerful perspective that has held sway for a long time in a number of fields. Might it not be of interest to investigate how other frameworks view the world of business, management and "decisions"? Such approaches as hermeneutics and phenomenology may re-frame some thorny issues, and allow for new insights and understandings, for both the actors involved, and the researchers (e.g. Preston, 1991).

- *Decision-making*

One of the strengths of the ethnomethodological programme that has been visible in CSCW has been its detailed and insightful accounts of how work gets done in organizations, as these accounts include descriptions and interpretations of local problem solving and decision making, as well as accounts of how larger, more formal, meetings are called, conducted and decisions arrived at. It would be a worthwhile exercise to organise a workshop between GDSS researchers, behavioural decision-making researchers and sociological researchers in CSCW to discuss their varied understandings of meeting processes, settings and outcomes. How do we reconcile their at times competing visions of how decisions are made?

- *Information Use in Organizations*

We have discussed a variety of issues around the nature and use of information in organizations and its role in decision-making. But the description above presents a rather static view on the concept and role of information in organizational life, that needs to be enriched and melded with other views. Just for example, how do we reconcile the view that good decision making is premised on large quantities of information with the view that managers only collect such information for political purposes, in order to show others how well prepared they are? What do we mean by "information" in any case?

- *Understanding Groups*

To what extent are groups as traditionally conceptualised, relevant to modern business functioning. Can we reconcile the results of studies done on group process in the lab with what seems to happen within organizations? Might we do better if we understand how decision making is actually occurring in organizations, in a distributed fashion, rather than in some centralised group fashion. Detailed, on the ground, studies would appear to be called for here.

- *Communication or Conversation ?*

How people interact and manage conversation in meetings is a complex skill, and if technology is to "support" this process it would appear to require richer models of communication embedded in it that is currently the case in some of the (G)DSSs that we have mentioned. As Robinson and Bannon (1991) note: " One particularly exciting area for further research lies in the exploration of "turn taking" and its support in CSCW systems. This complex yet universal aspect of human interaction, resting as it does on a mix of procedures, conventions and moral orders offers an interesting nexus for the concerns of many disciplinary communities within CSCW." - and I might add, GDSS. We also have a wide variety of other conceptual frameworks that could be applied here to enrich our concepts of communication and conversation. For example, the work of Gordon Pask on Conversation Theory, concepts from critical theory - Habermas' theory of communicative action, etc.

- *The role of models*

There are many issues that need to be addressed here. What is being modelled? Who constructs the model, who owns it, who can manipulate it, change it etc.? How do people relate to these models, work with them, in them.? What kind of language do we use to describe them, manipulate them, etc.? What role do models play in the support systems we generate? Do we model people in our systems, and if so, how? How do we handle the relation between individual and collective models? Are the models prescriptive or descriptive?

- *(Mis-) Use of tools*

Perhaps further investigation of how currently available GDSSs are actually used in practice could help us in understanding how people appropriate tools and also provide new insights for design. Creative misuse, or unanticipated use, can certainly provoke reflection and redesign (Mackay, 1990). I am not aware of much literature on the details of actual use of GDSSs in the material that I have to hand. Certainly, studies of use of (G)DSSs/CSCW systems by members other than the design team can produce striking results, as witnessed by the study on the Xerox PARC CoLab (Tatar, Foster and Bobrow, 1991). The pooling of experiences of use by both the CSCW and GDSS communities would be of great interest, as currently, even in CSCW, there is a dearth of such evaluative field studies (Bannon, 1996). The whole role of the support system in the context of the group task and context also needs to be investigated. For example, one of the facilitators who used (G)DSSs extensively confided to me how meetings where the technology played a secondary role, i.e. the focus is on the meeting conversations, with only intermittent use of the "support" technology, tended to be the ones perceived by the group as most satisfactory. So perhaps we need to reduce the emphasis on the structuring aspects of the technology and special-purpose setting throughout the meeting, and investigate its selective use. What this would imply for the whole concept of 'group support systems' is a moot point. Perhaps it would simply take away some of the fascination for large scale technical fixes for what are ultimately social problems, and encourage the development of simpler, more convivial computerised tools that can be picked up and discarded at will by the group participants during their mundane meetings.

7 ACKNOWLEDGEMENTS

I would like to thank first my colleagues Kjeld Schmidt and Mike Robinson, with whom I first charted the CSCW waters, and who have influenced my thinking over the years. The work of Rob Kling and John King of Irvine also had an impact from an early period. For the invitation to the IFIP 8.3 meeting that led to this paper, I wish to thank Patrick Humphreys. For useful, occasional, discussions on DSS and MIS, I would like to thank Dian Kjærgaard, Randall Whitaker, and Dick Boland. None of the above should be held responsible for anything that appears in the paper. Initial work on this paper was supported by a contract with the Cognitive Systems Group, Risø National Laboratory, Denmark as part of the Esprit Basic Research Action 6225 (COMIC). Further support from the EU TMR COTCOS Programme is also acknowledged.

8 REFERENCES

Bannon, L. (1990) A Pilgrim's Progress: From Cognitive Science to Cooperative Design. AI and Society, **4**, 1990, 259-275.

Bannon, L. (1993) CSCW: An Initial Exploration. Scandinavian Journal of Information Systems, August

Bannon, L. (1996) Use, Design, and Evaluation: Steps towards an Integration, in *The Design of Computer-Supported Cooperative Work and Groupware Systems* (eds. D. Shapiro, M. Tauber and R. Traunmueller) North-Holland, Amsterdam.

Bannon, L. (1997) Group Decision Support Systems: An Analysis And Critique, in *Proceedings of the 5th European Conference on Information Systems,* June, Cork, vol. 1, 526-535.

Bannon, L. and Bødker, S. (1997) Constructing Common Information Spaces, in *Proceedings ECSCW'97*, Lancaster.

Bannon, L. and Schmidt, K. (1991) CSCW: *Four Characters in Search of a Context, in Studies in Computer Supported Cooperative Work: Theory, Practice and Design.* (eds. J. Bowers and S. Benford) North-Holland, Amsterdam.

Boland, Jr., R. (1985) Phenomenology: A preferred approach to research on information systems, in *Research Methods in information systems* (eds. E. Mumford, R. Hirschheim, G. Fitzgerald, and A.T. Wood-Harper) North-Holland, Amsterdam.

Boland, Jr., R. (1987) The in-formation of information systems, in Critical Issues in Information Systems Research (eds. R.J. Boland, Jr., and R. Hirschheim) Wiley, New York.

Boland, Jr., R., Maheshwari, A., Te'eni, D., Schwartz, D., and Tenkasi, (1992) Sharing Perspectives in Distributed Decision Making, in *Proceedings of CSCW'92, Computer-Supported Cooperative Work Conference, Toronto* (eds. J. Turner and R. Kraut) ACM Press.

Checkland, P. (1984) Systems Thinking, Systems Practice. Wiley, Chichester.

Cicourel, A. V. (1990) The Integration of Distributed Knowledge in Collaborative Medical Diagnosis, in *Intellectual Teamwork: Social and Technological Foundations of Cooperative Work* (ed. J. Galegher, R. Kraut, and C. Egido,: Lawrence Erlbaum Associates, Hillsdale, N. J.

Davenport, T. (1994). Saving IT's Soul: Human-Centered Information Management. *Harvard Business Review,* March-April, 119-131.

De Vreede, J. and Muller, P. (1997) Why some meetings just don't work: Exploring success factors of electronic meetings, in *Proceedings of the 5th European Conference on Information Systems,* vol. 3, pp. 1266-1285.

Eden, C. (1989) Using cognitive mapping for strategic options development and analysis, in Rational Analysis for a Problematic World (ed. J. Rosenhead) Wiley, Chichester.

Elam, J., Jarvenpaa, S. and Schkade, D. (1992) Behavioral Decision Theory and DSS: New Opportunites for Collaborative Research, in *Information Systems and Decision Processes* (eds. E. Stohr and B. Konsynski) IEEE Computer Society Press, Los Alamitos, California.

Docherty, P. (Ed., 1992) CSCW/Groupware: A Promise soon to be realised? TELDOK Report No. 71, Stockholm.

Geertz, C. (1973) Interpretation of Cultures. Basic Books, New York.

Gerson, E. M. and Star, S. L. (1986) Analyzing due process in the workplace. *ACM Transactions on Office Information Systems,* **4**, 257-270.

Gray, P, Alter, S., DeSanctis, G., Dickson, G., Johansen, R., Kraemer, K., Olfman, L. and Vogel, D. (1992) Group Decision Support systems, in Information Systems and Decision Processes(eds. E. Stohr and B. Konsynski) IEEE Computer Society Press, Los Alamitos, California.

Grudin, J. (1989) Why groupware applications fail: problems in design and evaluation. *Office Technology and People,* **4,** 245-264.

Hoffman, L. (1978) Group problem solving, in Group Processes (ed. L. Berkowitz) Academic Press, New York.

Huber, G. (1980) Organizational science contributions to the design of decision support systems, in *Decision Support Systems: Issues and Challenges* (eds. G. Fick and R. Sprague) Pergamon, Oxford.

Humphreys, P.C. and Nappelbaum, E. L. (1997) Structure and communications in the process of organisational change: East European experience and its general relevance. *This volume.*

Johansen, R. (1988) Groupware: Computer Support for Business Teams. The Free Press, New York.

Jones, M. R. (1994) Information technology for Group Decision Support: Beyond GDSS. *Journal of Organizational Computing,* **4,** 23-40.

Keen, P. (1981) Information Systems and Organizational Change. *Communications of the ACM,* **24,** 24-33.

Kjærgaard, D. (1988) Decision Support and Organizational Learning: A Political - Cognitive Framework for Assessing Decision Support Systems. Ph.D. Thesis, Institute of Informatics and Management Accounting, Copenhagen Business School, Denmark.

Kjærgaard, D. (1989) A political-cognitive view of the knowledge-base for management support., in *Knowledge based Management Support Systems* (eds. G. Doukidis, F. Land and G. Miller) Wiley, Chichester.

Kling, R. (1980) Social Analyses of Computing: Theoretical Perspectives in Recent Empirical Research. *Computing Surveys,* **12,** 61-110.

Konsynski, B. , Stohr, E. and McGee, J. (1992) Review and Critique of DSS, in *Information Systems and Decision Processes* (eds. E. Stohr and B. Konsynski) IEEE Computer Society Press, Los Alamitos, California.

Kraemer, J. and King, J. (1988) Computer-based systems for cooperative work and group decision making. *ACM Computing Surveys,* **20,** 115-146.

Langley, A. (1989) In search of rationality: the purposes behind the use of formal analysis in organisations. *Administrative Science Quarterly,* **34,** 598-631.

Lyytinen, K., Maaranen, P. and Knuuttila, J. (1994) Groups are not always the same: An analysis of group behaviours in electronic meeting systems. *CSCW: An International Journal,* **2,** 263-286.

Mackay, W. (1990) Users and Customizable Software: A Co-Adaptive Phenomenon. Doctoral dissertation, Sloan School of Management, MIT.

March, J. (1991) How decisions happen in Organizations. *Human - Computer Interaction,* **6,** 95-117.

Marshak, D. (1990) Lotus Notes: A platform for developing workgroup applications. *Patricia Seybold's Office Computing Report,* **13,** 7(July), 1-14.

McDermott, R., Gospodinoff, K. and Aron, R. (1978) Criteria for an ethnographically adequate description of concerted activities and their contexts. *Semiotica,* **24,** 245-275.

Nunamaker, J., A. Dennis, J. Valacich, D. Vogel, and J. George, (1991). Electronic Meeting Systems to Support Group Work. *Communications of the ACM,* **34,** 40-61.

Orlikowski, W. (1992) Learning from Notes: Organizational Issues in Groupware Implementation, in *Proceedings of CSCW'92,* Toronto.

Poole, M.S. and DeSanctis, G. (1989) Use of group decision support systems as an appropriation process, in *Proceedings of the Twenty-Second Annual Hawaii International Conference on System Sciences,* Vol. IV, 149-157.

Preston, A. (1991) The "problem" in and of management information systems. *Accounting, Management, and Information Technology,* **1,** 43-69.

Robinson, M. and Bannon, L. (1991) Questioning Representations, in *Proceedings of the Second European Conference on CSCW* (eds. L. Bannon, M. Robinson, and K. Schmidt). Kluwer, Dordrecht.

Sachs, P. (1995) Transforming Work: Collaboration, Learning and Design. *Communications of the ACM,* **38,** 36-44.

Savage, C. M. (1987) Fifth Generation Management for Fifth Generation Technology (A Round Table Discussion), Society of Manufacturing Engineers, Dearborn, Michigan.

Schmidt, K. (1990) Analysis of Cooperative Work. A Conceptual Framework. Risø-M-2890. Risø National Laboratory, Roskilde, Denmark.

Schmidt, K. (1991). Riding a Tiger, or Computer Supported Cooperative Work, in *Proceedings of the Second European Conference on CSCW* (eds. L. Bannon, M. Robinson and K. Schmidt) Kluwer, Dordrecht.

Schmidt, K. and Bannon, L. (1992). Taking CSCW Seriously: Supporting articulation work. *Computer Supported Cooperative Work,* **1,** 7-40.

Stohr, E. and Konsynski, B. (1992) Information Systems and Decision Processes. IEEE Computer Society Press, Los Alamitos, California.

Strauss, A. (1985) Work and the Division of Labor. *The Sociological Quarterly,* **26,** 1-19.

Suchman, L. (1987). Plans and situated actions: The problem of human-computer communication. Cambridge University Press, Cambridge.

Tatar, D., G. Foster, and D. Bobrow, (1991). Design for Conversation: Lessons from Cognoter, in Computer-supported Cooperative Work and Groupware (ed. S. Greenberg)

Whitaker, R. (1992). Venues for Contexture: A critical analysis and enactive reformulation of group decision support systems, UMADP-RRIPCS 15.92, Dept. of Information Processing, Umeå University, Sweden.

Whitaker, R. (1994) GDSS' Formative Fundaments: An Interpretive Analysis. *CSCW: An International Journal,* **2**, 241-262.

Winograd, T. and Flores C. F. (1986) Understanding computers and cognition: A new foundation for design. Ablex, Norwood, N. J.

9 BIOGRAPHY

Liam Bannon is Director of the Interaction Design Centre, which includes the Computer Supported Cooperative Work (CSCW) Centre, and Senior Lecturer in the Department of Computer Science and Information Systems at the University of Limerick. His research interests include human-computer interaction, CSCW, multimedia design, and social and organizational aspects of computing. He is involved with IFIP Working Groups 8.2, 8.3, 8.6 and is an editor of the *CSCW Journal.* Previous publications include *Perspectives on the Computer Revolution* (1989) (with Z. Pylyshyn) and *Information Technology: Impact on the way of life* (1982) (with U. Barry and O. Holst).

8
Management developed DSS and organizational transformation

S. A. Carlsson
Department of Informatics
Lund University, Ole Römers väg 6
SE-223 63 Lund, Sweden
e-mail: sven.carlsson@ics.lu.se

Abstract

Management developed Decision Support Systems (DSS) are a major factor in business computing. Most of these DSS are developed using evolutionary approaches. These approaches stress continuous development of decision tasks. One drawback of continuous development of decision tasks is that it can lead to exploitation of old tasks instead of exploration of new possibilities. In an organization that experienced this problem, an intervention was made, using two approaches presented in this paper. As management developed DSS are becoming more important to organisations, it is critical to assess their value. For such an assessment we propose that the resource-based view of the firm might be useful.

Keywords

Decision support systems, management development, development approaches, resource-based view, organisational learning, organisational change and transformation, competitive advantage

1 INTRODUCTION

Management development of Decision Support Systems (DSS) is a major factor in business computing - see, for example, Brancheau and Brown's (1993) review of end-user computing research. There are several reasons, technical as well as managerial and organisational, for this phenomenon. The technical reasons, which have received most attention in the literature (Fahy and Murphy, 1996), include the DSS development backlog, greater computer literacy among managers, decreased software and hardware costs, increased hardware capacity, and higher hardware and software quality.

Some researchers have suggested that the more important reasons for management development of DSS are managerial and organisational. Fahy and Murphy (1996) found in a study that some of the technical reasons are valid but these do not give a full insight for management development of DSS. In summarising their study, they say: "...it is real management issues that are the key devices behind these systems [management developed systems] and that the development of these systems is an integral part of the activities of managers." (Fahy and Murphy, 1996, p. 140). Carlsson (1988) found, in a study of management development of DSS, that spreadsheet program usage by managers can be a means of changing a manager's experiential learning cycle[1] in two major ways. First, by using a spreadsheet program, some of the learning modes can be easier to accomplish and spreadsheet program usage can also lead to a higher quality in a learning mode. Second, the use of an spreadsheet program can speed up some of the learning modes and the whole learning process.

Although there are positive effects of management development of DSS, there are at the same time some "problems in paradise". One of the major problems is related to modelling errors (Panko, 1997a). For a good summary of the many studies on modelling errors see Panko, (1997b), a website on spreadsheet research with a focus on spreadsheet errors with implications for spreadsheet developers and development policies. In addressing such modelling problems, several recommendations, rules, and policies have been suggested by Panko (1988). Others have suggested validation procedures and frameworks (Finlay and Wilson, 1997). Although these rules, recommendations, etc., might lead to efficient development of error-free DSS there is no guarantee that they will lead to effective management development of DSS. They might just lead to *efficient* management development of DSS but the systems may be less effective or ineffective and, in some cases, meaningless. This suggests that we have to address the development process in context. Since management development of DSS, using an evolutionary DSS design approach, is common in many organizations, it is wise to examine the effects of such an approach to DSS design. In the following, some negative effects of management developed DSS will be pointed out, and some alternative approaches to DSS design will be discussed.

Another problem identified by researchers is the productivity problem, which can be exemplified by Edberg and Bowman's (1996) laboratory study of developer productivity. They found that surrogate IS professionals produced higher-quality applications and were much more productive than were end users. Studies like this

---

1 Kolb (1984) argues that an effective learning process can be "... described as a four stage cycle involving four adaptive learning modes - concrete experience, reflective observation, abstract conceptualization, and active experimentation" (ibid., p. 40). Concrete experience means that a learner is involved in new experiments - ideally a learner should involve himself fully, openly, and without bias in these experiments. Reflective observation takes place when a learner observes and reflects on his experiences. Abstract conceptualization means that a learner creates and changes concepts that integrate his observations into logically sound theories by, for example, developing and changing mental models. Active experimentation means that a learner uses these theories in the form of, for example, mental models to solve problems and make decisions.

one suggest that managers might be relatively less efficient in developing DSS. However, the studies by Fahy and Murphy (1996), Carlsson (1988), and others, suggest that managers can develop effective DSS.

Management development of DSS is also directly related to the discussion of empowerment and decentralisation of decision making. Malone (1997) suggests that empowerment is not just a fad that will soon pass away. He argues that greater decentralisation is "... a response to fundamental changes in the economics of decision making enabled by new information technologies." (Malone, 1977, p. 34). He argues that dependent, decentralised decision makers will be increasingly important to organisations in the knowledge-based economy (see Wyner and Malone, 1996, for a mathematical proof that changes in IT will lead to more connected, decentralised decision-making structures in organisations.[2]) A likely consequence of Malone's ideas is that management development of DSS will increase in importance but, as we will argue, researchers and practitioners should focus much more on managerial and organisational issues.

The remainder of this chapter is organised into five sections. The first section discusses some negative effects of management development of DSS. The second section presents alternative approaches that can be used to overcome some of the negative effects. The third section presents a case study where an intervention was undertaken to address some of the noted problems. In the fourth section we discuss what is the value of management development of DSS. The discussion is based on the resource-based view of the firm. The section opens up new challenges for practitioners on how to manage and assess management development of DSS. The section also raises new research questions. The final section provides a conclusion and a discussion on future research.

This paper is based on a more or less systematic series of studies of management development of DSS carried out over the last ten years - for some of the results, see Carlsson (1988, 1989, 1991, 1994). We have also profited from other researchers' qualitative and quantitative studies on management development of DSS, for example Avdic (1994) and Fahy and Murphy (1996).

2 MANAGEMENT DEVELOPMENT OF DSS: PROBLEMS IN PARADISE

It is widely believed that management development of DSS, as well as DSS development in general, requires an approach which is distinct from the traditional Systems Development Life Cycle (SDLC). Several authors have pointed out that SDLC approaches are not suitable for DSS development (see, for example, Keen and Scott Morton, 1978; Ginzberg, 1978; Sprague and Carlson, 1982; and Sprague and Watson, 1996). In his analysis of different schools of IS development,

---

2 It should be noted that Wyner and Malone mainly consider two dimensions: 1) the value of the remote decision information used, and 2) the costs of communicating the remote decision information.

Iivari (1991) suggests that the "...most significant contributions of DSS concern the IS development process. DSS directed the primary focus away from integrated MIS development governed by an overall MIS plan to a problem-oriented, small scale development of individual DSS applications. The very first DSS in the early 1970s also indicated the need for a flexible development process incorporating ideas of prototyping and in particular of evolutionary development" (ibid, p. 253).

Several alternative DSS approaches to SDLC have been launched, with names like *iterative and evolutionary design* (Lucas, 1978; Earl, 1978), *adaptive design* (Keen, 1980), *middle-out design* (Ness, 1975; Hurst et al., 1983), *l'approche évolutive* (Courbon, 1996), and *expanding subsets* (Moore and Chang, 1983).

Early research and experimentation in evolutionary design was done at the University of Grenoble by Courbon and associates (Courbon, 1996; Courbon et al., 1978). Courbon *et al.* suggest that an evolutionary design approach is characterised by the building of a version of the DSS, using it, evaluating it, refining it, and so on. There are several essentials to remember when developing an evolutionary design. First, it is critical to identify an important decision task. Secondly, the identified decision task has to be broken down into subtasks. This means identifying a part of the decision task that the potential user (manager) thinks is important and critical and for which it is possible to "quickly and easily" build a DSS. It is the potential user who is in the "driver's seat" while identifying the decision task and the subtasks. Thirdly, a "small" but useful DSS for the subtask(s) is developed. Fourthly, the DSS is used in "daily life", evaluated, and enhanced and modified.

From the experience of our own studies, as well as other researchers studies of management development of DSS where evolutionary DSS design have been used, it seems that this design approach can lead to several problems and negative effects. For example:

- A manager can get carried away by the technology at the expense of his primary tasks. We have seen highly-paid managers building and changing their DSS instead of having an assistant do the job to a lower cost and probably with a better result.
- A manager can get carried away by the "bells and whistles" of his DSS Generator - building what he thinks is a fancy DSS - instead of concentrating on the content of the DSS.
- Managers are in many cases "barefoot modelers."
- Managers have limited ability to identify complete and correct requirements for their DSS.
- A manager's lack of knowledge and acceptance of application assurance procedures for development and operation can lead to problems in the form of: 1) reluctance to test a system, 2) reluctance to document a system, 3) reluctance to include validation, especially validation of input data, 4)

reluctance to include audit trails, including processing trails, and 5) reluctance to have operating controls, e.g. to check that all input data have been entered and results are compared to independent control figures (Davis, 1989).

Although the above problems are serious in themselves, we feel that a more serious problem, in the long run, is that evolutionary design and continuous development of decision tasks seem to lead to exploitation of current decision tasks. Henderson and Ingraham (1982) point out that evolutionary design seems more often to be a convergent process than a divergent process - see, also Davis (1989) and Cooprider and Henderson (1990/91) for the same point.

Evolutionary design and continuous development can be characterised as an *anchoring and adjustment* design approach. The concept of anchoring and adjustment is borrowed from Kahneman *et al.* (1982). They suggest that "anchor and adjust" can be a problem solving bias and hence in many DSS design situations a less good way to behave as a designer. Anchoring and adjustment in DSS design means that a developed DSS tends to be the result of minor adjustments of the current decision tasks (the anchor point). Stabell (1983) points out that, in prototyping and evolutionary design, there is no direction of the changes to be achieved. In using this design approach, it is easy to "...fall into a 'usability trap', the development of systems that are useable and used, but not very useful" (Stabell, 1983, p. 228). Carlsson (1984) and Marsden and Pingry (1986a, b, 1988) also criticise such approaches as non-directed change processes which do not make use of explicit purposes and goals to guide the design process.

In recent years, system restrictiveness has been discussed (Silver, 1991) mainly in terms of physical system restrictiveness. This "...signifies that system restrictiveness can be understood by examining the presence or the absence of certain system features, and that the system restrictiveness can be easily manipulated by including or excluding particular features." (Chu and Elam, 1990, p. 195). Chu and Elam propose another type of system restrictiveness: *induced restrictiveness*, which is a form of restrictiveness that "...manifests itself when the users of a DSS predominantly employ a particular decision process or a small set of decision processes, even though the system also physically permits a complementary process or an array of other decision processes which somehow tend to be ignored by the users. The presence of this effect would indicate that the system users are induced toward employing a particular process or processes." (Chu and Elam, 1990, p. 195).

In a laboratory study, Chu and Elam found that a spreadsheet program (Lotus 1-2-3) tended to induce an incremental decision process. Our own field studies suggest that in decision situations where there are no strong pressures for a synoptic decision process[3], use of a DSS Generator to build a DSS is likely to induce an

---

3 A synoptic decision process is characterized by an unbiased search for a solution and makes no use of an existing solution. In many cases, an existing solution is seen as a hindrance to discovering innovative solutions.

incremental decision process, i.e., anchor and adjust. On the other hand if, in a decision situation, there is strong pressure to do so, the DSS user can choose a synoptic decision process and employ a DSS Generator to build a DSS that can be used in that decision process.

Our studies suggest that, in general, a DSS Generator does not induce a synoptic decision process. Tentatively, it can be suggested that in a decision task in which there is some kind of anchor point - an existing solution or procedure - a DSS Generator will induce an incremental decision process unless a DSS designer deliberately chooses a synoptic decision process.

If the above is true, the question if this is good or bad for an organisation is an important one. Perusing the organisational learning literature, we suggest that, from an organisational point of view, DSS design as exploitation of current decision tasks might in the long run lead to some unwanted consequences. For example, March, in discussing organisational learning, points out that a "... central concern of studies of adaptive processes is the relation between the exploration of new possibilities and the exploitation of old certainties." (March, 1991, p. 71). Broadly, exploration "...includes things captured by terms such as search, variation, risk taking, experimentation, play, flexibility, discovery, innovation" and exploitation "...includes such things as refinement, choice, production, efficiency, selection, implementation, execution." (ibid., p. 71). An organisation must engage itself in both exploration and exploitation to survive in the long run. March says, "...maintaining an appropriate balance between exploration and exploitation is a primary factor in system survival and prosperity" (ibid., p. 71).

In discussing the pros and cons of exploration and exploitation, March points out that "...adaptive processes characteristically improve exploitation more rapidly than exploration. These advantages for exploitation cumulate. Each increase in competence at an activity increases the likelihood of rewards for engaging in that activity, thereby further increasing the competence and the likelihood." (ibid., p. 73). Still, for an organisation it is critical to sustain a reasonable level of exploration. According to organisational learning theories, the tendencies to increase exploitation and reduce exploration are likely to become effective in the short run but potentially self-destructive in the long run (ibid.). If we take March's words on the relationship between exploration and exploitation seriously, the tendency to use DSS for exploitation, ceteris paribus, can in the long run be a disadvantage to an organisation. In other words, management development of DSS (exploitation of decision tasks) can be a powaqqatsi.[4] It consumes resources that should have been used for exploration. This means that too much continuous development (exploitation) of decision tasks can in the long run be hazardous to an organisation.

---

4 Powaqqatsi. From the Hopi language, powaq (sorcerer) + qatsi (life). n. an entity; a way of life, that consumes the life forces of other beings in order to further its own life.

3 ALTERNATIVES TO CONTINUOUS DEVELOPMENT OF DECISION TASKS

In one of the organisations we have been working with, the problem of convergent continuous management development of DSS design had become a problem. The question for the organisation was: How can we handle the situation in a positive way. For the organisation it was not possible to invest in more information technology and it needed its DSS. Before presenting the case, we discuss alternatives to continuous development of decision tasks. We focus on alternatives to evolutionary DSS design. We will discuss two concepts: strategic opportunistic DSS design (Section 3.1) and radical redesign of decision processes (Section 3.2). The purpose of these alternatives are that they should increase the likelihood of the development of effective DSS in an efficient way and also lead managers to avoid developing less effective or meaningless DSS.

The design and building of DSS can be described and discussed from what we call a macro and a micro perspective. In the micro perspective the focus is on the design and building process of a specific DSS, i.e. once a person has decided to build a DSS, how does he go about designing and building it? At the micro level, we can identify several system analysis and design approaches. One way to classify these approaches is on a scale with two end points. One end point is *pure top-down design and building,* where one starts with high-level goals for the system to be designed and built and breaks them down into smaller and less complex problems. Each of these smaller problems is then in turn broken down until one reaches a level of achievable actions. The other end point of the scale is *pure bottom-up design and building*, where one starts with identifying the bottom-level objects and actions that are required and then figures out how to put them together.

In the macro perspective, the focus is on building and using a DSS in the context of other information sources. It focuses on questions such as: When and why does one build a DSS? A new or redesigned DSS can be viewed as a new or changed information source. White (1975) made a distinction between primary and secondary decisions. A secondary decision is defined as a decision that is related to the choice of information and methods to be used in addressing the primary decision problem. Our notion of macro level design falls under White's definition of a secondary decision. Stabell (1975, 1983) also discussed the relationship between secondary decisions and the design of DSS, stressing that a DSS designer should also consider what other information sources - beside the DSS - a decision maker uses or might use in his primary decisions.

3.1 Strategic opportunistic DSS design

The concept of *strategic opportunistic DSS design* has its roots in work by Hayes-Roth and Hayes-Roth (1979), Anderson (1983), and Isenberg (1988). Hayes-Roth and Hayes-Roth (1979) used the concept of *opportunistic planning* to describe multiple asynchronous processes that a person uses when planning whereby he or she can act opportunistically as the current situation suggests various opportunities for development. Anderson (1983) used the concept of *opportunistic model* in his discussion on human cognition and especially control of cognition, i.e. how human cognitive systems choose, consciously or unconsciously, what to process. In writing on managerial thinking, Isenberg (1987, 1988) used a related concept, *strategic opportunism,* to describe "... the ability to remain focused on long term objectives while staying flexible enough to solve day-to-day problems and recognise new opportunities." (Isenberg, 1987, p. 92). Isenberg's research suggests that effective managers strike this balance.

Here, we introduce *strategic opportunistic DSS design* as an approach for management development of DSS. In the macro perspective, the concept refers to a process characterised as follows:

- The manager has an overall long-term focus, i.e. a focus on overall organisational purposes and goals, and on the purposes and objectives of different tasks. This long-term focus is guided by the manager's mental models, for example, of information sources, etc. Such mental models might be intuitive and implicit, but can also be explicit and externalised.
- The manager is flexible: he can solve problems not foreseen and anticipated, which is of special interest here when this is done by building a DSS.
- The manager can recognise new opportunities and he must be reflective. This means, for example, that during task accomplishment the designer can recognise new opportunities a DSS can give in handling the task. In other words, the manager has a strategic perspective to guide him; at the same time he also acts opportunistically.

In the micro perspective, strategic opportunistic DSS design refers to a process characterised by the following:

- The designer/builder (manager) focuses on the overall objectives and purposes of a DSS, although these objectives are not stated in the same form as those discussed in top-down approaches, and it might not be possible to use them in a traditional top-down process.
- The designer has a mental model of the DSS to be built before he starts to build it; this model might in part be externalised, for example, sketched on a piece of paper. The designer is flexible in that he can solve problems not foreseen in the incomplete mental model and/or in the externalised model; the design and building process is flexible. The designer can also see new opportunities while designing and building the DSS.

The most important aspects of strategic opportunistic DSS design are as follows First, the process is guided by an overall understanding of the situation at hand: it is strategic. The designer is guided by mental models of the situation. These models can be intuitive and implicit, but they can also in part be externalised. Secondly, the design process is opportunistic in that it is a flexible process that can be adapted to new circumstances, problems, opportunities, etc. The adaptation process is guided by the overall understanding of the problem, i.e. by the designer's mental models. Adaptation should not be interpreted as more or less defensive adjustment; instead adaptation should be interpreted as adaptable development, improvement, and growth. These two features make strategic opportunistic design different from other DSS design approaches. In discussing DSS design, Ginzberg and Ariav present a classification scheme for DSS design methods; the methods can be classified along a continuum (Figure 1).

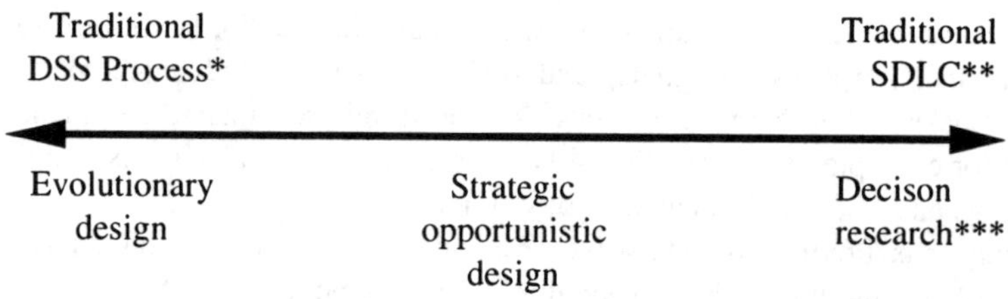

* i.e., those often put forward as the most suitable DSS design methods.
** like traditional SDLC in that it emphasises analysis and is prescriptive and design-oriented.
*** see Stabell (1983).

Figure 1 DSS design methods: Evolutionary design, strategic opportunistic design, and decision research.

Ginzberg and Ariav say, "Moving from left to right on this continuum generally implies (1) more effort (e.g., time) spent 'up-front'; (2) decreasing 'respect' for the current decision making process; (3) an increasingly normative approach; (4) increasing attention to ultimate 'decisional impact,' i.e., change in actual performance; and, as a result, (5) potentially more radical impact on the decision situation and outcomes" (Ginzberg and Ariav, 1986, pp. 52-53). Moore and Chang (1983), in discussing DSS design, distinguish between "weak" and "strong" design: "The 'weak' versus 'strong' design dimension distinguishes those designs that follow the user's preferences and personal decision-making style from those that consciously attempt to manipulate or refine the user's approach to problem solving" (ibid., p. 188). Weak design methods will be on the left of the continuum and strong design methods on the right of the continuum. On the left hand side of the continuum we have prototyping and evolutionary design. As discussed above, these approaches have been put forward as suitable DSS approaches, more or less as panaceas. These approaches can be regarded as mainly opportunistic design approaches. *Strategic opportunistic design* is placed in the middle of the continuum and should be seen as mainly an approach to enhance evolutionary design. How one can get a manager DSS designer to become a strategic opportunistic designer will be discussed in Section 4. Meanwhile, the next section takes a closer look at macro level design.

3.2 Radical redesign of decision processes

In recent years, we have witnessed a growing interest in *business process redesign.* This growing interest can be found among researchers as well as among practitioners. Some researchers and practitioners have suggested that continuous, incremental product and process improvements, though still essential, are in many cases no longer sufficient if an organisation will stay or become competitive and effective - see, for example, the discussions in Davenport (1993), Hammer (1990), Davenport and Short (1990), Handy (1990), and Hammer and Champy (1993). The goals of business process redesign and process innovation are, for example, to achieve major reductions in process cost or time, or major improvements in flexibility, quality, or service levels. Davenport suggests a five steps approach to business process innovation: "identifying processes for innovation, identifying change enables, developing a business vision and process objectives, understanding and measuring existing processes, and designing and building a prototype of the new process and organisation." (Davenport, 1993, p. 25). It should be noted that when Davenport talks about processes he has in mind broad and inclusive processes. He proposes that most companies, even very large and complex ones, can be broken down into fewer than 20 major processes.

Using what we have presented and discussed above we propose a taxonomy for DSS design approaches. The taxonomy uses two dimensions: level of change (outcome) and frequency (Figure 2). In the figure we have classified various DSS design approaches. It is important to note that incremental improvements and radical innovations are not really distinct types, but a whole continuum, with low incremental improvements at one end of that continuum and highly radical innovations at the other end. We can find changes of all shades of grey along the continuum. Continuous improvement can also be viewed as a continuum. From situations where it only takes a couple of hours or days to design, build, implement, and use a new or different version of a DSS to situations where one uses an approach that is close to traditional systems development.

The lines that separate the cells are, in reality, hard to draw. Traditional SDLC approaches (Cell A) have been used to successfully design and implement DSS (Hogue and Watson, 1984; Findley, 1983). DSS design approaches that are like traditional SDLC - different forms of life cycle and waterfall models - seem to lead to incremental improvements. These approaches often take, as a starting point, existing decision tasks. They often have a "narrow" functional scope, for example, they often take current tasks, functional units, and responsibilities as given. The approaches are "single shot" approaches: development of a DSS is carried out as a project with a relatively clear start and end.

However, even if a DSS is developed as a project it will, as most CBIS do, require maintenance: there will be a need for changes in the DSS. This may include "...*reactive maintenance*, or bug fixes; *interactive maintenance*, or maintenance that better supports present user interaction with the system; and *proactive maintenance*, or maintenance that will enable the DSS to keep abreast of needs and technology as each evolves over time." (Sage, 1991, p. 187). The latter type of maintenance is close to continuous improvement. One problem with Cell A approaches is that, since they do not make radical changes in old decision processes and tasks, it is easy to end up speeding up messy tasks and processes.

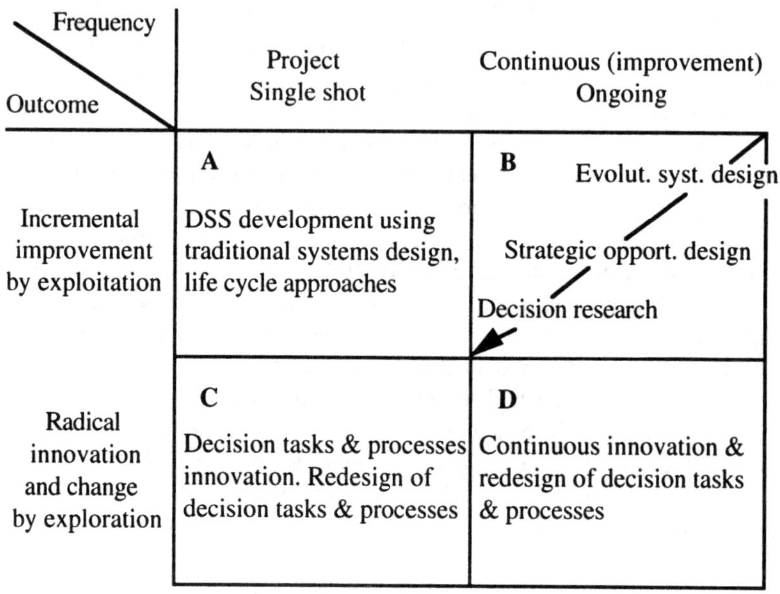

Figure 2 DSS design approaches to decision improvement.

The ideas underlying this the taxonomy can be found in Davenport (1993), who focused on business improvement, but we have adapted his ideas here to decision processes and decision improvement. The various DSS design approaches we classified above, according to the scheme suggested by Ariav and Ginzberg (1986), can be considered as approaches likely to lead to incremental improvements. Hence these approaches are placed in the cell *incremental improvement and continuous improvement,* that is, Cell B. Moving from the right upper corner to the left lower corner in this cell generally implies that more effort is spent up-front; a decreasing respect for the current decision making process; an increasingly normative approach; an increasing attention to ultimate decision impact (change in actual performance); and, as a result, a potentially more radical impact on the decision tasks and outcomes.

Approaches in Cell C are intended to achieve radical decision improvement. At the heart of innovation in, and redesigning of, decision processes lies the notion of *discontinuous thinking* (Handy, 1990), that is, identifying, questioning, and abandoning those outdated rules and fundamental assumptions that underlie current decision processes. The approaches in Cell C would focus on an organisation's decision processes infrastructure, working on it. to change the organisation's ability to make decisions and take action. As far as we know, there are no such DSS design approaches in existence at present. There are, however, CBIS approaches that can be considered total or global, in that they focus on a whole organisation or a major part of the organisation. These approaches can be considered as *enterprise modelling approaches*. Examples are IBM's Business Systems Planning (IBM, 1984) and information engineering (Finkelstein, 1992).

Enterprise modelling and information engineering approaches have in common that they view data and information as corporate resources. These resources must be managed from an overall organisational view. In *Business Systems Planning* (BSP), the goal is to discover a stable information architecture that supports all of the business processes. One of the first steps in BSP is to define business processes where business processes are defined "...as *groups of logically related decisions and activities required to manage the resources of the business*" (IBM, 1984, p. 29). As long as the business processes remain basically the same, then the information architecture will be stable. An assumption is that as long as an organisation stays in the same business, the business processes will remain relatively constant. The approaches use the information architecture as a basis for future information systems planning, that is, to identify the CBIS that should be developed in the next years. As we see it, approaches like BSP take a *workflow view* of an organisation. Important in a workflow view is to create structures and administrative processes that fit an organisation's production processes and operations.

Cell C approaches are to a large extent based on the assumptions of stability and continuity. Some writers on management and organisation design suggest that these assumptions are unrealistic. Tapscott (1996), writing about innovation, says that in the "new digital economy", continuous improvement or single shot radical redesign will not be enough. He suggests that many organisations have to continuously innovate new products and services, and hence redesign many of their business processes continuously. Nohria and Ghoshal (1997) say that an increasing number of firms must continuously innovate to maintain and enhance their performance. Boynton (1993) suggests that managers in organisations that face frequent, rapid, unpredictable changes in their competitive environments must create organisations that are dynamically stable. These are organisations that are capable of serving the widest range of customers and changing products and service requirements (dynamic) and at the same time build on long-term process capabilities and the collective organisational knowledge (stable). Boynton says that one of the most critical steps in building these organisations is strategic management of information. An implication of the above for management development of DSS is that infrastructural issues will become even more critical.

In Cell D, the challenge is to develop approaches that can be used to create DSS supported decision processes, that can rapidly be radically redesigned, and that build on previous process capabilities and the collective knowledge of the organisation. This means that IS and DSS managers will have to focus much more on organisational and managerial issues.

On the other hand it, should be noted that several *business process redesign* writers believe that radical levels of processes innovations are difficult to maintain and co-ordinate on a continuous basis (Davenport, 1993; Hammer and Champy, 1993). They say that employees and organisations need periods of rest and stability between radical innovation initiatives. These in turn may be no more than management fads (Jackson, 1995).

Having presented the framework and the alternative approaches we now turn to our case study to illustrate two of the concepts, strategic opportunistic DSS design and radical redesign of decision processes.

4 A CASE STUDY ON STRATEGIC OPPORTUNISTIC DSS DESIGN AND RADICAL REDESIGN OF DECISION PROCESSES

The organisation (Alfa) in our case study is a public sector organisation. Its main field of action is to provide child care. In the mid 1980s, there was major frustration in the organisation due to the development backlog for its CBIS/DSS The few DSS that had been implemented - mainly for budget simulations - had been developed using a traditional SDLC approach (State I in Figure 3). At that time, it was decided that personal computers should be installed - this was a major investment for the organisation. Approximately a quarter of the 150 personal computers that were installed replaced dumb terminals and stand-alone word processing machines. The personal computers were equipped with suitable software. The basic software for DSS applications were a spreadsheet program, a database package, and a statistical program. A computer education programme for all personnel working with administrative tasks was launched. The goal of the programme was that all personnel working with administrative tasks should become computer literate. This goal was fulfilled.

By the beginning of the 1990s, personal computers were being used fairly well in the organisation. Many management developed DSS were in use. Most of the managers (users) were satisfied with the situation. They had been able to build DSS that they felt were useful. The approach used to build and rebuild the individual DSS was evolutionary design (State II in Figure 3). At the same time, it had become apparent to Alfa's executive team and various managers that, from an organisational perspective, the situation was less than satisfactory. The individual DSS were built from the task perspectives of the individual builders (managers) rather than from a common organisational perspective. For example, those DSSs which should reflect Alfa's goals and policies did so in quite different ways, and some DSS reflected personal views that were contradictory to the organisation's goals and policies. Thus, decisions that should be consistent across the organisation were not at all consistent. This meant that the situation, from an organisational perspective, was a little bit too anarchistic and chaotic.

At the same time, there was external pressure on the organisation. During the late 1980s and early 1990s, there were major changes in the city's administration and in the public sector in general. Discussions, decisions, and implementation of privatisation and outsourcing were taking place. Privatisation and outsourcing meant changes in goals and boundaries of different public sector organisations, as well as of other organisations. Although this was a slow process, these changes progressively led to changes in decision authorities, responsibilities, etc., that is, changes in decision processes.

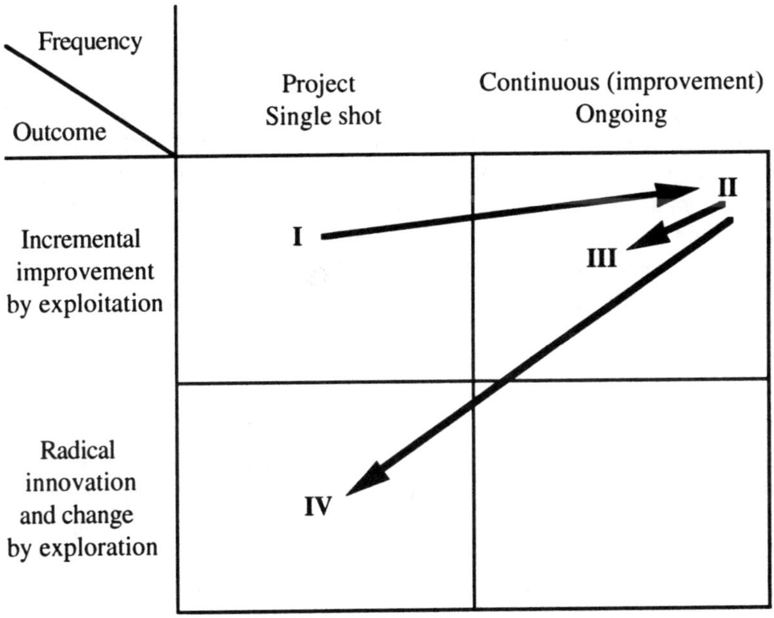

Figure 3 DSS design approach used in the organisation prior to user DSS design (I). User DSS design approach used in the organisation (II) and intended changes (III and IV).

It should be noted that Alfa had and has scarce resources which meant that there were, and are, few resources to support the "transformation process". Since Alfa is a public sector organisation, it is not allowed to do what ever changes it would like to do: laws, agreements, political decisions, stakeholders, etc., are restricting the decisions and actions Alfa can take. After discussions in Alfa - during the summer of 1993 - it was decided by the executive team that the two approaches discussed above should be tried in order to address Alfa's problems with management development of DSS. This means that two different approaches would be used. The first approach would be employed to try to get the manager DSS designers to become *strategic opportunistic designers,* that is, a move to State III in Figure 3. The second approach would be employed to prepare the organisation for radical redesign of decision processes (a move to State IV in Figure 3). A small project team (5 persons) was established with the responsibility to start the change programme.

4.1 Learning to become a strategic opportunistic DSS designer

The purpose of this intervention was to get the managers to become more strategically minded in their DSS design, in other words, to move to state III.

With regard to micro level design, it was decided by the project team that different means should be used. In Alfa, there were no formal controls on DSS design, building, or use. As seems to be typical, the planning and control mechanisms that existed focused on hardware and software issues. The control mechanisms addressed problems like: what hardware and software should be used in the organisation, how hardware should be maintained, and how a new version of a software should be distributed. This means that there was no support to help managers act as good DSS designers. Panko (1988) and Ronen et al. (1989) have proposed rules, guidelines, and principles of good practice with respect to designing and building small DSS using a spreadsheet program. These rules, etc., cover such subjects as proper design, screen design, and construction of equations. Ronen et al.'s suggestions resemble suggestions for using structured techniques in "traditional" systems development using, for example, hierarchical or modular design. So far, these kinds of techniques have not been on the agenda in Alfa's spreadsheet program courses. The team expected that Ronen et al.'s approach has to be properly packaged - taught in courses, for example, and supported by handbooks and software - in order to have any impact.

The project team assessed that the DSS manager- designers had a passive knowledge of the actual DSS Generators. They decided that, instead of taking a traditional approach in the course, three specific means should be used. First, a DSS design handbook for users was developed. Second, good DSS examples, developed in the spreadsheet program, were distributed to the DSS manager-designers. The DSS examples were all related to administrative tasks in Alfa and were distributed on local area networks and disks. Third, a "train the trainee" approach was used to increase the likelihood that the handbook and the examples would have an impact on the designers.

With regard to macro level design, it was decided that a "train the trainee" approach should be used. The same persons were educated as were for micro level design. In all, 20 persons were taught strategic opportunistic DSS design in a two day course. The DSS handbook contained a short discussion on what a secondary decision means and two short cases. The cases were written to show the differences between *strategic opportunistic DSS design* and opportunistic DSS design, and showed what methods and techniques that could be used in strategic opportunistic DSS design.

These ways of educating and influencing the DSS manager-designers to become strategic opportunistic designers were implemented during the last months of 1993. No formal follow up study was done, but semi-structured interviews conducted with some persons suggest that there were changes in the behaviour of the DSS manager-designers and that these changes were in the desired direction.

4.2 Preparing for redesign of decision processes

A second task for the team was to start a process that in the end should lead to the redesign of Alfa's decision processes and the design of new decision processes (state IV).

It was decided that a high-impact approach should be used, which meant deciding which business processes were most in need of redesign.[5] The first step was to identify or establish the existing decision processes, which would then provide the basis for identifying which decision processes to change. As pointed out in the redesign literature, a process, to be improved, must first be understood and regularised. We found that what Davenport says about management processes was quite true in the case of Alfa: "...of all the processes in an organisation, management processes are the most poorly defined, and least likely to be viewed in process terms" (Davenport, 1993, p. 275).

From our initial discussions and interviews with the personnel we found that the fundamental issue was: what are the purposes of Alfa's different decisions and decision processes? We used Brunsson's (1985, 1989) alternative interpretation of decision making as our base for this issue. The "standard" view of decision making is that the purpose of decision making is to choose. Brunsson proposes three alternative purposes of organisational decision-making: 1) decision making as a

---

[5] Davenport (1993) says that the main generic business processes potentially in need of process innovation include product and service development and delivery (including research, design, engineering, logistics, and manufacturing); customer-facing activities (including order management and marketing); and management activities (including strategy formulation, performance measurement and reporting, planning and budgeting, human resource management, resource allocation, and infrastructure building).

mobiliser, 2) decision-making as responsibility allocation, and 3) decisions as legitimisation. A problem in Alfa, as in many organisations, is how to achieve co-ordinated and collective actions. Decision-making and decisions can sometimes be used for this purpose. The key is to secure commitment from actors, and hence link actors to action in advance.

Several decisions which had, as their main purpose, to establish and maintain commitments were identified in Alfa. In many decision situations goals, alternatives, etc., can be uncertain, but uncertainty can also concern decision-makers (decision-making as responsibility allocation). Decision-making is sometimes used for clearly pointing out who are the decision-makers. In Alfa we found decisions that were employed for allocating responsibility by making the decision-makers visible. Alfa can, in part, be considered a decision-oriented organisation. This means that decision making constitutes important activities and decisions are important outputs. Normally it is assumed that there is a connection between decisions and actions, but sometimes decision-oriented organisations, like governments and public organisations, are eager to publicly declare some of their decisions, although they might not be connected to actions (decisions as legitimisation).

The result was that several decision processes were identified and described, and the purposes of these decision processes were pointed out. Although the descriptions of the decision processes were fairly crude, they led to intensive discussions. This work also led to changes in the personnel's mental models of tasks and decisions processes. The project was halted in the spring due to an upcoming election. The project was not restarted after the election. The main reason was that other issues and problems had to be addressed and solved.

Having presented the framework, the alternative approaches, and the case study, we will address, in the next section, the question: what is the organisational value of management development of DSS, and what is its relationship to firm performance?

5 ASSESSING MANAGEMENT DEVELOPED DSS: A RESOURCE-BASED VIEW

In trying to address the question of value, we looked for theories and frameworks that could suggest when management development of DSS matters, and in what way it matters. Most of the writing on the relationship of IT to performance of the firm has been based on an external view, focusing on the ways IT affects or might affect a firm's competitive environment. It has been suggested that this is not enough. The focus must also be on strengths and weaknesses of a firm. The *resource-based view* of the firm, developed by Wernerfelt (1984), Barony (1991, 1995), and others, has this focus. This view makes two assertions about firms. The first is *resource heterogeneity,* which means that resources and capabilities[6] may be heterogeneously distributed across competing firms. The second is *resource immobility,* which means that these differences in resources and capabilities may be stable over time. A firm's resources and capabilities include all financial, human, physical, and organisational assets utilised by a firm to develop, manufacture, and deliver services and products to its customers. According to Barney (1994, 1997), the following four questions may be asked about any resource or capability to assess whether or not it can be a source of competitive advantage:

- "*The Question of Value.* Do a firm's resources and capabilities enable the firm to respond to environmental threats or opportunities?" (Barney, 1997, p. 145)
- "*The Question of Rareness.* How many competing firms already possess particular valuable resources and capabilities?" (ibid., p. 148).
- "*The Question of Imitability.* Do firms without a resource or capability face a cost disadvantage in obtaining it compared to firms that already possess it?" (ibid., p. 150).
- "*The Question of Organisation.* Is a firm organised to exploit the full competitive potential of its resources and capabilities." (ibid., p. 160).

Barney used these four questions to form a Value, Rareness Imitability and Organization (VRIO) framework to understand the potential competitive implications of exploiting any of a firm's resources and capabilities (Table 1).

The VRIO framework can be used to evaluate the competitive implications of management development of DSS. For any specific DSS, decision task, or decision process, it is possible to assess these implications. A specific DSS may be vied as consists of three components 1) the data component, 2) the model component and 3) the dialogue component (Sprague and Watson, 1996). For each of the three components, and for the total DSS, it is possible to evaluate: if they are valuable, if they are valuable, if they are costly to imitate, and if they are exploited by the firm.

We have seen DSSs where the data component and the model component ,when exploited by the firm. have given that firm a competitive advantage. In one firm, the management developed a DSS whose data base contained sales data that helped the firm make better marketing decisions. Since this data was not costly to collect, it gave the firm a temporary competitive advantage. It took the firm's competitors about one year to establish their own data bases in response.

In another firm the management developed a DSS which, when exploited by the firm, gave it a sustained competitive advantage. The firm spent several years developing various market indices which were incorporated as models in the DSS.

---

6 Writers on the resource based view define these and related concepts differently but for our purposes they can, and will, be used interchangeable.

These indices were better predictors of market changes than were the official indices, available to all the firms in the industry. The DSS was used in several contexts: from tactical decision processes, like production planning, to strategic decision processes, like production capacity investment decisions. The DSS, and its use in the various decision processes, was valuable to the firm. The competitors did not have this resource and they could not imitate it in an inexpensive way, or substitute it. The resource was exploited well by the firm.

Table 1 The VRIO framework for evaluating the competitive implications of a firm's resources and capabilities (Barney, 1997, p. 163).

Is a resource or capability . . .

Valuable?	Rare?	Costly to imitate?	Exploited by the organization	Competitive implications	Economic performance
no	—	—	no	competitive disadvantage	Below normal
yes	no	—		competitive parity	Normal
yes	yes	no		temporary competitive advantage	Above normal
yes	yes	yes	yes	sustained competitive advantage	Above normal

Although the resource-based view of the firm, and the VRIO framework, are powerful, they have limitations (Barney, 1997). First, rapid and unpredictable changes in a firm's environment can change the value of a firm's resources. In the case that a firm has gained a sustained competitive advantage, because of its decision process and DSS, this advantage will not last forever. It can be displaced through revolutionary change in the firm's environment.

One way for a firm to prepare itself for such a change would be to design and develop decision processes and DSS that can support the firm in becoming dynamically stable (c.f. the discussion in Section 3.2). Second, the VRIO might suggest that firms and managers have a limited ability to create sustained competitive advantages. Obviously, this is not true. Third, data necessary for a VRIO analysis can be hard to collect and several things are hard to measure.

6 DISCUSSIONS, CONCLUSIONS, AND FURTHER RESEARCH

In this chapter we have focused on management development of DSS - a major factor in business computing - and how this is in different ways are related to organisational change and transformation. Many management -developed DSS are developed using an evolutionary design approach. Even if evolutionary user DSS design has many positive effects, it seems that it can lead to too much exploitation of current decision tasks and, in the long run, be harmful to an organisation. We presented two approaches that could be used to overcome some of the problems with evolutionary design. The *strategic opportunistic design approach* can be seen as an enhancement of traditional evolutionary design. The aim is that managers should become more strategically oriented in their secondary decisions as well as in their DSS building activities. If we assume that strategic opportunistic DSS design can be effective for management development of DSS, there, of course, remain several unanswered questions and research topics such as: How do we best teach managers to become strategic opportunistic DSS designers? Can such a design approach be "formalised" and supported? Is it possible to design DSS generators that can support a user to act more strategically when designing?

A second approach discussed was *redesign of decision processes*. Unless a very expert-oriented approach is used, the first step would be to have the members of an organisation change their perceptions of decision tasks and processes. This is in line with the Scandinavian tradition of organisational change and CBIS development. Our case study suggests that the two approaches can be useful in overcoming some of the negative effects of management development of DSS. The goals of the two approaches are quite different. The goal of the first approach is to change the behaviour of the DSS user-designers without radically changing an organisation's decision processes. The goal of the second approach is to challenge and strive for radical changes in an organisation's current decision processes.

Looking at the history of DSS, one sees that the focus has changed over the years: from group and organisation to the individual and back to the group and organisation. Early DSS studies, like Scott Morton's (1971) study, focused on non-individual DSS. This was partly due to the high cost of hardware, software, and cost per line of code generated for the DSS - it was not economically justifiable to build individual DSS. The advent of personal computers made it possible to build small individually oriented DSS without too much effort and high costs. Hackathorn and Keen (1981) were among the first to distinguish among individual, group, and organisational DSS. In recent years, we have witnessed a growing interest in group and organisational DSS (see, for example, Lee *et al.*, 1988, and Nunamaker et. al., 1992). So far, most of the writings on organisational DSS have been on how to conceptualise and define ODSS and on the IT to be used in building ODSS. Very little has been done on the development of specific approaches for designing ODSS.

We feel that there is a need to develop DSS design approaches that are single shot approaches, but where the purpose is to achieve radical improvements through redesigning and reengineering decision processes. If we want such approaches to be based on decision making theories, one starting point could be the work of Huber and McDaniel (1986). They propose a decision-making paradigm of organisation design and provide sensitising concepts. They give guidelines, for example, on designing decision management systems. However, Huber and McDaniel do not provide any methods and techniques that can be used in design.

An interesting DSS development approach, more or less in line with Huber and MacDaniel's ideas, has been suggested by Adam (1996, 1997). This approach is based on social network analysis and stresses the multi-manager nature of most important organisational decision processes. It could be interesting to also look at workflow management approaches (Sherr, 1993) and approaches based on an organisation change view (Ferioli and Migliarese, 1996, Migliarese and Ferioli, 1997). These approaches could be complemented with more cognitively oriented approaches. At the same time, it should be noted that the research community do not seem to know exactly what constitutes management processes. A management process is often semi- or unstructured, more or less discontinuous, often ad hoc, in many cases based on intuition, and cognitive. This means that, in general, management processes are not a target for the same kind of process innovation that can be found for standard order management or manufacturing. There is a need to develop ways to combine *decision process reengineering,* as a discrete (project based) initiative with incremental initiatives for development of ongoing decision processes: i.e., taking an approaches that marries radical innovation and strategic opportunistic design.

In the case study above, we focused exclusively on Alfa's internal decision processes, but it is also possible to take a broader view on decision processes. concerning business process redesign, Short and Venkatraman (1992) suggest that it might be of greater strategic importance to an organisation to redesign business networks, that is, to reconceptualize the roles of the organisation and its key business processes within the larger business network. Short and Venkatraman's ideas can be transferred to *decision process redesign.* Instead of focusing on an organisation's decision processes infrastructure, one can focus on how to reconceptualize and redesign an organisation's decision processes within the larger decision network. It seems that Adam's (1996, 1997) approach could be useful to develop DSS within a larger decision network.

A relevant research issue to address in future is, of course, how the relationship between exploitation and exploration can be changed by providing different forms of easy-to-use computer-based tools. It should also be interesting to see if certain computer-based tools induce exploration or exploitation. Using a DSS for exploration of new alternatives may reduce the likelihood of learning and improvement of existing products/services and processes. Designing and implementing DSS for improvements of existing decision processes may make exploration less likely and attractive. A trend that is very clear is that IT and software for DSS generation is becoming cheaper, more powerful, and easier to use. Thus it is likely that DSS-supported exploitation will become easier and cheaper in the future. DSS-supported exploitation will probably be more rewarding than it used to be, at least in the short run. As far as we know, these issues have not been addressed in the literature, and there are no reported studies that have investigated them empirically. Another problem with the DSS design approaches in cells A and B, in figure 2, is that too much focus and efforts on developing stand-alone applications might lead to a neglect of the design and creation of a technology platform in an organisation which should be capable of supporting a variety applications, most of which have not yet been designed, or even foreseen.

In the previous section, we focused on the question of the value of management developed DSS. We suggested that one way to address this question could be through the *resource based view*, using the VRIO framework. while other researchers have suggested the use of the framework in IS research and practice (Andreu and Ciborra, 1996a, b; Mata et al. 1995), empirical research on its usefulness is needed. An implication of the resource base view of the firm is that managers and DSS personnel have to become more managerial and organisational oriented. Meanwhile, the standard view of DSS in the literature has been too technically oriented - the same point has been made by Murphy (1994).

7 REFERENCES

Adam, F. (1996) Experimentation with Organisation Analyser, a tool for the study of decision making networks in organisations, in *Implementing systems for supporting management decisions* (eds. P. Humphreys, L. Bannon, A. McCosh, P. Migliarese and J.-C. Pomerol), Chapman & Hall, London. 1-20.

Adam, F. (1997) Can social network analysis provide a new analytical approach for DSS development and DSS research. *Proceedings of the 5th European Conference on Information Systems*, 413-426.

Anderson, J. R. (1983) *The architecture of cognition.* Harvard University Press, Cambridge, MA.

Andreu, R. and Ciborra, C. (1996a) Core capabilities and information technology: an organizational learning approach, in *Organizational learning and competitive advantage* (eds. B. Moingeon and A. Edmondson), Sage, London, 121-138.

Andreu, R. and Ciborra, C. (1996b) Organizational learning and core capabilities development: the role of IT. *Journal of Strategic Information Systems*, **5**, 111-127.

Avdic, A. (1995) Work-integrated systems development with spreadsheet programs. Unpublished Licentiate dissertation, Linköping University, Linköping, Sweden (in Swedish).

Barney, J. B. (1991) Firm resources and sustained competitive advantage. *Journal of Management*, **17,** 99-120.

Barney, J. B. (1994) Bringing managers back in: a resource-based analysis of the role of managers in creating and sustaining competitive advantages for firms, in *Does management matter? - on competencies and competitive advantage* (ed. A. T. Malm), Lund University Press, Lund, Sweden, 1-36.

Barney, J. B. (1995) Looking inside for competitive advantage. *Academy of Management Executive*, **9,** 49-61.

Barney, J. B. (1997) *Gaining and sustaining competitive advantage.* Addison-Wesley, Reading, MA.

Boynton, A. C. (1993) Achieving dynamic stability through information technology. *California Management Review*, **35,** 58-77.

Brancheau, J. C. and Brown, C.V. (1993) The management of end-user computing: status and directions. *ACM Computing Surveys*, **25,** 437-482.

Brunsson, N. (1985) *The irrational organization: irrationality as a basis for organizational action and change.* John Wiley & Sons, Chichester.

Brunsson, N. (1989) *The organization of hypocrisy: talk, decisions and actions in organizations.* John Wiley & Sons, New York.

Carlsson, S. A. (1984) Decision support systems: a critical assessment of two approaches for developing decision support systems, in *Systems development - by whom, for whom, and how?* (ed. H.-E. Nissen), Swedish Work Environment Fund, Stockholm, 99-113 (in Swedish).

Carlsson, S. A. (1988) A longitudinal study of spreadsheet program use. *Journal of Management Information Systems*, **5,** 82-100.

Carlsson, S. A. (1989) Why Johnny can't or won't spreadsheet. *Scandinavian Journal of Information Systems*, **1,** 118-142.

Carlsson, S. A. (1991) DSS and unlearning: taking organizational environments into account, in *Environments for supporting decision processes* (eds. H. G. Sol and J. Vecsenyi), North-Holland, Amsterdam, 371-385.

Carlsson, S. A. (1994) Continuous development of decision tasks versus redesign of decision processes, in *Proceeding of the IFIP WG8.3 conference on Decision support in organizational transformation* (eds. B. Mayon-White, S. Ayestarán and P. Humphreys), San Sebastian, Spain, 137-154.

Chu, P.C. and Elam, J. J. (1990) Induced system restrictiveness: an experimental demonstration. *IEEE Transactions on Systems, Man, and Cybernetics*, **20**, 195-201.

Ciborra, C. (1994) The grassroots of IT and strategy, in *Strategic information systems: a European perspective* (eds. C. Ciborra and T. Jelassi), John Wiley & Sons, Chichester, England, 3-24.

Cooprider, J. G. and Henderson, J. C. (1990/91) Technology-process fit: perspectives on achieving prototyping effectiveness. *Journal of Management Information Systems*, **7**, 67-87.

Courbon, J. C. (1996) User-centred DSS design and implementation, in *Implementing systems for supporting management decisions* (eds. P. Humphreys, L. Bannon, A. McCosh, P. Migliarese and J.-C. Pomerol), Chapman & Hall, London, 108-123.

Courbon, J. C., Grajew, J. and Tolovi, J. (1978) Design and implementation of decision support systems by an evolutive approach. Working Paper, Institut d'Administration des Enterprises, Université des Sciences Sociales, Grenoble, France.

Davenport, T. H. (1993) *Process innovation: reengineering work through information technology*. Harvard Business School Press, Boston, MA.

Davenport, T. H. and Short, J. E. (1990) The new industrial engineering: information technology and business process redesign. *Sloan Management Review*, **31**, 11-27.

Davis, G. B. (1989) CAUTION: User-developed systems can be dangerous to your organization, in *End-user computing: concepts, issues and applications* (ed. R. R. Nelson), John Wiley & Sons, New York, 209-228.

Earl, M. J. (1978) Prototype systems for accounting, information and control. *Accounting, Organizations and Society*, **3**, 161-170.

Edberg, D. T. and Bowman B. J. (1996) User-developed applications: an empirical study of application quality and developer productivity. *Journal of Management Information Systems*, **13**, 167-185.

Fahy, M. and Murphy, C. (1996) From end user computing to management developed systems. *Proceedings of the 4th European Conference on Information Systems*, 127-142.

Ferioli, C. and Migliarese, P. (1996) A DSS design method based on organizational change, in *Implementing systems for supporting management decisions* (eds. P. Humphreys, L. Bannon, A. McCosh, P. Migliarese and J.-C. Pomerol), Chapman & Hall, London, 160-181.

Findley, J. J. (1983) Critical success factors for DSS implementation. Presentation at the Third International Conference on Decision Support Systems, DSS-83, June 27-29, Boston, MA.

Finkelstein, C. (1992) *Information Engineering*. Addison-Wesley, Reading, MA.

Finlay, P.N. and Wilson J. M. (1997) Validity of decision support systems: towards a validation methodology. *Systems Research and Behavioral Science*, **14,** 169-182.

Ginzberg, M J. (1978) Redesign of managerial tasks: a requisite for successful decision support systems. *MIS Quarterly*, 2(1), 39-52.

Ginzberg, M. J. and Ariav, G. (1986) Methodologies for DSS analysis and design: a contingency approach to their application. *Proceedings Seventh International Conference on Information Systems*, 15-17 December, San Diego, CA, 46-56.

Hackathorn, R. D. and Keen, P. G. W. (1981) Organizational strategies for personal computing in decision support systems. *MIS Quarterly*, **5,** 21-27.

Hammer, M. (1990) Reengineering work: don't automate, obliterate. *Harvard Business Review*, **68,** 104-112.

Hammer, M. and Champy, J. (1993) *Reengineering the corporation: a manifesto for business revolution*. Harper Business, New York.

Handy, C. (1990) *The age of unreason*. Harvard Business School Press, Boston

Hayes-Roth, B. and Hayes-Roth, F. (1979) A cognitive model of planning. *Cognitive Science*, **3**, 275-310.

Henderson, J. C. and Ingraham, R. S. (1982) Prototyping for DSS: a critical appraisal, in *Decision support systems* (eds. M. J. Ginzberg, W. Reitman and E. A. Stour), North-Holland, Amsterdam, 79-96.

Hogue, J. T. and Watson, H. J. (1984) Current practices in the development of decision support systems. *Proceedings Fifth International Conference on Information Systems*, November 28-30, Tucson, AZ, 117-127.

Huber, G. P. and McDaniel, R. R. (1986) The decision-making paradigm of organizational design. *Management Science*, **32,** 572-589.

Hurst, G. E., Jr., Ness, D. N., Gambino, T. J. and Johnson, T. H. (1983) Growing DSS: a flexible, evolutionary approach, in *Building decision support systems* (ed. J. L. Bennett), Addison-Wesley, Reading, MA, 111-132.

IBM (1984) *Business systems planning: information systems planning guide*. International Business Machines Corporation, GE20-0527-4, White Plains,

Iivari, J. (1991) A paradigmatic analysis of contemporary schools of IS development. *European Journal of Information Systems*, 1(4), 249-272.

Isenberg, D. J. (1987) The tactics of strategic opportunism. *Harvard Business Review*, **65,** 92-97.

Isenberg, D. J (1988) Managerial thinking: an inquiring into how senior managers think. Book manuscript.

Kahneman, D., Slovic, P. and Tversky, A. (eds.)(1982) *Judgement under uncertainty: heuristics and biases*. Cambridge University Press, New York.

Jackson, M. C. (1995) Beyond the fads: systems thinking for managers Systems Research, **12**, 25

Keen, P. G. W. (1980) Adaptive design for decision support systems. *Data Base*, **12,** 15-25.

Keen, P. G. W. and Scott Morton, M. S. (1978) *Decision support systems: an organizational perspective*. Addison-Wesley, Reading, MA.

Kolb, D. A. (1984) *Experiential learning: experience as the source of learning and development.* Prentice-Hall, Englewood Cliffs, NJ.

Lee, R. M., McCosh, A.M. and Migliarese, P. (eds.)(1988) *Organizational decision support systems.* North-Holland, Amsterdam.

Lucas, H., Jr. (1978) The evolution of an information system: from key-man to every person. *Sloan Management Review*, **19,** 39-52.

Malone, T. W. (1997) Is empowerment just a fad? Control, decision making, and IT. *Sloan Management Review*, **38**, 23-35.

March, J. G. (1991) Exploration and exploitation in organizational learning. *Organization Science*, **2,** 71-87.

Marsden, J. R. and Pingry, D. E. (1986a) Problem structure and DSS design. *Proceedings of the Nineteenth Annual Hawaii International Conference on Systems Sciences*, 603-608.

Marsden, J. R. and Pingry, D. E. (1986b) Generating an optimal information system: PMAX-SLDC and the redirection of MIS research (or how to help Joe eat salmon). *Journal of Management Information Systems*, **3,** 32-51.

Marsden, J. R. and Pingry, D. E. (1988) End user-IS design professional interaction - information exchange for firm profit or end user satisfaction?. *Information & Management*, **14,** 75-80.

Mata, F. J., Fuerst, W. L. and Barney, J. B. (1995) Information technology and sustained competitive advantage: a resource-based analysis. *MIS Quarterly*, **19,** 487-505.

Migliarese, P. and Ferioli, C. (1997) The Organizational Relational model: proposal and results. *This volume*, 121-146.

Moore, J. H. and Chang, M. G. (1983) Meta-design considerations in building DSS, in *Building decision support systems* (ed. J. L. Bennett), Addison-Wesley, Reading, MA, 173-204.

Murphy, C. (1994) Decision support systems - putting emphasis on personnel rather than technology, in *Proceedings of the IFIP WG8.3 Conference on Decision support in organizational transformation* (eds. B. Mayon-White, S. Ayestarán and P. Humphreys) San Sebastian, Spain, 106-120.

Ness, D. N. (1975) Interactive systems: theories of design. Paper presented at the Joint Wharton/Office of Naval Research Conference on Interactive Information and Decision Support Systems, November 4-7, Department of Decision Sciences, The Wharton School, University of Pennsylvania, Philadelphia, PA.

Nohria, N. and Ghoshal, S. (1997) *The differentiated network.* Jossey-Bass, San Francisco, CA.

Nunamaker, J. F., Applegate, L. M., Culnan, M. J., Fedorowicz, J., George, J. F., Gutek, B., Henderson, J. C., King, J. L., Konsynski, B. R., Star, S. L., Swanson, E. B., Valacich J. S. and Mud, R. W. (1992) Organizational decision support systems (ODSS), in *Information systems and decision processes* (eds. E. A Stohr and B. R Konsynski), IEEE Computer Society Press, Los Alamitos, CA, 137-166.

Panko, R. R. (1988) *End user computing: management, applications, and technology*. John Wiley & Sons, New York.

Panko, R. R (1997a) Spreadsheet on trial: a survey of research on spreadsheet risks. *Proceedings of the 29th Hawaii International Conference on Systems Sciences*, 326-335. URL http://www.cba.hawaii.edu/panko/research/risks/h6trial.htm

Panko, R. (1997b) Spreadsheet research. URL http://www.cba.hawaii.edu/panko/ssr/

Ronen, B., Palley, M. A. and Lucas, H. C., Jr. (1989) Spreadsheet analysis and design. *Communications of the ACM*, **32** 84-93.

Sage, A. P. (1991) *Decision support systems engineering*. John Wiley & Sons, New York.

Scott Morton, M. S. (1971) *Management decision systems: computer-based support for decision making*. Graduate School of Business Administration, Harvard University, Boston, MA.

Sherr, A. L. (1993) A new approach to business processes. *IBM Systems Journal*, **32,** 80-98.

Short, J. E. and Venkatraman, N. (1992) Beyond business process redesign: redefining Baxter's business network. *Sloan Management Review*, **34,** 7-21.

Silver, M. S. (1991) *Systems that support decision makers: description and analysis*. John Wiley & Sons, Chichester, England.

Sprague, R. H., Jr. and Carlson, E. D. (1982) *Building effective decision support systems*. Prentice-Hall, Englewood Cliffs, NJ.

Sprague, R. H., Jr. and Watson, H. J. (1996) *Decision support for management*. Prentice-Hall, Upper Saddle River, NJ.

Stabell, C. B. (1975) Design and implementation of decision support systems, some implications of a recent study, in *The implementation of computer-based decision aids* (ed. P. G. W. Keen), Proceedings of a Conference Sponsored by the Center for Information Systems Research, Massachusetts Institute of Technology, Cambridge, MA, April 3-5.

Stabell, C. B. (1983) A decision-oriented approach to building decision support systems, in *Building decision support systems* (ed. J. L. Bennett), Addison-Wesley, Reading, MA, 221-260.

Tapscott, D. (1996) *The digital economy: promise and peril in the age of networked intelligence*. McGraw-Hill, New York.

Wernerfelt, B. (1984) A resource-based view of the firm. *Strategic Management Journal*, **5**, 171-180.

White, D. J. (1975) Coordinating paper: the nature of decision theory, in *The role and effectiveness of theories of decision in practice* (eds. D. J. White and K. C. Bowen), Hodder & Stoughton, London, 3-16.

Wyner, G. M. and Malone T. W. (1996) Cowboys or commanders: does information technology lead to decentralisation? *Proceedings of the Seventeenth International Conference on Information Systems*.

8 BIOGRAPHY

Sven A. Carlsson is assistant professor at Department of Informatics, Lund University, Sweden. He has a Ph.D. in Informatics from the School of Economics and Management at Lund University. His research interests include the use of information technology to support both individual and group decision making, strategic information systems, organizational transformation through information technology, and knowledge management. He has been a visiting scholar at University of Arizona, Tucson, University of Southern California, and National University of Singapore. He has published in *Journal of Management Information Systems*, *Information & Management*, *Journal of Decision Systems*, *Scandinavian Journal of Information Systems*, and international conference proceedings.

9

The Organizational Relational model: proposal and results*

P. Migliarese
Università della Calabria e Politecnico di Milano
P.zza Leonardo da Vinci, 32 - 20133 Milano - Italy
Fax +39.2.2399.2720
e-mail migliare@mail.ecopro.polimi.it

C. Ferioli
Politecnico di Milano
P.zza Leonardo da Vinci, 32 - 20133 Milano - Italy
Fax +39.2.2399.2720
e-mail ferioli@mail.ecopro.polimi.it

Abstract

The paper proposes a new method, the Organizational Relational model, based on the new concept of Relation, for the analysis of innovative organizational models like the network organization . The proposal is supported through results and through the evidence from some applications in real situations. Two different basic elements can be distinguished in the innovative organization: nodes (i.e. organizational units or agents) and links among nodes (i.e. organizational relations, contracts, communication channels or architectures). This paper explains the important role of IT in providing tools for the innovative organizations. IT and especially GDSS extend the autonomy of nodes and provide instruments for supporting the links between two (or more) nodes. The proposed method describes the relation according to four elements: the tools supporting the link, the goals of the node, the organizational rules and norms of the organizational group and the organizational culture. Moreover, the proposed method provides a "guide" based on the oppositions *formal versus informal and society versus community* for describing the role of IT (especially GDSS) in innovative organizational models. The method has been applied in different organizational contexts, like public health and various industrial companies. While the specific applications are described and detailed in other papers, the empirical evidences and the synthetic results obtained

---

* The paper is due to the collaboration of the authors. Nevertheless, par. 1, 4 and 5 are common, par. 2 is mainly due to Piero Migliarese, par. 3 is mainly due to Claudio Ferioli.

are described in this paper as a confirmation of the proposed organizational framework and method.

Keywords

Innovative organizational models, network organizational models, relational organizational model, organisational networks, job modification, organisational culture

1 INTRODUCTION

In the research on new models of organization, network enterprise or network organizational models are emerging and largely successful concepts. Two different types can be distinguished with respect to the network organization: *external networks,* in which several distinct companies are linked in various forms and *internal networks,* in which distinct organizational units of the same company have particular managerial autonomy and are linked by complex relations apart from the hierarchical one.

In the last few years research on dynamic networks has grown rapidly and valuable results have been achieved in industrial organization theory with regard to the forms of networks in different enterprises and the causes that lead to the growth and development of inter-firm networks (Miles and Snow, 1986). External networks have been described and analysed in detail, and many examples and theories have been provided in the literature. However, internal networks research has given fewer results and few studies have been provided.

Nevertheless, many recent signals from companies suggest that a model of network organization is really emerging in the industrial world. Many companies have brought changes and innovation in their organizations: we think that in many cases the model of internal network organization can describe the resulting organizational forms.

Some of these changes involve the use of self-managed teams such as, in the manufacturing area, the U.T.E.s (Technological Elementary Units) of F.I.A.T., the use of the internal market mechanism to regulate interchanges among different organizational units in the same company, the disappearance of clear firm borders with the growth of units located neither inside nor outside the factory, such as some suppliers of FIAT Auto, which are neither inside the organization, since they are legally autonomous, nor completely outside, since they physically work in the area of the customer (Cesaria, 1993).

It is possible to say that actual trends in organizations are towards information-based as well as knowledge-based organizations, and that organizational units are largely composed of specialists. Employees are encouraged to act in an entrepreneurial way, as they have to achieve the objective assigned to their organizational unit; in particular they can obtain the know-how and the ability required for the assigned objectives through relations with colleagues and through interchange of services or information with other organizational units (Drucker, 1988).

In the present competitive environment, innovative organizational forms seem to enlarge the autonomy of nodes and seem to foster the establishment of complex links among nodes for improving know-how, flexibility and capacity to react rapidly to environmental changes.

The internal network organization is considered here with reference to two basic elements: the autonomy of nodes and the link complexity.

Nodes can be defined both as organizational units and as agents. The need for enlarged *autonomy of nodes* is one of the most relevant aspects of the new organizational forms which have emerged in the last few years. The need for autonomy is due to the new competitive features in the present economic environment. The enlarged autonomy requires improvement of the skills and the know-how of every node. This paper explains the role of IT in supporting autonomy of nodes. In particular, DSS and GDSS provide methodology for problem solving, tools for decision making and instruments for sharing knowledge: in this way they increase the capacity and the know-how of the nodes and they allow the enlargement of the autonomy of nodes.

The second aspect of network organization regards the capability of nodes in creating complex *links*. Every node can obtain the capacity and the know-how required for its objectives through making links with other nodes: the link allows the exchange of information, services, know-how, etc., between two (or more) nodes through complex organizational relations or communication architectures and channels or special contracts. The paper explains the role of IT and GDSS in supporting the links in network organizations: IT establishes a channel of communication between two (or more) nodes and provides facilities for the exchange of information. For this reason, IT as well as GDSS is one of the most powerful instruments for creating links among nodes.

Moreover the paper describes a specific method for the analysis and the design of network organizations based on the concept of *relation* (a relational approach to the network organization). A relation is the result of the connection of two nodes: schematically, the relation is made up of the two nodes together with the links that connect the two nodes. The relation considers both properties of the nodes and characteristics of the link itself. The paper proposes a method for the analysis of relations derived from the AGIL model (Adaptation, Goal, Integration, Latency). This model, proposed by T. Parsons for sociological analysis, has been modified for the analysis of the relation in the network organization at micro-analysis level.

In the proposed modified AGIL method, the relation is described according to four components: the *tools* that support the connection, and that enable organizational units. to react to the environmental variables (Adaptation to the environment); the *goals* of the nodes for which the relation is created; the *organizational rules and norms* that allow the Integration of individuals in organizational groups, and the Latent *organizational culture.*

Concerning the design of IT systems within a network organization, the paper proposes two basic dilemmas: formal/informal and community/society. The dilemma formal/informal considers the presence in each of the four components of formal elements and of informal ones. The opposition community/society was introduced by F. Tonnies for sociological analysis. The word *community* indicates aggregations based on traditional behaviour and common will of people, while *society* considered to be based on common accords, on legal rules and on contracts. The paper proposes to examine the role of GDSS and IT in designing the relations in network organizations: along the two basic dilemmas. Information Technology amplifies formal characters and societal aspects, and reduces informal and community ones. In this way IT improves the efficiency of the relation, but reduces the richness of the interaction: the design of IT tools has to solve the trade-off between these two aspects.

The paper is organized as follows: *section two* describes the two basic elements of the network organization: the nodes and the links among nodes. A method (the *relational method*) is proposed for the analysis and the design of network organization, based on the concept of relation. The concept of relation refers both to the link and to the nodes connected by the link. First of all, the proposed method provides the scheme of the four basic elements of the relation: the *tools,* the *goals,* the *organizational rules,* the *organizational culture.* Secondly, the proposed method suggests a guide for the analysis of the four basic elements of the relation, based on the opposition *formal/informal* and on the opposition *community/society.*

In *section three,* the paper explains the role of IT in the network organization. IT (especially DSS and GDSS) provides support both to autonomy of nodes and to the establishment of links. As regards autonomy of nodes, IT (especially DSS and GDSS) improves the know-how, the problem solving ability and the decision making capacity of nodes. The paper describes the example of Delta methodology, a technique implemented in Digital and based on distributed data bases connected with the computer network. As regards links, IT and especially GDSS provide different tools that support the creation of links between two (or more) nodes and facilitate the communication through the links.

In *section four,* applications of the proposed relational model are briefly outlined. In particular a successful IT application, used in the health service sector is presented as well as some applications in manufacturing enterprise environments. The use of the relational method was helpful in the design process of an IT system for analyzing the modification of the "organizational relations" among the main actors in the health service organization. Other successful applications concern empirical research conducted in a sample of enterprises (AT&T, Olivetti, Digital) for analyzing of an existence and effectiveness of network organizations. This empirical research revealed that the presence of network organization was positively correlated with effectiveness described in the section , moreover, a case study conducted in the Italian company Olivetti, in which the existence of several "relations" among organizational units can be discovered and explained with the proposed Relational Model. While the concept of network organization is somehow not totally defined, the "relational organizational model" shows a great explanation power and the concept of relation proved very helpful in analyzing traditional as well as innovative organizational forms. Conclusions follow.

2 THE RELATIONAL MODEL: A NEW MODEL PROPOSED FOR ORGANIZATIONAL ANALYSIS

New competitive and environmental features require new models for organizational analysis. Traditional models miss some of the new requisite for organizational design. For example, managers have to design flexible organizations, based on dispersed organizational units located in all over the world; Information Technology has became the main system for co-ordination and communication; companies adopt new mixed strategies of collaboration *and* competition.

Organizational designers need to integrate their competencies with new tools and new perspectives. Traditional organization charts represent only hierarchical lines of control and communication: they are no longer adequate for describing organizations composed of semi-autonomous organizational units, that can create several links with other organizational units (as well as with other companies) through lateral mechanisms of co-ordination and communication.

New *client-supplier* links provide another example. In several cases the reduction of *slack-resources* has drastically changed this tie from the classical market exchange to a new mechanism. New client-supplier links are based on several aspects, such as: (i) the definition of some common goals (partial economic-risk sharing, objectives of product quality improvements, etc.), (ii) long period contracts, (iii) strong interpersonal trust, (iv) organizational exchange (knowledge sharing, information exchange, etc.), (v) technical links, such as computer networks, etc. (Lamming, 1993).

Traditionally, client-supplier links have been studied through the analysis of economic exchange based on the concept of economic transaction (Williamson, 1975; Jensen and Meckling, 1976; Alchian and Demsez, 1972). But nowadays the transaction-costs model can provide only a partial description of these new links, because it considers only economic elements and disregards technical, social and organizational aspects.

2.1 The proposed Relational model for organizational analysis

We propose a new model for organizational analysis, the *relational model* of organization. The researches on this new model are still in progress, nevertheless some significant theoretical and practical results have been achieved. The Relational model for organizational analysis describes the organizations as *networks* of *nodes* linked through *organizational relations*.

Nodes are composed of organizational actors. Several criteria may be defined for the location of nodes: formal borders of organizational units, similarity in technical activity, equality in hierarchical position, similarity in professional qualification, etc. The choice of the best criteria may vary according to the purpose of the analysis.

For example, for the design of a Decision Support System supporting technical activities, organizational actors will be grouped in nodes according to their technical qualifications. Instead, if the purpose of the analysis is the implementation of an IT support for lateral communication, the best criteria might be the relational homogeneity of nodes, i.e., defining the nodes so that all the components of a node have the same set of relations with every other organizational actor (Baker, 1992).

Moreover the width of the nodes varies in relation to the size of the analysis (Ferioli and Migliarese, 1994). For example, if the analysis covers a whole organization with many divisions located in several countries, a local factory may be considered a node; whereas if the analysis is limited to a shop floor, the size of nodes is restricted to the individual employee.

Each node is linked with other nodes through a complex set of connections (see for example the previously described client-supplier link), that is described as *organizational relation.*

The word "relation" was firstly introduced in organization theory by Elton Mayo and his Human Relations school. Even if nobody can deny the importance of this school in organization studies, the concept of relation is used here with a limited meaning: (1) only interpersonal relations are considered; (2) the analysis is centred on the organizational climate, whereas the relation remains only in the background. Some other authors (Gabarro, 1990; Granovetter, 1992; Ferioli and Migliarese, 1994) have proposed instead the concept of *organizational relation* as the *basis* for organizational analysis.

The *organizational relation* is defined as a link between two organizational actors (individuals and/or organizational units and/or different companies) with the following characteristics: (a) it is orientated toward a (partially) common goal, (b) it is not trivial, (c) it is not an occasional link, (d) it is supported by several tools.

(a) Two economic actors establish an *organizational relation* for pursuing a (partially) shared goal. For example, the client-supplier link becomes an *organizational relation* if client and supplier identify a common objective (such as a product quality improvement; a reciprocal economic aid; etc.). If the shared goal disappears, the *organizational relation* dies or changes to another mechanism (for example to a classical market contract).

(b) The shared goals of the *organizational relation* are jointed to the objectives of the organization (for example productivity objectives, market objectives, etc.). This means that the *organizational relation* is not "trivial", but created by the nodes in order to obtain their organizational objectives. This not "trivial" feature distinguishes organizational relations from pure phenomenological, interpersonal interactions, that (roughly speaking) are not linked to any organizational objectives.

(c) A link requires a medium/long period to become an *organizational relation.*

(d) The *organizational relation* is supported by several tools, such as: formal contracts, interpersonal links, exchange of materials/services, exchange of information, etc.

Table 1 The definition of relation

- It is based on a (partially) common goal
- It is not trivial
- It is not an occasional link
- It is supported by several tools

2.2 The design method of organizational relations

A method for the design of organisational relation has been proposed by the authors. This method describes *organizational relations* through four axes: the *tools* supporting the relation, the *goal(s)* common to the economic actors, the *norms* regulating the behaviour of actors within the relation and the *cultural background* associated to the relation. They represent the four base elements common to every *organizational relation,* whereas they do not provide the *real* description of *organizational relations* (For example a client-supplier relation has a different "shape" from a relation between two single employees. Nevertheless the four axes position the analysis and the design for both relations)

Tools

The axis of tools regards the necessary instruments for a relation to take place or the support to improve relation effectiveness. Different kinds of tools are used in organizations for supporting collaborative relations or for enabling the creation of relations:

Inter-personal contacts are the main instruments for many collaborative relations, so that many personnel executives try to promote this type of interaction. Some of the instruments for fostering interpersonal contact are (Hastings, 1993):

- periodic meetings for people from different divisions;
- residential training periods for new employees (6-9 months);
- personnel rotation (also for limited period); etc.

Group management techniques and working group methodologies are tools that improve group work collaboration, and they are required for every group leader.

IT instruments are tools for supporting and creating communication channels among economic/organizational actors.

The *price system* in the internal market mechanism provides instruments for establishing relations among organizational units, so it can be classified as a tool.

According to Miles and Snow (1992), various companies are using an internal market mechanism for regulating internal interactions: some organizational units play the role of brokers and buy services/goods from other organizational units. Through this new rule system, the brokers create some particular product required by clients.

Goals

The axis of goals explains the purposes and the objectives for which an *organizational relation* is established and maintained. The presence of a shared goal is the *raison d'être* of the organizational relation: no effective relation can survive without defined goals. The previously described client-supplier *relations* are different from classical client-supplier market contracts because they are based on (partially) common objectives (common design of new products, shared objectives of quality improvement, joint investments in new plants, etc.). If the goal disappeared, the relation would change into another type of link (for example in a simple market exchange).

Moreover, the relation goals influence the remaining characteristics of the relation: they determine the amount of information to exchange, the need for negotiating mechanism and the required cultural background common to the actors involved in the relation (if the goals of the two persons/organizational units are different, the relation will require a negotiation and the creation of complex contractual norms and rules).

Rules

The axis of rules and norms defines the set of implicit as well as explicit rules that govern relations. Relational norms define the accepted behaviour: in this way they allow/prevent the integration of (new) actors in the group created through the relation. Relations are regulated either by general organizational rules and values, and by specific norms defined among involved organizational actors.

For example, the organizational relations based on internal market mechanisms are regulated through: (i) specific contracts -negotiated by the organizational units that create the relation, and (ii) general rules, that the headquarters has decided (for example) in order to promoting some company areas.

In most cases, many organizational rules are "implicit" and based on unwritten social values. In some organizations hierarchic relations are very formal and "cold", while in others they take place in an informal and friendly way.

Cultural background

The cultural background is composed of the organizational culture common to the two economic/organizational actors involved in the relation, i.e., the values, the traditions and the customs the two actors share.

The cultural background forms the base knowledge shared by the actors of the relation, i.e., the common assumptions that do not require any negotiation or contractual definition (Schein, 1984). A largely shared cultural background improves the effectiveness of organizational relations, as it reduces the need for negotiation and information exchange.

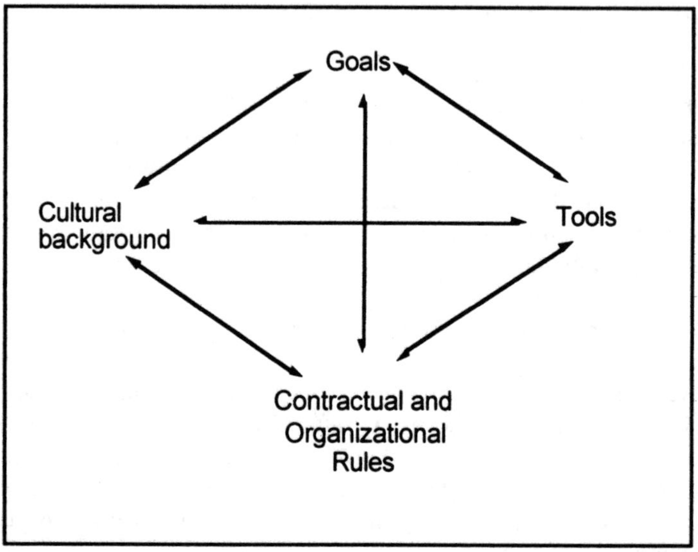

Figure 1 The four axes of the organizational relation according to the proposed method (Ferioli and Migliarese, 1994)

3 THE NEW ROLE OF IT AS RELATIONAL TECHNOLOGIES

The proposed Relational Perspective for the analysis of organizations provides indications for the design of IT supports and for their introduction in organizations. Information Technology plays the new role of *relational technologies* in new organizational models because it facilitates the *creation* of a *network* of organizational relations.

3.1 IT support for creation of nodes

IT based tools foster the constitution of semi-autonomous nodes, through providing support to technical and managerial decisions (DSS, MIS, EIS, etc.) that improve the decisional capabilities of managers as well as the competencies of organizational units.

Decisional support for management should facilitate managers to play the new role of *small businessman*, assigned to them by new competitive features (Leidner and Elam, 1993). Roughly speaking, these systems should provide two kinds of information:

- Data about organizational units subordinate to the manager in order to facilitate the control over a large number of employees (increased span of control) and the monitoring of the performance of organizational units (through economic and/or technical indicators);
- Data from outside the organizational unit, in order to facilitate the middle manager to act as an "entrepreneur". This requires the capability to respond to new opportunities/ties from the environment (that can be fostered for example with information about the economic environment, the technical/scientific community, etc.) as well as behaviour in line with the strategy and the main decisions of the company (that can be facilitated through data about main company decisions, market/economic company results, etc.).

Decisional supports for organizational units enlarge the capability of autonomous problem solving and decision making. Organizational units require an enlarged amount of information and know-how for solving complex but well-known problems. Decision Support Systems provide partial solutions to this need for knowledge (Ferioli and Migliarese, 1994). Roughly speaking, knowledge based DSS can provide organizational units with the technical capability for complex problem solving, through the "collection" of existing expertise and know-how. For example, a maintenance team whose activity is supported by a DSS has less need for interactions with other maintenance units for problem solving or sharing experience. All the know-how required is collected in the IT support, and the team is completely autonomous.

Moreover, organizational units need to improve their expertise and creativity, for finding valid solutions for new problems. Tools based on Artificial Intelligence can improve the capability of discovering new solutions for emerging problems, that were never faced before. For example, applications based on "neural networks" or on "genetic algorithms" can find hidden dependencies among data, build new models, etc.

3.2 IT support for the creation of organizational relations

IT can facilitate the creation of organizational relations among nodes, mainly through providing support to lateral mechanisms of communication and co-ordination. These mechanisms are based on the exchange of information among organizational units through channels different from hierarchy-based links. Lateral mechanisms are established by organizational units in order to pursue some specific organizational goal (for example: to buy services, to obtain information/solutions about a technical problem, etc.). The goal influences the "pattern" of the link. For example a production team (liable for a part of the production process, for example door assembling in a car production process) may establish links with:

- (link-1) the engineering office and the quality manager, for suggesting a door modification (this link may be based on a meeting);
- (link-2) the maintenance team, for planning plant servicing (this link may be based on a periodic planned meeting);
- (link-3) a similar production team, located in another plant, for solving a technical problem (this link may be based on interpersonal contact); etc.

Two main problems may affect communication in these links: (a) organizational units may be located in remote places and (b) the identification of "suitable" organizational units sometimes may be difficult (for example in link-3).

The elimination of communication obstacles (first problem) is one of the main areas of IT based application: IT communication tools solve the time and space constraints of communication among organizational units or even among different companies. Research on the field of Group Decision Support Systems (Nunamaker, Vogel and Konsynski, 1989; Gallupe, Bastianutti and Cooper, 1991) and on Computer Supported Cooperative Work (Bannon, 1997) provide important tools in this area.

Information Technology may also provide (partially) solutions for the problem of identifying the "suitable" organizational unit (second problem). In particular, Organizational Decision Support Systems (Lee, McCosh and Migliarese, 1988) collect information about the organizational units and the personnel belonging to the organization, their expertise, the organizational rules and procedures, etc. They provide a "map" of the organization and facilitate the research of the unit/person with particular characteristics.

An example of ODSS, provided by British Petroleum (Hastings, 1993) is outlined in figure 2. The BP high technology environmental department (called HSE technology team) provides knowledge and expertise for solving environmental problems and for preventing disasters. Those kinds of solutions are used by BP itself and are sold to BP's market client .The HSE technology team is composed of three research laboratories, located in three different places (two in UK and one in US); in spite of the fact that the HSE activities require great collaboration among all researchers. For improving integration, they have connected the three laboratories through a distributed personnel database, accessible by every researcher. The database memorises skills, specialisation, know-how and previous project experiences of all employees of the three laboratories, so that everybody in the department can access the information about researchers as if they were working in a unique small group. For example, it is possible to identify who was previously involved in a specified problem, who has the required expertise, etc.

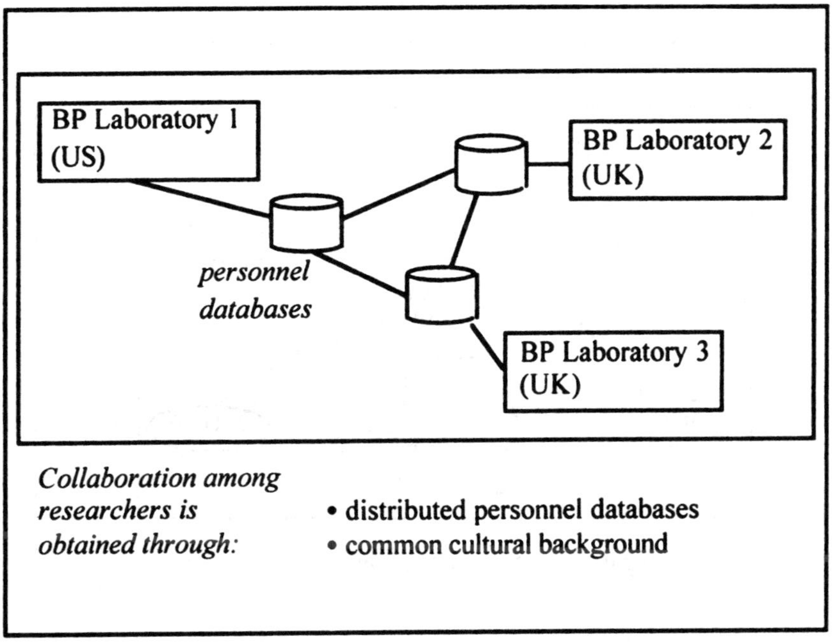

Figure 2 The ODSS of British Petroleum

3.3 IT as enablers of organizational relations

The previous example has shown the capability of IT to foster the creation of organizational relations. According to the proposed relational method for organizational analysis, Information Technology can be considered as a *tool;* just like many others mechanisms. Nevertheless, due to its great possibilities, IT is a *special tool*, able to foster organizational relations. New IT tools could be enablers of modern organizational mechanisms, based on flexible and effective relations. In some cases the *network* of *organizational relations* would not be possible without IT based *tools*.

An Italian example is provided by the network organization of Benetton, outline in figure 3. This company is composed of a central node, situated in Treviso, about 500 small factories, and a lot of shops all over the world. The small factories and the shops are linked to the central node by different kinds of formal contracts (most of them are franchising contracts) and by a computer network. The computer network supports the collection of orders from the shops to the head office, so as to make the production planning easy. Through the information network, the central node informs the linked factories about the quantity and the quality of goods to be produced. Without IT tools, the network of organizational relation in Benetton would perhaps be very different: it would involve a limited number of nodes and the exchange of information would not be as easy as now.

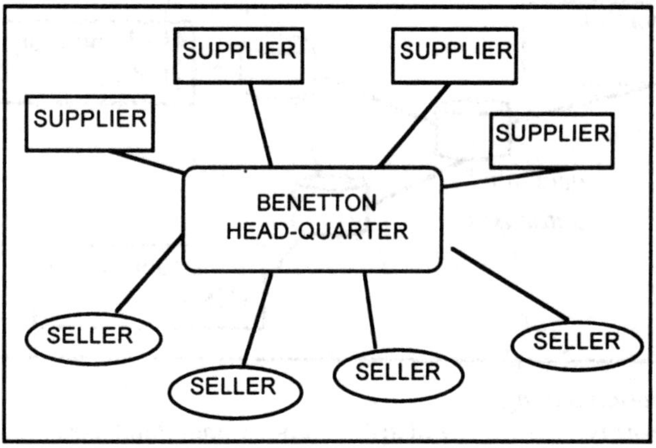

Based on:
- legal contracts (such as franchising)
- IT network

Figure 3 The Benetton network organization

But the design of IT tools is not enough for the implementation of effective organizational relations. The proposed method of analysis of *organizational relation* prescribes a coupled design of the four axes: *tools, goals, norms, cultural background.* In particular the design of Information Technology for supporting *existing organizational relations* may fail when the technical design of the tools is not joined to the analysis of the remaining three axes of the relation. The relational method provides two main design principles for preventing IT failures:

Coherence among tools

Effective relations use several tools at the same time. This means that IT design should look for the coherence of IT tools with the other ones. For example one of the most natural tools in group decision activities is interpersonal contact: the design and introduction of Group Decision Support Systems (IT tools) has to look for integration with the existing interpersonal contact tool, for example by planning periodic face-to-face meetings (Vogel and Nunamaker, 1990). The main causes of failure of most GDSS are that they do not respect the required coherence: often groups using GDSS are "co-located yet remote" (Whitaker, 1994); participants in electronic meetings "report a feeling of dissociation from others, due to the lack of interaction" (Bannon, 1997).

IT tools (as well as the other tools) need to be coherent with the remaining axis of goals, norms, cultural background.

For example, the organizational relations of franchising (among a central company and several dispersed shops) generally have the following characteristics: formal and easy to measure *goals*, standard *norms* (all the norms are clearly defined in the franchising contracts), limited *cultural background* (the two actors must share a limited knowledge about the product and about some marketing techniques). This franchising organizational relation may be supported through a computer network, that enables the exchange of a limited set of structured data (for example data about sales, catalogues, etc.). On the contrary the organizational relation among two remote R&D units is based on: non rigidly defined *goals*, formal and informal *norms* (they ca not negotiate a rigid contract), a vast *cultural background* (that continuously changes with new information/discoveries). IT support must enable the non structured exchange of information, data and hypertext documents(E-mail is a proper form of support).

3.4 Two dilemmas for organizational relation design: formal/informal and community/society.

Each of the four components of a relation proposed with the AGIL adapted model can be described along two axes: *formal/informal* and *community/society*. This classification allows a better description of the four elements of the relation and the analysis of the role of Information Technology in defining the characteristics of relations in network organizations.

The axis *formal/informal* underlines that in every relation there are both formal and informal elements (Donati, 1991). A hierarchic relation uses for example both formal tools (such as rewards, reproof, punishment, etc.) and informal tools (authority, influence, etc.); it follows both formal goals (formal objectives, co-ordination and control of subordinates, etc.) and informal ones (encouraging, stimulating, etc.). Every relation has aspects of both types, but in some cases there are more formal elements in the relation, in some cases more informal ones.

The binomial *community/society* was introduced by F. Tonnies (1887) in the social field. The word *community* (Gemeinschaft) indicates an aggregation based on traditional behaviour and on the common will of people. In a simple way, the community is the most basic and primary form of association of people. Key words for understanding the meaning of community are friendship, village, solidarity, etc.

Society (Gesellschaft) is based on common accords, on legal rules and on contracts. It is a more complex form of aggregation and requires a formal agreement on the way it takes place.

Organizations are aggregations of societal type: they are based on *accord* and *contract* among individuals that follow their *interests* in the *rational* way. Nevertheless, in an organization there are also some aspects of community type, since organizations answer some basic human needs (the need for communication, the need for association, etc.).

Table 2 Examples of social norms and legal rules are born in community and in society (Donati, 1991)

	Community	*Society*
Social order	Consensus	Contract
Law	Custom (Tradition)	State, Government

These two criteria (formal/informal, society/community) are the basis for the definition of *different* types of relations as exemplified in table 3.

Table 3 Example of intersection between formal/informal and community/society.

	Formal	*Informal*
Community	Relation between a trade union officer and a worker	Relation between two friends
Society	Relation between a supervisor and a subordinate in an assembly line	Relation among the members of a surgical team.

The two proposed oppositions are particularly relevant for the analysis of the role of IT in the innovative network organizational model, which represent one of the main goals of this paper. Information technology instruments are, in fact, formal and, at the same time, societal tools: IT pushes a relation from formal to informal and from community to society. IT tools are based on standards of communication (protocols) that specify the form of messages to exchange. IT-based connections have to respect the limits of electronic media; communication regards only keyboard (or mouse) imputable data and screen suitable information. Through IT tools, interaction become more efficient and more oriented to organizational objectives (society purpose) than "face-to-face relations". Communication become colder and less rich: only formal messages are exchanged among nodes.

Groups using electronic brainstorming tools are, for example, more productive than the ones using traditional brainstorming and with electronic brainstorming tools groups generate more good ideas, that are the formal and society purposes of those teams. At the same time, in brainstorming supported by electronic tools, there is not more oral communication: participants can talk if they want but they choose not because they are concentrating on their screen. This is a disadvantage because it reduces the opportunity for personal interaction while the richness of oral communications gets lost (i.e. the informal and community aspects are lost) (Gallupe and Cooper, 1993). The introduction of electronic brainstorming is good for the efficiency of the group (number of ideas produced), but it is not good for the ability of the group to work outside the computer structured logic schema, i.e. the team is less flexible.

Roughly speaking, IT causes change from a man-to-man relation to a triple connection: man-to-machine, machine-to-machine, machine-to-man. For this reason, it has been seen that in groups using GDSS periodic face to face meetings are required to improve the quality of decisions and the efficiency of communications (Vogel and Nunamaker, 1990).

4 APPLICATIONS OF THE PROPOSED RELATIONAL MODEL AND A CASE STUDY.

Empirical research have been conducted in order to reveal the presence and the effectiveness of network organization in a sample of manufacturing companies. The analysed organizations have been decomposed in nodes (organizational units with similar objectives and belongings to the same organizational process) and the links among nodes have been discovered for analysing existence and effectiveness of *network organizations*. *Relational matrices* were used in order to summarise the networking propulsion of each company. Empirical research revealed that the presence of network organization was positively correlated with effectiveness and flexibility. Moreover the analysis discovered an extension of propulsion toward network organizational forms in last few years. More detailed case studies have been conducted in two organizations: in the Italian company Olivetti and in an Italian Health Service. These case studies have tested the proposed relational model for organizational analysis and have proved its validity.

4.1. The DSS design for an Italian health agency

In this section we will describe the application of the proposed relational method for implementing a managerial DSS in an Italian public health agency. The case regards the psychological and social division of the health agency. This division provides a town of about 120,000 persons with psychological services and social work.

An expert psychologist is the manager of the division. His task is very broad and regards the technical supervision of other employees, the institutional deputation of the division, the psychological consulting, the planning and control of the division activities. This psychologist is one of the four top managers of the health agency: so he is always very busy with his work. The other psychologists and social employees of the division are organized in nine teams. Three teams deal with child patients (from 0 to 14 years old), three with adolescent patients (from 14 to 18 years old) and three with senior patients (more than 18 years old). Each group of three teams has a sector-head psychologist and each team has a team-head psychologist. Moreover, the division is composed of some administrative employees, working on a central office under the direction of an administrative boss.

At the beginning of 1994, the division manager asked a consulting-team (composed of the authors of this paper) to design and to implement a managerial DSS. The introduction of a managerial DSS in this psychological and social division required a complex process of organizational change and political mediation in the organization. The initial decisional user requirements were modified and completed with other features in order to make the organization accept the new system.

The analysis of decisional and information needs

The division manager asked for a managerial DSS to support his planning activities. He wanted an IT based tool providing help for decision making to create the annual plan as well as the three-year activity planning. The manager needed an accurate and synthetic description of the past activities of his division (data such as: the number of patient with certain diseases, the frequency of certain psychological treatment, the correlation between external conditions and certain diseases, etc.) in order to formulate a good organizational plan for the future.

A DSS was designed, based on data collected about the team's activities. At least once a week, each psychologist and social employee would have provided data about his own patients (diagnosis, therapy, results, etc.), through structured interfaces for data entry. Through the tool, the manager would have extracted the required statistical information from data collected.

Uncertainty about which data to collect was one of the main problems in this design phase. The information required by the manager may vary in relation to new planning needs. This necessitates designing a flexible system. Thus the possibility for handling new user-defined queries was introduced and the data base was built in order to be easy to modify.

When the news of the introduction of the new DSS circulated in the organizations, psychologists and social employees expressed their strong opposition against the new IT system. Some causes of opposition were easy to foresee while others were less clear. In order to prevent system failure, the division was analysed according to the users' perspective on their job changes, and according to the *Relational Perspective.*

The analysis of job modification.

The DSS introduction would have changed the job and the work habits of the psychological and social employees. First, most of the psychologists and social employees had no expertise in computer usage. Even if the data entry interfaces were user friendly and easy to use, the DSS would have required some minimum computer learning. In most employees the need for a training process caused an "a priori" refusal of the system: some employees refused to have to learn a new subject. Second, the DSS was designed for managerial planning activities. Psychologists and social employees would have obtained no direct benefits from the system, whereas they would have taken on the data entry activity. Even if interfaces were designed in order to minimise the time required for data entry, psychologists and social employees had to modify their work organization for maintaining the data base. This caused a diffused refusal of the new DSS.

The analysis of the network of organizational relational.

The analysis of the network of relations in the division revealed a third cause of opposition against the DSS. Four nodes were detected with the criterion of relational homogeneity:

- the manager.
- the administrative employees
- the team head psychologists and some few other social employees
- the remaining psychologists and social employees.

The discovered relations among the four nodes are complex and composed of several dimensions. In the following, we provide only a synthetic description for case understanding (Figure 4 and Table 4, below). The relational method proposed in section 4 is used.

Relations among node 2 and nodes 1, 3, 4.

The node 2 is linked with a similar relation to all the remaining nodes.
Tools: First of all, the relation is based on the work flow of documents from/to administrative office to/from psychological teams (technical dimension). Second, there is an important social link. Psychologists appreciate administrative

employees, because they relieve psychologists from all the fastidious bureaucratic problems and duties. Administrative employees hold psychologists and social employees in esteem, because of their professional preparation and their ability to deal with patients.

Goals: The organizational goal of this relation is to provide psychology and social employees with administrative and bureaucratic support.

Rules: The flow of document has to respect some formal rules, decided by the health-agency top-management as well as by external public agency (for example national or regional government). The social esteem link has established also unwritten rules of mutual help.

Cultural background: Employees belonging to node 2 share with the rest of the employees the same organizational culture: assumptions about top management, stories and legend regarding the public health, etc. As a result, the emerging organizational relation is characterised by a mutual liking that enables a good work collaboration.

Relations between node 1 and node 3.

Tools: The relation between node 1 and node 3 is based on three main tools: (a) hierarchical link: node 1 is the supervisor of the components of node 3; (b) periodic meetings. The division manager (node 1) gives psychological consulting to team head psychologists (node 3): face-to-face meetings take place at least once a week. The number of these meetings is considered insufficient by the team's head psychologists: in fact, the division manager is very busy also with his institutional task (he is one of the top managers of the health agency). (c) psychological link of esteem: the psychologists and social employees of node 3 recognise the professional capability of the division manager and his psychological expertise.

Goals: Two main organizational goals are assigned to this relation: (a) the operational control of psychological teams; (b) the psychological consulting to team-head psychologists. This relation between the division manager and the team-head psychologists should ensure the quality of the psychological cares.

Rules: There are a number of sources of rules: (a) formal hierarchy rules, (b) authority rules, deriving from the professional capabilities of the division manager, (c) professional rules, due to general practice and theoretical models in psychological consultancy.

Cultural background: The division manager and the team head psychologists share the same organizational culture (such as in the relation between node 2 and nodes 1,3,4) and a common psychological background. The resulting relation may be defined "neutral". There is coherence among the four dimensions of tools, goals, rules and cultural background that enables an effective work collaboration. Nevertheless, the limited number of meetings causes frequent small conflicts, so that the relations remain quite cold.

Relations between node 1 and node 4.

Tools: The relation between node 1 and node 4 is based on the hierarchical authority of the manager.

Goals: The organizational goals of this relation are the same as in the relation between node 1 and node 2.

Rules: The formal hierarchical norms regulate the relation.

Cultural background: The two nodes share a common organizational background. Moreover some of the employees belonging to node 4 are psychologists and they share a common psychological culture with the division manager.

Table 4 The analysis of the network of relations through the proposed relational method

	1<=>3	*1<=>4*	*3<=>4*	*2<=> 1,3,4*
Tools	- Hierarchy link -Psychological consulting meeting	- Hierarchy link	- Hierarchy link - Cooperation for patients caring - "Clan" links	- Flow of documents - Interpersonal links
Goals	- Control and support of psychological teams	- Control and support of psychological teams	- Support of psychologists and social employees	- Administrative support
Rules	- Hierarchical rules - Psychological competence of the Division Manager - Professional rules on psychological consulting	- Hierarchical rules	- Hierarchical rules - Professional rules regarding psychological methodologies - Mutual help rules	- Hierarchical and bureaucratic rules - Mutual help rules
Cult. Bkg.	- Organizational culture - Psychological background	- Organizational culture - Psychological background	- Organizational culture - Psychological-team culture	- Organizational culture

The analysis reveals a low coherence among the four dimensions: in particular the important organizational goals are not coherent with limited hierarchy based tool. This relation should be similar to the relation between node 1 and node 3, but because of work load problems, the division manager gives direct psychological consulting only to the team head psychologists. The remaining psychologists and social employees (node 4) have few opportunities for working together with him.

This causes a feel of mistrust of node 4 toward node 1. In the resulting relation, work collaboration is very difficult.

Relations between node 3 and node 4.

Tools: The link between node 3 and node 4 is based on: a) hierarchical supervision of members of node 3 toward components of node 4; (b) technical interdependencies. Between the activities of the two nodes there are complex interdependence as they work together in the teams for patients caring; (c) social links: the team based organization and the particular task (the care of social and psychological disease) has developed a strong cohesion among team members. These teams may be correctly defined as "clans" (Ouchi, 1980).

Goals: Node 3 has the organizational goal to control and to support the node 4, in order to ensure the quality of the psychological team activities.

Rules: Formal hierarchical rules exist but they are scarcely used. The team-working has developed unwritten rules of trust, commitment to mutual help, friendship. Moreover psychological methodologies provide a framework for regulating the teamwork.

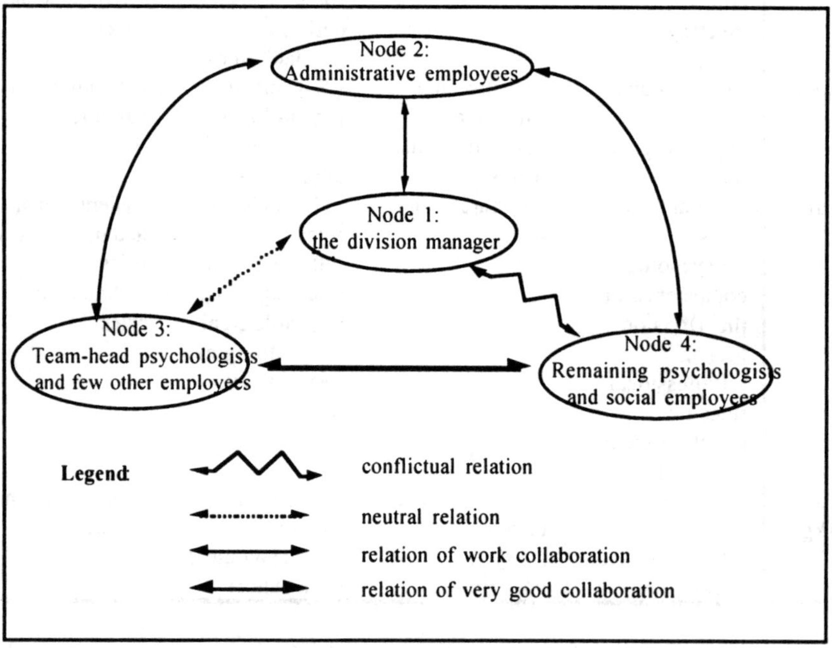

Figure 4 A synthesis of the network of relations in the social and psychological division.

Cultural background: The two nodes share the common organizational culture.

They are also unified by the team specific culture: for example stories, past "epic" episodes and "legend" regarding the team circulate among team members. Moreover the daily working together has developed a specific slang.
The resulting relation is very warm and it enables a strong work collaboration.

Conclusions of the network of relations analysis in the Health Agency

The managerial DSS was perceived as a relational instrument. Existing relations influenced the "political" judgement to its introduction in the organization. Psychologists and social employees of node 4 were particularly against the DSS. Because of the existing relation between node 4 and node 1 (Figure 5), they saw the new IT tool as an instrument of control of their activity imposed by the manager.

The opposition of other psychologists and employees (belonging to node 3) was less strong, and limited to work habits change reasons. Nevertheless the warm relation linking node 3 to node 4 prevent psychologists belonging to node 3 from taking sides in favour of the DSS.

4.2 A case study of a big Italian company: Olivetti DCI

In the following section, we will describe a simple application of the relational approach to network organizations. The aim of this description is to show how a relational approach can explain the complex aspects involved in an internal network organization. For this purpose we describe the case study of a big Italian company.

As we have seen, internal network organizations are among the new trends in organization form. Organizational unity of internal network organizations are partially autonomous and can connect to one another in some way. In the Italian Commercial Department of Olivetti (Olivetti DCI), every organizational unit has a budget of its own, that it can increase by selling its performances to other organizational units or decrease by buying services from other nodes. In this way, an *internal market* develops among organizational units. This quasi-market joins to the existing hierarchical relations.

A network model can describe the contemporary presence of both hierarchy and market. We can model organizational units as nodes connected by two kinds of relations: hierarchical relations and market ones. The formal *tools* of hierarchical relations are the usual instruments of an authority/dependency connection, as punishment and rewards; their main goals are control and co-ordination of employees. The formal *tools* of market relations are the contracts of internal exchanges; their *goals* are sales and/or purchases of services, so as to increase the organizational unit's budget. But, in fact, connections among organizational units are more complex than market or hierarchy relations: those relations still exist also when market transactions are finished and they create a valid system of collaboration among the different employees of the firm.

Comprehension of these phenomena requires the knowledge of the *organizational culture* of Olivetti DCI, which presents the following characteristics:

it is oriented to collaboration and informal contacts; individual competition is low; the considered and examined relations use also informal tools and follow community purposes. Thus, beside the introduction of internal market, a complex network of organizational and interpersonal relations exists.

Roughly, we can propose the following developing cycle in this case study, explaining the two elements for this partial network organizational model (internal market and interpersonal relations):

- At the beginning relation is built by two organizational units, with the objective of sales (or purchases) of services (society goal). Instruments are internal contracts (formal tools).
- After the two organizational units have drawn up the contract, interpersonal contacts emerge and become the main tool of the relation (people belonging to the two different organizational units work together).
- Social values and organizational culture change the goals of relations: collaboration among individuals becomes informal and of a community-type: the two organizational units collaborate not only for market exchange but also for every kind of problem solving.
- When contractual objectives have been achieved, formal tools stop working but informal ones remain still alive. A community-type relation connects the two organizational units at least for some months (sometimes persistently).

A description of the various different relations revealed and discovered in the simple case study at Olivetti DCI, is summarised in Table 5, along the parameter society/community.

Table 5 The characteristics of relations in Olivetti DCI

	Society	*Community*
Tools	- market contracts	-interpersonal contacts
Goals	- efficiently sale and/or purchase of services	- problem solving
Organizational rules and culture	- rules and norms of behaviour	- collaboration - informality

As a result of this process, every member of Olivetti DCI is a node of a complex network: he or she can use relations with other nodes for problem solving, for finding information and contacting experts. Some employees are appreciated fundamentally either because they are able to connect a great number of nodes or because of their capacity to use the best relation for solving the worst problems. The set of relations they can establish changes and enlarges their role in the network.

The use of the proposed relational analysis has made clear the complex dynamics of Olivetti DCI internal network. From the given description indications for the management can be obtained, both for operative aspects and for IT design: as regards operative aspects, relational analysis for example finds out the key nodes (i.e. people or organizational units connected to the large number of nodes): those nodes for example have an important role in the most important projects because of their connection capability.

As concerns IT design, the analysis shows for example that the introduction of an *information network* in Olivetti DCI could sort positive effects as regards the interchange of information among organizational units, but it may not (and it must not) eliminate the described interpersonal contacts that give an important support to the capacity of problem solving and decision making in Olivetti DCI.

5 CONCLUSION

Internal network organizations are among the most innovative forms of organizations; IT and especially DSS and GDSS play an important role in their design and development A network is made up of two components: nodes and links. The new competitive features of the present economic environment require enlargement the autonomy of the nodes. The enlarged autonomy requires the improvement of the skills and the know-how of every node and it needs to extend the amount of available information on environmental variables and opportunities. One of the ways to obtain the capacity and the know-how required by every node is to establish links with other nodes: a link allows the exchange of information, services, know-how, etc., between two (or more) nodes, through organizational relations, information channels, interpersonal contacts.

This paper has proposed a method for the design of a network organization based on the concept of *relation*. A relation is made by two nodes connected by a link. The concept of relation regards both the characteristics of the two nodes and the properties of the link itself. The basic elements of a relation are the *tools* that support the relation, the *goal* of the nodes, the *organizational rules* of the organization group and the *organizational culture*. Each of these four elements can be described along two axes: the opposition formal/informal and the opposition community/society.

In the paper, the role of IT in the network organizations has been analysed according to three aspects. First of all, IT (especially DSS and GDSS) improves the *autonomy* of every node: it allows the sharing of information and experience among organizational units, it provides a common set of problem solving methodologies and increases the knowledge of the node. The Digital Delta methodology for example allows the sharing of experience among the organizational units, and so it improves the know-how and the capacity of every node. Secondly, IT provides tools for *creating links and relations.* Computer networks permit the exchange of data among remote points. GDSSs provide a lot of facilities to improve communications and to establish relations, for example with remote conferences, decision rooms, electronic brainstorming instruments.

The network of Benetton is an example of how IT can support the relations in network organizations. Thirdly, the impact of the use of IT is *to push a relation from informal to formal and from community to society.* The paper shows that this improves the efficiency of the relation, but reduces the richness of the interaction: the design of IT tools has to solve the trade-off between those two aspects. The choice of the degree of the introduction of IT depends on the importance of existing informal and community aspects and/or on the lack of communication links.

6 REFERENCES

Applegate, L. M., Cash J. I. Jr. and Mills D. Q. (1988) Information Technology and Tomorrow's Manager, *Harvard Business Review.*

Bannon, L. (1997) CSCW - A challenge to certain (G)DSS perspectives on the role of decisions, information and technology in organisations. *This volume.*

Ciborra, C. (1993) Teams, Markets and Systems. Cambridge University Press, Cambridge.

Ciborra, C., Migliarese, P. and Romano P. (1984) A methodological inquiry of Organizational Noise in Socio-technical Systems, *Human Relations*, **37**, 565-88.

Donati, P. (1991) Teoria relazionale della società, Franco Angeli, Milano.

Drucker, P. F., (1988), The Coming of New Organizations, *Harvard Business Review*, January-February.

Ferioli, C. and Migliarese P. (1996a) A DSS Design method based on organizational change, in *Implementing Systems for Supporting Management Decisions* (eds P. Humphreys, L. Bannon, A. McCosh, P. Migliarese and J. C. Pommerol). Chapman and Hall, London.

Ferioli, C. and Migliarese, P. (1996b) Supporting organizational relations through information technology in innovative organizational forms. *European Journal of Information Systems* **3** No. 5.

Ferioli, C. and Migliarese P. (1994) The role of IT and GDSS in internal network organizations. in *Proceedings of IFIP WG 8.3 Working Conference on Decision Support in Organisational Transformation* (eds. B. Mayon-White, S. Ayestaràn and P. Humphreys) San Sebastian.

Gallupe, R. B. and Cooper W. H. (1993) Brainstorming Electronically, *Sloan Management Review.*

George J. F. and Nunamaker, J. F. (1992) ODSS Information Technology for Organizational Change, *Decision Support Systems*, **8**

Humphreys , P., Bannon, L., McCosh, A., Migliarese, P. and Pommerol, J. C. (1996) Implementing Systems for Supporting Management Decisions Chapman and Hall, London..

Lee, R. M., McCosh A.M. and Migliarese P. (1988) Organizational Decision Support Systems, North Holland, Amsterdam.

Miles, R. E. and Snow, C. C. (1986) Organizations: New Concepts for New Forms, *California Management Review*, **3,** Spring.

Migliarese, P. (1984) Knowledge representation and organizational noise: an organizational framework about Decision Support Systems, in *Knowledge representation for decision support systems* (ed. J. Hawgood), North Holland, Amsterdam..

Migliarese, P. (1992) Sistemi di supporto per i processi decisionali, in *Progettare e gestire l'impresa innovativa* (eds. R. Filippini, G. Pagliarani and G. Petroni), ETAS Libri, Milano.

Migliarese, P., *et al.* (1995) Improved communications and collaborations among tasks induced by Groupware. *Decision Support System Journal*, **14,** 237-250.

Parsons, T., Smelser N. J., (1956), *Economy and Society*, Free Press, New York.

Tonnies, F, (1887), Gemeinschaft und Gesellschaft, Leipzig.

Vogel, D., Nunamaker, J. F., Jr, George, J. F. and Dennis, A. R. (1988), Group Decision Support Systems, in *Organizational Decision Support Systems* (eds. R. M. Lee , A.M. McCosh and P. Migliarese) North-Holland, Amsterdam.

Vogel, D. and Nunamaker, J. F. (1990) Group Decision Support Systems impact: multi-methodological exploration, *Information and Management*, **18.**

Zigurs, I. (1989) Interaction Analysis in GDSS Research: Description of an Experience and Some Recommendations, *Decision Support Systems*, **5.**

7 BIOGRAPHIES

Piero Migliarese graduated in electrical engineering at Politecnico of Milano. He is full Professor of Managerial Economics and Organizational Systems and teaches at Politecnico of Milano, Italy and at University of Calabria, Italy. He is a founding member of IFIP 8.3 Working Group on Decision Support Systems. His research interests are regarding innovative organizational models, information systems, group decision support systems and work support systems. At present he is proposing conceptual models regarding co-ordination and co-operation support coming from information technologies. He has published various papers on these subjects in national and international journals. He has edited two books on the organizational perspective of Decision Support Systems, published by North Holland and Chapman and Hall.

Claudio Ferioli graduated in Electrical Engineering at Politecnico of Milano and worked in the field of Information Technology as a CASE expert. Since 1993 he has been working in the research activities of the Department of Economics and Production, Politecnico of Milano. He participates in a number of research projects about the emergence of new organizational models and the role played by information technologies in implementing organizational changes. He collaborates with public health organizations for management consultancy and software implementation. He is a member of the IFIP 8.3 Working Group on Decision Support Systems.

10

Inter organisational systems as a backbone for organisational DSS: scope, impact, examples

C. Loebbecke
University of Cologne
Wilh.-Backhaus-Str. 23, 50931 Koeln, Germany
Tel./ fax: +49-221-444 900
e-mail claudia.loebbecke@uni-koeln.de

P. Powell
Information Systems Research Unit
Warwick Business School
University of Warwick
Coventry, CV4 7AL, UK
Tel: +44-1203-524658
e-mail orspp@razor.wbs.warwick.ac.uk

P. Finnegan
Executive Systems Research Centre
University College Cork
Ireland
Tel: +353 21 276871
e-mail lect2.ersc.ucc.ie

and

W. Golden
University College Galway
Ireland
Tel: +353 91 75030
e-mail willie.golden@ugc.ie

Abstract

Organisations have had links with others and have operated globally for decades. However, these links were largely at arm's length, though now information systems linking organisations are emerging. Recent technological developments in communications and networking and management moves such as outsourcing, partnerships and just-in-time production have given a new capability and impetus to these issues. This chapter discusses inter-organisational systems (IOS) and identifies why managers need to consider them differently from other, internal, information systems. It looks at different types of IOS along the dimensions of functional scope and IOS-autonomy, IOS-induced business transformation, and issues of IOS planning and design. Further, the chapter outlines new business opportunities afforded by combining the mutually interdependent strategy of co-operation and IOS which span corporate boundaries.

Keywords
Inter organisational systems, flexibility, management implications, business scope

1 INTRODUCTION

IT will play a major role in the development and operation of inter-organisational co-operation (Venkatraman, 1991). In addition to databases holding information, telecommunications facilities are required to facilitate the sharing and use of data as well as to link businesses processes. Thus IT is central to inter-organisational co-operation as information is central to any sort of co-operation, and IT is valuable for manipulating information. By linking procedures within and between companies and enhancing the co-ordination and controlling function, information systems (IS) enable and enhance co-operation between companies in many ways.

From a technical perspective, telematics and telecommunication infrastructures, analogous to inter-organizational physical logistic systems termed information logistical infrastructures (Szyperski, Klein, 1993), are the basis for the efficient operation and cooperation of transactions and support the reorganisation and development of efficient and effective business relationships.

Inter-organisational systems (IOS) is a general term given to IT systems which enable the transfer of information across organisational boundaries. There are a number of specific IOS technologies, the best known and most prevalent is electronic data interchange (EDI), the Internet is another, well-known example. It is estimated that in 1995 over 50% of all business documents in the US are exchanged electronically.

2 ORIGINS OF IOS

Rockart and Short (1989) suggest that IT's impact on organisations can be classified into five types. First, technology changes the organisation's internal structure (see, for example, the case of Gerling, an international insurance company, Loebbecke, Jelassi, 1997); second, it results in team-based, problem-focused work groups; third, inter-organisational systems are causing firms to become nebulous - that is they are shifting to a market rather than a hierarchical orientation by linking electronically or legally with suppliers, customers and potential competitors. Fourth, the technical perspective suggests that continuing improvements in computer and communications capabilities will lead to further systems integration within the business allowing organisations to think or act globally rather than locally if they wish. Last IT provides a new approach to managing interdependence.

Thus, organisations are being transformed from single location hierarchical structures with well-defined boundaries to more flexibly organised and dispersed configurations. The main drivers of this are information and communications technology, globalisation, customer service, a desire for risk and cost reductions and an increasingly competitive environment, all of which decompose organisations into smaller, focused units (see, for example, the case of the French bank CORTAL, the first fully IT-based bank in Europe, which has been successful since its foundtion in 1984, Loebbecke, Jelassi, 1994). Collaboration occurs on an inter-organisational basis as partnerships with suppliers and customers are increasingly important.

The co-ordination of activities by electronic markets and hierarchies has led to the emergence of electronic brokerage firms and electronic integration between organisations. Such markets reduce the costs and time required to acquire information. Bakos (1987) distinguishes between electronic information links and electronic markets. The former is a value added chain between two organisations while the latter have many buyers and sellers, usually with an intermediary. These intermediaries reduce search costs and can create critical mass.

These developments give rise to extended, or virtual, organisations where external boundaries are obscured by inter-organisational dependencies (e.g. the case of KHD, a German diesel engine manufacturer, see Loebbecke, 1996). The sharing of information, ideas and expertise becomes central to the success of such businesses. However, equally important is co-ordination and control. Decision making by geographically separated managers and teams is possible as concurrent access to data and communications using IT is available (Rockart, Short, 1989). However, difficulties of control and co-ordination mechanisms across organisational barriers have long been recognised as making transactions subject to substantial inefficiencies (Williamson 1975). Yet it is proposed that IT may improve co-ordination of these activities.

3 OVERVIEW: INTRA-INDUSTRY SYSTEMS AND CUSTOMER SUPPLIER SYSTEMS

There is no doubt that systems that cross organisational boundaries offer the possibility of doing business in new ways through collaborating with competitors and working more closely with customers and suppliers. Celebrated cases such as American Airlines and American Hospital Supplies fuelled excitement in the 1980s about using IT to gain competitive advantage along the lines advocated by Porter (1980). These cases illustrate the two types of IOS that exist, intra-industry systems and customer/supplier systems.

An early example is how American Airlines gained advantage by the introduction and control of an airline reservation system *(intra-industry systems)*, the rules of which could be set to favour American. As the first in the field (along with United), American was able to establish a presence in travel agents' offices, and competitors were faced with the option of participating in the established system or an uphill struggle to develop and introduce their own system. Many airlines chose the former and the seat reservation business became more profitable for American than running the airline. When the great shakeup occurred in the US after deregulation few airlines survived, but American and United did. United then attempted to use their reservation capability to redefine their business by extending into car and hotel reservation, though this was less successful.

In the case of American Hospital Supplies (AHS) the key was to get on-line terminals into the purchasing offices of hospitals. The simplicity and immediacy of the system *(customer supplier systems)* encouraged purchasers to buy from AHS, with AHS (now Baxter Healthcare) allowing its competitors as well as other producers access to their customers through the system. Increasingly it is the norm in particular industries for orders and invoices to be transmitted between customers and suppliers via EDI. There is the potential for much closer and broader links, including for instance, technical and logistical issues (e.g. Loebbecke, Jelassi, 1995). Engineering data can be shared between companies.

Retailers and manufacturers are also keen to improve responsiveness and reduce inventories through JIT delivery systems. Close cooperation is required between customer and supplier. JC Penny, the largest US retail department store chain, has tied in a number of apparel and fabric manufacturers, including JP Stevens, Milliken and Dupont, all giants in their own right. JC Penny automatically transmits orders to the fabric and fibre manufacturers, which then deliver the needed materials to the apparel manufacturers through a JIT delivery system. While each participant in the value-added information network benefits, the bulk of the benefits have accrued to JC Penny, whose profits reflect the wisdom of the investment (for a further example of a retail store chain, see Loebbecke, Kronen, Jelassi, 1996; Loebbecke, Kronen, 1994).

4 IOS PECULIARITIES (IOS VERSUS INTERNALLY-USED IS)

Although technically IOS may not always differ from those systems that organisations use internally, there are a number of reasons why it is necessary for management to view them differently (Sprague and McNurlin, 1993; Cash et al, 1993):

- IOS require partners which implies a willingness and ability to interact.
- Standards play a key role, and these allow reuse of systems and hence economies of scale.
- Education is important and is often more of a hurdle than is the technology.
- 3rd parties are often involved who have roles in educating, developing or provide links.
- Work must be synchronised especially when systems and processes are upgraded.
- Work processes are often re-evaluated.
- Technical aspects are often not the major issue
- Efforts cannot be secretive - this might be taken to imply that competitive advantage from IOS is not sustainable.
- IOS introduce new and different challenges to the organisation's internal control, planning and resource allocation systems.
- Legal issues may arise in terms of replacement of physical entities such as orders by electronic exchanges.
- New roles for IOS facilitators as co-ordinators or providers of the IOS services may exist.
- IOS generally have a broader and more potential competitive impact than traditional internal uses of IT.

5 MOTIVATIONS FOR AND RISKS OF IOS

Beyond the possibility of doing business in new ways through collaborating with competitors and working more closely with customers and suppliers, and a suggested IOS-based movement from hierarchies (firms doing things themselves, internally) to markets (firms trading with others for a wider range of goods and services) with value-added partnerships, participants get the benefits of vertical integration and economies of scale, yet can remain small. Furthermore, the motivations for IOS include a desire to (Cash et al., 1993):

- reduce paper work and improve transaction efficiency,
- improve control of inventory or suppliers,
- strengthen channel control - that is, to improve distributor product awareness, or raise entry barriers. Though, virtually any IOS that works to strengthen a channel can also be designed to eventually bypass that channel,
- improve customer relationships,
- share resources or risks,

- gain synergy from collaboration.

Of course, IOS are not without *risks* which must be set against these motivations, and which may be grouped as:

- technical - a lack of experience, the expense, the multitude of partners, and the geographical scope, organisations may join on efficiency grounds but actually find themselves with less bargaining power,
- legal and regulatory - most are not written with IOS in mind,
- organisational - the intended and unintended IOS impact on structure, control systems, and people.

To come to terms with the risks and to obtain the benefits organisations contemplating joining or establishing IOS need to (Neumann 1994):

- recognise the realities of the marketplace including
  - the embedded information in products, structure etc, and the value of IT infrastructure
  - the strategic necessity of leveraging information and IT that leverage requires co-operation,
  - that IOS becoming infrastructure,
- recognise the realities of the firm:
  - before entering an IOS understand the capabilities of the organisation,
  - assess the values, commitment and capabilities of partners.

IOS-based alliances should be managed like separate companies and core operations should be changed to learn from alliances. In terms of managing IT, the IT infrastructure is a central asset in any IOS initiative, the development costs and risks are large and there is a need to decide whether activities are better performed less expensively or more flexibly by outside suppliers.

6 IOS TYPOLOGY

Reality shows a wide range of IS which are used jointly by companies which have joined forces. Depending on the functional scope[1] and the IOS autonomy[2],

---

1 What is the functional scope of the system? Is it the information backbone of a whole business, or is its use limited to specific functional segments? Does it support planning and/or operational activities? Does it focus on businesses the partners are already engaged in, or does it intend to develop new business opportunities?

2 What is the degree of autonomy of the IOS? IOS autonomy refers to the independence of the IOS of other IS implemented by the cooperating partners. If most functions of a CIS are distributed among the operational IS of the partners, IOS autonomy is low (e.g. EDI embedded in proprietary systems of the cooperating partners), while a IOS supporting a wide range of functions within a separate system possesses a higher degree of autonomy (e.g. carrier reservation systems). Generally, a high degree of IOS autonomy is observed in cooperations

Loebbecke, Kronen (1996) suggest to distinguish three types of IOS on a horizontal level: (1) IOS that focus on the operation of inter-organisational activities, (2) IOS that stress the management of inter-organizational activities, and (3) IOS that trigger inter-organizational activities (see Figure 1).

6.1 IOS Focusing on Operational Activities

IOS that focus on the operation of inter-organisational activities are usually linked to other operation systems of the partners, they are characterized by a low to medium degree of autonomy. They support the operational business processes between cooperating partners, which can be linked only if information processes are also linked in a corresponding manner.

These systems occur in two different forms: They are either composed of several modules which belong to the proprietary operation systems of the cooperating partners, or they are a separate system which builds the integrating bridge between the partners' operation systems.

A range of purposes of IOS which focus on the operation of inter-organisational activities can be distinguished depending on the goals of a cooperation. Examples include order and delivery systems, production planning systems, or electronic sales support systems (see Table 1).

In a cooperation in the area of research and development, the partners' needs concentrate on the free flow of project-specific information. Systems which support groupwork, such as Lotus Notes, are readily available solutions to fulfill this objective. Procurement cooperations which aim at bundling buying volumes need features which support separate accounting and individual links to the partners' inventory systems. The fashion information planning system (FIPS) of a large European department store chain (see Loebbecke, Kronen, Jelassi, 1996) is a prominent example for such a system. Marketing cooperations, on the other hand, usually require IS for exchanging, retrieving and analyzing market information and customer data. The marketing cooperation of a gardening retailer and a book distributor is supported by IS: the gardening retailer forwards data on its customers with specific information about the products ordered to a book distributor who compiles and mails highly individualized offer lists with books of interest to the gardening retailer's clients. Management functions in cooperations, such as project management and controlling, still lack an IS support which fulfills cooperation-specific requirements.

---

which are business-idea driven. These settings are created to support a diversification strategy and therefore cannot be based upon existing IS.

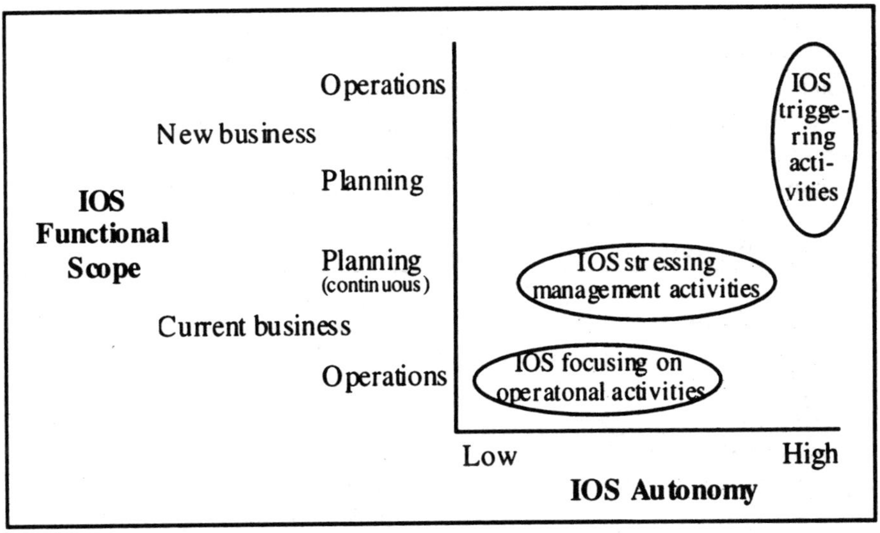

Figure 1 IOS Typology (after: Kronen, Loebbecke, 1996).

Practically speaking, cooperations are hardly restricted to only one of the functions mentioned in the table. In much cooperation, several functions of the value chain or separate systems are linked. For example, companies making joint bids or developing an interdependent range of products cooperate simultaneously in the areas of research, production and sales. The corresponding multiplication of interfaces between the partners' systems and the bi-directional, multiple data flow leads to sophisticated IOS requirements.

Further IOS requirements result from the structure of business processes: activities are often executed simultaneously in a decentralized manner. IOS therefore have to trigger and coordinate the sub-processes carried out by the partners as well as monitor the completeness of all activities.

Another well-known example of an IOS that focus on the operation of inter-organisational activities are just-in-time systems among suppliers in the automotive industry. Due to the pyramidal structure of the supplier industry, the main contractor uses just-in-time systems to coordinate the delivery and assembly of modules. In such a context, competitive IOS constitute a valuable asset for the partners and contribute to survival of the supplier shake-out.[3]

A co-operation aiming at bundling functions or products from a customer's point of view is characterised by the interdependence of multiple functions. For instance, outsourcing, increasingly employed to manage a company's IT function, consists

3 The number of suppliers in the automotive industry generally decreases as the necessary relation-specific investments are increasing (for CAD/CAM systems, JIT systems). Bakos; Brynjolfsson (1993) emphasize the decreasing number of suppliers especially in a quality-oriented competition.

of bundling functions specific to a company's needs. The outsourcer acts as an integrator and combines several services and products (hardware, system and application software, service, training), and thus reduces the company's transaction costs. Not only companies, but also consumers are developing a preference for 'one-stop shopping' instead of dealing with numerous providers (e.g., reservation systems for airline, hotel, and rental car; package tour; insurance broker).

Table 1 IOS focusing on the operation of inter-organisational activities

Area of Co-operation/ Operative Function	*Available Applications*	*Co-operation-specific Requirements*	*Examples*
research and development	• e-mail • data bases • CAD	• unlimited access to project-specific information	• Lotus Notes
procurement	• procurement systems • order entry system	• joint procurement • separate accounting • link to partner's inventory control	• FIPS
production	• production planning - systems (PPS)	• locally distributed, timely linked production • joint venture production	• just-in-time system among suppliers of a dashboard system
sales and distribution (pooling / swapping sales forces, products, distribution channels)	• joint customer data base • joint management of sales force	• customer data pools, differentiated along regions and other criteria • linked route planning	• code sharing among airlines (e.g. Lufthansa / United Airlines co-operation, using Galileo

marketing	• market analysis tools • communication tools	• exchange of socio-demographic data • joint compilation of market data	• exchange of buyers' data between gardening retailer and book distributor[4]
service	• joint data base • dispatching of service personnel	• single data base with decentralised input and feedback of availability and errors • co-ordination of joint service force	• PICA[5]
project management	• project planning software	• link to each partner's time / resource planning	NOT DOCUMENTED
controlling	• MIS • EIS • reporting systems	• multi-client capability	

Source: Kronen, Loebbecke, 1996.

6.2 IOS Stressing Management Activities

Due to the low degree of integration with other applications, IOS stressing the mangement of inter-organizational activities posses a high degree of autonomy. They support mainly planning activities during the start-up phase as well as along the entire life-cycle of a cooperation.

The focus of activities in the phase of acquiring a cooperating partner and setting up the cooperation rests on strategic planning functions. IT provides numerous tools to support these tasks within a single enterprise. To manage a cooperation, already existing systems for internal strategic planning can be used. Examples

4 Cash, McFarlan, McKenney, 1992)

5 PICA (Project for Integrated Catalogue Automation) is an IOS of the Dutch public libraries to support the joint cataloguing and archiving activities (Wierda, 1991).

include IS-based strength-weakness analyses, applications to segment strategic business units, and tools for project management or budget planning or control.

In order to be used in cooperation, these applications must fulfill cooperation-specific requirements. Therefore, their features have to be enlarged along three dimensions:

(1) Contents

Applications have to cover contents and details relevant to the cooperation/joint management activities. Models embedded in an application must allow for cooperative activities instead of only permitting competitive relations with other enterprises. An example is using an IT-supported competitor analysis for profiling and identifying potential cooperating partners. Electronic checklists, a convenient tool for strategic planning, must be enriched to contain cooperation-specific items for analyzing the company's needs for a cooperation or for selecting a cooperating partner.

(2) Multi-Client Capability

All applications in cooperation must be able to treat the cooperative structure as a separate unit of analysis. The system has to be capable of recognizing the cooperation as a separate structure and the partner companies as the cooperation's 'clients', it must allow for several 'views' on the cooperation. In this context, data specific to the cooperation must be identified, manipulated and stored without being mingled with the partners' own business data.

Another requirement is to verify the compatibility between the cooperation's planning and project management data with each partner's figures and capacity restrictions. Shifting resources between partners gives each cooperation additional flexibility which should be fully exploited by a high-performing IOS.

(3) Communication

A final requirement of IOS that stress the mangement of inter-organizational activities is to permit links between the systems of all cooperating partners. In the case of informal communication, electronic mail provides a relatively stable and convenient tool based on wide-spread standards on the transportation layer of the OSI 7-layer model. A communication link on the application layer, however, is more difficult to implement, especially when striving for distributed applications, which require open system architectures.

Most applications for strategic planning provided on the market lack any form of integration. They are difficult to link with other applications, data cannot be imported from operations, etc. Cooperating partners, who want to use IS to support their cooperation management, have to make firm efforts to develop the required IOS features.

Unfortunately, the IOS features discussed above are neither wide spread nor available on the market. Table 2 summarizes specific requirements for IOS that stress the mangement of inter-organizational activities.

Table 2 Requirements for IOS stressing the management of inter-organisational activities

Management Function	*Available Applications*	*Co-operation-specific Requirements*
strategic analysis	• portfolio systems • value chain simulation • other simulation	• competitor analysis • profiling potential co-operating partners
planning and project management	• project management software • planning systems for certain functions (e.g. sales, budgeting, procurement) • electronic checklists	• link with time / resource management of partners • co-operation-specific items
communication	• groupware • e-mail	• inter-organisational
controlling	• MIS • EIS • reporting systems	• multi-client capability • joint control of co-operation, including feedback to partners

Source: Kronen, Loebbecke, 1996.

6.3 IOS Triggering Inter-Organisational Activities

IOS that trigger inter-organizational activities drive cooperation and are therefore their purpose and focus; they show a high degree of IS autonomy and usually cover a wide range of planning and operational functions. They are often the result of innovative business ideas and lay the ground for an IS-based diversification providing a new business opportunity unrelated to the sponsor's / participants' field of business.

Cooperation which aim at bundling functions, products or services are especially prone to use such systems. IOS that trigger inter-organizational activities facilitate to jointly offer the products of several suppliers and thus to offer convenience from a customer's point of view. American Airlines, Hilton hotels and Budget Rent-A-Car have joined forces and IS resources in order to offer a full range of travel services to customers. The customer enjoys one-stop-shopping for all needs in air travel, accommodation and transportation. The reservation systems of all three partners have to be able to access a joint customer data base.

Cooperating partners in an information partnership draw conclusions from their joint data base which might lead to offering new products and services; thus such an IOS can be the starting point for highly differentiated services. For example, a carrier reservation system may be extended into specialized travel services for corporate clients. To fully exploit the strategic potentials of such an IOS, the continuous development and maintenance of information has to be a priority from the very beginning. At the same time, the cooperation's compatibility with the corporate strategy of each partner is crucial.

Most IOS that trigger inter-organizational activities are separate systems with clearly defined interfaces to the IS of the cooperating partners. In many cases, the operation of the IOS has been outsourced to the IS specialists of the system's sponsor, to a jointly funded company, or to an external service provider. Solving security problems in an adequate manner is a mandatory prerequisite for all of these arrangements.

Crucial for the success of such an IOS is the fast implementation of a new business idea while, due to the high degree of autonomy, technical integration with the partners' operation systems is not a top priority. Common procedures and standards are defined during the development phase of such an IOS, common codes for product and customer data have to be agreed upon. While an external service provider can make valuable contribution in this phase, the definition of functional requirements remains with the partners. Furthermore, the task to monitor and trigger the necessary adaptation of the IOS to the changing content of the cooperation must be fulfilled by the partners themselves.

7 IOS IMPACTS

Companies may cooperate for a number of reasons. In a cooperative arrangement, the balance between competitive and cooperative behavior is crucial for stability. The advantages of cooperating motivate the partners not to endanger the existence of the cooperation or its functionality by opportunistic behaviour. Two main desired effects, which are discussed below, provide a strong incentive to cooperate and obey the rules. These desired effects also explain why cooperation built around an IOS that trigger inter-organizational activities regularly involve more than two cooperating partners:

Table 3 IOS triggering inter-organisational activities

Strategic Intent	***Available Applications***	***Co-operation-specific Requirements***	***Examples***
procurement pooling	• order collection system (with invoicing component)	• provider of information (price; freight space) identifiable • commission accounting • bulk orders • joint analysis of suppliers' behaviour • joint quality control	various electronic market systems, e.g. • TRANSPOTEL[6], • IKARUS[7]
bundling (Sales / Distribution Alliance)	• carrier reservation systems (CRS, e.g. SABRE)[8] • information partnerships	• joint customer data base with separate access	• SABRE • American Airlines / Hilton and Marriott Hotels / Budget Rent-A-Car[9] • MAC (ATM Network of Philadelphia National Bank)

6 TRANSPOTEL is a Swiss electronic market for available freight space (Hohagen, Schmid, 1991).

7 IKARUS is an EDI-based network for the allocation of freight space, sponsored by a consortium of the Irish air freight industry (Commission of the European Communities, 1992).

8 Hopper, 1990.

9 Cash, McFarlan, McKenney (1992).

market research	• product data base	• decentralised input; central market research channelling results to partners	• AA / Citibank / MCI • Insurance[10]
marketing alliance	• CRS	• separate accounting • routing of bonuses, conditions, discounts (frequent flyer miles)	• AA / Citibank / MCI • SWISSLINE[11]
service alliance	• software for dispatching service personnel	• mutual access to service personnel • joint customer data base	• RIA[12] (linking customer files) • Cash Management Alliance[13]

Source: Kronen, Loebbecke, 1996.

(1) Virtual size and virtual diversity

Cooperation based on IOS that trigger inter-organizational activities try to lever the bargaining power of the cooperating partners. A procurement cooperation can expect better conditions than a single member if the cooperation results in a higher procurement volume. A sales cooperation, offering a high volume or a wide range of products can lever its power over customers.

MUSIK (Commission of the European Communities, 1992) is an example of a sales cooperation of small suppliers in Europe, in which a new distribution channel is opened by cooperation. In MUSIK, small independent producers of

10 Porter; Millar (1985) discuss the example of an insurance company which extracts market research data from its contract data base to sell them as a separate product.

11 SWISSLINE is an accomodation reservation system, in which the Swiss Tourist Board, several regional Swiss tourist associations, and the Swiss Railroad cooperate (Ritz, 1991).

12 RIA's initiator Rosenbluth is an American travel service corporation for corporate travelling. All members of Rosenbluth International Alliance (RIA) have access to the sponsor´s specific IS in order to provide world-wide customer service. RIA uses a widely-spread CRS as the carrier system for its proprietary system and thus utilizes the CRS geographic presence (Clemons, Row, Miller, 1992).

13 Cash; McFarlan; McKenney, 1992).

classical music labels cooperate to produce and maintain an electronic catalogue which contains the products of all partners and it is updated directly. Orders and invoices are exchanged with wholesalers and retailers using the EDIFACT standard. The virtual range of products and the use of EDI reduce the transaction costs for music wholesalers and retailers to carry MUSIK products in their line. MUSIK increases the chances of carrying the stock, even if none of its individual members could succeed. At the same time, MUSIK acquires new customers who would not have dealt with individual members.

To jointly overcome market barriers to entry, IOS in service cooperation bundle the partners' service personnel to virtual service networks, guaranteeing geographical presence from a customer's point of view.

Furthermore, such IOS are often the 'backbone' in marketing cooperation. This cooperation type bundles complementary products and services to a functional unit from the customer's viewpoint. The customer can book a flight, reserve a hotel room and order a rental car by 'one-stop shopping'. In addition, marketing cooperation can increase customer loyalty for all partners by awarding the purchase of their products with low transaction costs or special discounts. From the suppliers' point of view (airline, hotel chain, car rental company), the IOS is a separate distribution channel.

The potential of marketing cooperation can be fully exploited only by building and using joint customer databases. The joint database accumulates during the life of cooperation and supplies valuable marketing data which could not be provided by external market researchers. Thus, the advantages of the cooperation reach far beyond increased customer loyalty and increased sales.

(2) Scale effects

Developing and operating an IOS that triggers inter-organizational activities usually causes high fixed cost, whereas the number of users only marginally affects operating cost. Therefore, the more partners use the system, the lower will be the cost for each partner, and the greater the spreading of the financial risks involved. The amortization of the IOS development cost - which is a sunk cost - is easier for a consortium, since the total is divided by all partners. However, the choice between founding a consortium and single sponsoring the IOS constitutes an entrepreneurial decision because the cost as well as the IOS-generated income have to be shared.

7.1 Organisational Implications

One fundamental consequence of IOS is that the cost of transactions between organisations is being reduced. The result is that there is less incentive to integrate businesses vertically or horizontally, businesses can operate on a smaller scale and extended, networked organisation become possible. A further consequence is that organisation and geography become separable. Businesses are no longer defined by their geography. Cash et al. (1993) suggest that the winners in using IOS will be small, flexible organisations that take advantage of IT-driven integration and synergy. Economies of scale· may no longer be sufficient to offset the disadvantages of size and complexity.

At a general level IOS will enhance flexibility in terms of productivity and competitiveness (Cash, Konsynski, 1985). Specifically, IOS may increase and decrease an organization's flexibility in a number of ways (Golden, Powell, 1995).

Organisational implications resulting from IOS may include that the entire organisational units may be disbanded while others are created; and that new management challenges of control, the flow of information and knowledge, legal, intermediaries, strategic participation, etc arise (Neumann, 1994). Changes will have to take place in procedures, style, culture, structure and strategy and the extent of these changes may depend on the reactive or proactive stance of management. If these implications turn out to be true, then managers must prepare for a fundamental shift in the way that they do business.

7.2 Altered Business Relationships

IOS enable electronic integration of the elements of a value chain. This provides possibilities for shortcutting by eliminating some stages such as distribution. Fewer stages should result in a more flexible value chain given that response time should be reduced. A second form of restructuring takes place as a result of organisations creating closer links with a reduced number of trading partners. Moves to fewer preferred suppliers creates longer-term, co-operative relationships, which enable the entire value chain to be more flexible.

7.3 Restructuring of Organisational Boundaries

Organisational boundaries are restructured by IOS because of the increased capability for co-ordination-intensive business structures which they provide (Davenport, Short, 1990). This may lead to a return, in certain industries, to small family networked organisations as in the pre-Industrial Revolution (Malone, Rockart, 1992). This may, in turn, lead to an increase in outsourcing and the creation of flexible business networks, to which trading partners can be added and subtracted easily (Venkatraman, Zaheer, 1994). Thus vertical integration becomes possible without the disadvantage of inflexibility due to ownership.

7.4 Electronic Delivery of Business Documents

Given that 70% of business data that is manually entered into a computer is the output from another computer, delivering business documents through IOS results in a reduction in the time taken between ordering and dispatch of goods, and may enable organisations to introduce just in time purchasing. This increases flexibility to adapt to market demands since a reduced amount of inventory is held in the complete value chain. The electronic delivery of business documents may also increase flexibility due to the increased availability of information leading to better decision making.

7.5 Increased Dependence on Information Technology

Conversely, the adoption of IOS may lead to a decrease in flexibility. By introducing IOS an initiator organisation becomes more dependent on technology. Increased use of IT may reduce flexibility because of the inability of information systems to change.

7.6 IOS Messaging Standards

In order to exchange business documents electronically specific messaging standards are needed. The variety of standards has been blamed for the slow development and application of EDI (Edwards, 1987). Standards are set by bodies whose main aim is to design message standards which possess a great deal of flexibility to ensure that the needs of different organisations can be expressed. But in order to achieve flexibility, standards have become too all inclusive. This increases the investment required by each set of trading partners to enable electronic understanding and may inhibit or at least delay in EDI diffusion. A way of reducing the investment is to introduce a sub-set of standards, but this eliminates the flexibility of an open, universal standard (Horluck, 1994).

7.7 Non Inter-operability of Communications Networks

Organisations who conduct EDI using an accepted non-proprietary standard normally communicate using an independent value added network (VAN) which provides the telecommunications facilities which enable the partners to exchange messages. VANs enable flexibility at the level of the network because they provide facilities which enable trading partners to be added or deleted. Yet, the inability to exchange messages between VANs restricts an organisation's trading partners to those using a particular VAN and thus reduces flexibility.

Participants in a value chain may differ in the extent to which each benefits by the introduction of IOS. Flexibility derived from EDI adoption is dependent on the size of the organisation, the IT expertise of the organisation and whether the organisation is the initiator of the project (Swatman et al., 1994).

7.8 Shift towards Markets Structures

IOS can enable low transaction costs, provide communications capabilities that overcome geography and provide easy access to information which reduces the cost of search. These are the ingredients required to allow creation of electronic markets which can offer convenience, speed and automated administration to handle volumes of business that could not be contemplated with manual systems.

Some markets, such as stock and commodity markets, are natural candidates for electronic systems. Less obviously the capability of IT to support electronic marketplaces translates into economic forces which encourage single source sales channels to evolve into electronic markets (Malone et al, 1989). Often a dominant player is well positioned to create an electronic market, but if no single player is sufficiently powerful, an industry association may be the initiator.

8 IOS PLANNING AND DESIGN

Existing IS reflect organizational structures which are often outdated. In order to support cooperations, the functional scope of existing IS has to be extended. Especially flexible and project-oriented forms of the division of labor between companies were not taken into account when the present IOS generation was designed. Communication audits, often the empirical base for IS design, do not routinely examine communication flows across the border of the organization. While numerous developments on the technical level support working in distributed architectures, current enterprise models do not emphasize these recent developments and therefore show deficits in designing flexible boundaries of the firm.

IOS often evolve in an organisation from automating paper-based transactions to process integration between the partners. Such an evolution requires that processes be altered to take account of the potential of IT, which involves altering working practices and responsibilities among network participants. IOS designers need to recognise that these systems affect organisations at many levels, and that linkages must go beyond electronic data interconnection to deal with people, policies and procedures (Konsynski, 1992). IOS tend to be implemented on an ad hoc basis, hindered by an absence of appropriate planning. This is not surprising given that many IOS tend to start operational (eg EDI) and become strategic. The lack of planning is the result of inadequate experience of multi-organisational planning environments and poor methodological guidelines.

Though IOS affect organisational structure, strategy, style, systems, skills and staff, the order that these effects occurs in depends on strategic intent and the planning involved in the systems introduction. If an organisation participates in an IOS agreement in an ad hoc manner, there is generally no broad management participation and no explicit planning or consideration given to the implications of participation. Hence, the initial effect that participation has is on systems such as procedural reports and routine processes. Also the skills or distinctive capabilities of key personnel or perhaps of the entire organisation will change. Finally, there will be effects in relation to organisational style, structure and strategy as managers alter the organisation's goals and how these are achieved as a result of IOS participation (Cash, 1985).

Typically IS planning has focused exclusively on the internal functions of the business. This conventional view targets information systems applications at an organisation's planning and control processes. While such perspectives have served well in the past, a different type of IS planning method is required for IOS. Such methods should have foundations in competitive strategy rather than in planning and control.

IOS planning has distinct characteristics that differentiates it from internal IS planning. Essentially, IOS planning can be undertaken by adopting planning approaches for telecommunications, EDI, groupware, and business process redesign. However IOS deal with a large number of people, policies and procedures and, therefore, require more extensive planning than internal IS planning or planning for individual technologies. In addition no integrated methodology exists which guides planning for IOS in their entirety. This is in contrast to intra-organisational IS planning.

For example, EDI is a complicated technology and many organisations do not recognise it is a business issue that requires more than just "hooking a couple of computers together and starting to send data" (West, 1994); the successful implementation of groupware requires more than installing the software as multiple participant involvement and organisational considerations are paramount (Bullen, Bennet, 1990). However, planning guidelines for group technology are more limited that those for EDI. Most guidelines emphasise an iterative approach, relying more on pilot projects than on planned introductions. However, certain aspects such as the support of top management and the alignment of the technology with organisational objectives are recognised as important (Opper, 1994). Nevertheless, while such planning guidelines are largely inadequate on an individual organisational basis, they are impossible when multiple independent organisations, with often conflicting objectives, are involved, as in IOS.

Although IOS designers often minimise changes to business processes in an attempt to minimise resistance to the new system, some form of structural integration involving the redesign of business processes is required to fully benefit from inter-organisational cooperation (Benjamin et al, 1990). In fact, BPR efforts that focus on the market network are potentially more important than their internal counterparts (Short and Venkatraman, 1992). Particularly on an inter-organisational basis, multiple participant organisations with disparate objectives need more precise plans before moving towards process redesign and structural integration.

In the future, IOS design has to take into account new models of intercorporate links in order to support the emerging number and variety of cooperations. Corporations cannot afford to let the opportunities pass which can be exploited by joining forces, just because their information systems lack capabilities of IOS or even do not allow links to any form of IOS.

The value of IOS-based cooperations stems partially from their potential for restructuring and rationalizing internal structures and processes, known as BPR. Designing IOS and organizational structures is a highly mutual adaptation process.

On the one hand, IOS should be customized to specific needs of an organization, on the other hand, they should not be adapted to existing structures without questioning them thoroughly.

9 SUMMARY AND CONCLUSION

Inter-organisational systems (IOS) have received much attention recently by both business and researchers. This is not to say that organisations have not had links with others over the last few centuries, nor that firms have not operated globally for decades. Rather, it is technological developments in communications and networking and management moves such as outsourcing, partnerships and just-in-time production which have given a new capability and impetus to these issues.

This chapter discussed inter-organisational systems and identified why managers need to consider them differently from other, internal information systems (IS). It looked at different types of IOS along the dimensions of functional scope and IOS-autonomy, IOS-induced business transformation, and issues of IOS planning and design. Furthermore, this chapter outlined new business opportunities by combining the mutually interdependent strategy of cooperation and IOS which span corporate boundaries. It therefore intended to encourage practitioners to identify the chances provided by the cautious development of IOS and by conceptualizing new businesses which are fully leveraged by the creative use of IOS.

10 REFERENCES

Bakos, J. Y. (1987) Inter-organisational Information Systems: Strategic Opportunities for Competition and Co-operation. Ph.D. Dissertation, MIT Sloan School of Management.

Bakos, J. Y., Brynjolfsson, E. (1993) Why Information Technology Hasn't Increased the Optimal Number of Suppliers, in *Information Systems: Collaboration Technology, Organisational Systems and Technology,* (eds. Jay F. Nunamaker; Ralph H. Sprague) Proceedings of the Hawaii International Conference on System Sciences **26**, Vol. IV, 799-808.

Benjamin, R., DeLong, D., Scott Morton, M. S. (1990) Electronic data interchange: How much competitive advantage?. *Long Range Planning*, **23** 29-40.

Bullen, C.V., Bennett, J. L. (1990) Learning from user experience with groupware, Proceedings of the Conference on Computer-Supported Co-operative Work, 291-302.

Cash, J. I. (1985) Inter organisational systems: An information society opportunity or threat?. *The Information Society*, **3**, 199-228.

Cash, J. I., Konsynski, B. R. (1985) IS redraws competitive boundaries. *Harvard Business Review*, **2**, 134-142.

Cash, J., McFarlan, W.F., McKenney, J. L. (1992) Corporate Information Systems Management: The Issues Facing Senior Executives, 3rd ed., University of Illinois Press, Homewood, Ill.

Cash J., Eccles R., Nohria N., Nolan R. (1993) Building the Information-Age Organisation, Irwin, New York.

Clemons, E. K., Row, M. C., Miller, D. B. (1992) Rosenbluth International Alliance: Information Technology and the Global Virtual Corporation, in *Information Systems: Collaboration Technology, Organisational Systems and Technology* (ed. Jay F. Nunamaker; Ralph H. Sprague), Proceedings of the Hawaii International Conference on System Sciences **25**, Vol. IV, 678-688.

Commission of the European Communities (1992) *TEDIS - Technical, Organisational and Managerial Aspects of Implementing EDI - Results and Experiences of 12 EDI Pilot Projects*, Brussels.

Davenport, T. H, Short, J. E. (1990) The New Industrial Engineering: Information Technology and Business Process Redesign, *Sloan Management Review*.

Edwards D. W. (1987) Electronic Data Interchange: A Senior Management Overview, ICIT Briefing Paper.

Golden W., Powell, P. (1995) The Effects of Inter-Organisational Information Systems on Flexibility, Working Paper.

Hohagen, U., Schmid, M. (1991) Stand und Entwicklungstendenzen Elektronischer Märkte in der Logistik, Working Paper No. IM2000/CCEM/7 of the 'Institut für Wirtschaftsinformatik', Hochschule St. Gallen, Switzerland.

Hopper, M. D. (1990) Rattling Sabre - New Ways to Compete on Information. *Harvard Business Review*, May-June, 118-125.

Horluck J. (1994) The Pragmatics of Electronic Data Interchange: The Use of EDI will Unify Business Procedures. *International Journal of Information Management,* **14**, 330-343.

Konsynski, B. R. (1992) Issues in design of inter-organisational systems, in *Challenges and Strategies for Research in Systems Development* (eds. Cotterman, W. W., Senn, J. A.) Wiley, Chichester, England.

Kronen, J., Loebbecke, C. (1996) Co-operation Information Systems (CIS) - Typology and Illustrative Examples, EDI-IOS (Electronic Data Interchange - Inter organisational Systems) Conference, Bled, Slovenia.

Loebbecke, C. (1996) Innovative IT-based Logistics - KHD's 'Vision 2000' engine factory, EDI-IOS (Electronic Data Interchange - Inter organisational Systems) Conference, Bled, Slovenia.

Loebbecke, C., Jelassi, T. (1994) Home Banking: An I. T. Based Business Philosophy or a Complementary Distribution Channel CORTAL versus Crédit Comercial de France', in: *Strategic Management of Information Technology: Some European Case Studies* (ed. T. Jelassi), Prentice Hall, New York - London - Toronto - Sydney - Tokyo - Singapore.

Loebbecke, C.; Kronen, J. (1994) FIPS - An Innovative IT Application for Fashion Purchase in a European Department Store. *Association of Management Conference Proceedings*, Dallas, USA.

Loebbecke, C., Jelassi, T. (1995) Business Process Redesign at CompuNet - Standardising Top Quality Service Through Information Technology. *Journal of Strategic Information Systems* (forthcoming).

Loebbecke, C., Kronen, J., Jelassi, T. (1996) The Role of IT in Retailing: The Case of Supporting Fashion Purchasing at a European Department Store Chain. *Journal of Strategic Information Systems*, **5,** 67 - 78.

Loebbecke C. and Powell P., (1997) Inter-organisational Systems: Scope, Impact and Competitiveness, in *Inter-organisational Systems* (ed. S. Strzelczak),

Loebbecke, C., Jelassi, T. (1997) Concepts and Technologies for Virtual Organising: the Gerling Journey. *European Management Journal*, **15**, 138-146.

Malone, T. W., Yates, J., Benjamin, R. I. (1987) Electronic Markets and Electronic Hierarchies. *Communications of the ACM*, **30**, 484-497.

Malone, T. W., Rockart J. F. (1992) Information Technology and the New Organization. *Proceedings of the Hawaii International Conference on System Sciences IV*, 636-643.

Neumann, S. (1994) Strategic Information Systems, Macmillan, New York.

Opper, S. (1994) Choosing and implementing a groupware system, Datapro.

Porter, M. E. (1980) Competitive Strategy: Techniques for Analysing Industries and Competitors, Free Press, New York.

Porter, M. E., Millar, V. E. (1985) How Information gives you competitive Advantage. *Harvard Business Review*, July-August, 149-160.

Ritz, D. (1991) Aktuelle Entwicklungen bei touristischen Informations- und Reservierungssystemen, Working Paper No. IM2000/CCEM/9, Institut für Wirtschaftsinformatik, Hochschule St. Gallen, Switzerland.

Rockart, J. R., Short, J. E. (1989) Information Technology in the 1990s: Managing Organisational Interdependence. *Sloan Management Review*, Winter, 7-17.

Short, J. E., Venkatraman, N. (1992) Beyond business process redesign: Refining Baxter's business network. *Sloan Management Review*, Fall, 7-21.

Sprague, R., McNurlin B, (1993) Information Systems Management in Practice, Prentice-Hall International, Englewood Cliffs.

Starkey, K., Wright, M., Thompson, S. (1991) Flexibility, Hierarchy, Markets. *British Journal of Management*, **2**, 165-176.

Stoneman, P. (1986) Technological Diffusion: The Viewpoint of Economic Theory. Ricerche Economiche, **XL**, 4, 585-606.

Swatman, P. M. C., Swatman, P.A., Fowler, D. C. (1994) A model of EDI integration and strategic business reengineering. *Journal of Strategic Information Systems*, **3,** 141-160.

Szyperski, N., Klein, S. (1993) Informationslogistik und virtuelle Organisation - Die Wechselwirkung von Informationslogistik und Netzwerkmodellen der Unternehmung. *DBW*, **53**, 187-209.

Venkatraman, N (1991) IT Induced Business Reconfiguration, in *The Corporation of the 1990s: Information Technology and Organisational Transformation* (ed. M. S. Scott Morton), Oxford University Press, Oxford.

Venkatraman N., Zaheer A. (1994) Electronic Integration and Strategic Advantage: A Quasi-Experimental Study in the Insurance Industry, in *Information Technology and the Corporation of the 1990's* (eds. Allen, M. S. Scott Morton), Oxford University Press, 184-201.

West, L. J. (1994) Breaking down the barriers to EDI implementation. *TMA Journal*, **14**,10-15.

Williamson, O. (1975) Markets and Hierarchies, Free Press, New York.

Wierda, F. W. (1991) Developing Inter organisational Information Systems, Dissertation at the University of Delft, Netherlands.

11 BIOGRAPHIES

Claudia Loebbecke received a Master in Business and a PhD from the University of Cologne, Germany, and an M.B.A. from Indiana University. She worked as Consultant with McKinsey & Co. in Germany, as Research Assistant at INSEAD in Fontainebleau, France, as Research Consultant at the Hong Kong University of Science and Technology (HKUST), and as Visiting Professorial Fellow at the University of New South Wales, Sydney. She regularly presents at international IS conferences, teaches master sutdents and executives in Cologne and abroad, and participates in several national and international research and consulting projects.

Philip Powell received his PhD from Southampton University. He is Director of the Information Systems Research Unit, Warwick Business School and an ICAEW Academic Fellow. He has authored books on information systems and financial modelling, and has published in Omega, JORSBritish Journal of Management, Organizational Computing, Journal of Strategic Information Systems, Journal of Management Systems, and Decision Support Systems amongst others. He is Managing Editor of the Information Systems Journal.

Pat Finnegan is a lecturer in Information Systems at University College Cork, Ireland, and a senior researcher with the Executive Systems Research Centre (ESRC). His research interests include IS Planning, Inter-Organisational Systems, Electronic Commerce and Information Systems for multinationals. He is completing a PhD at Warwick Business School.

William Golden is lecturer in the Department of Accountancy and Finance at University College Galway, Ireland. His research interests include Inter-Organisational Systems, Electronic Commerce and issues of flexibility. He is completing a PhD at Warwick Business School.

11

A strategic partnership in outsourcing: a public sector case study

C. A. Davies, T. Campbell
School of Management,
Queens University,
Belfast,
Northern Ireland.
Tel 01232 273204
Fax 01232 248372
e-mail a.davies@qub.ac.uk

Abstract

This paper presents a case study of the outsourcing process in the Central Information Systems Division of the Northern Ireland Civil Service. This was one of the earliest examples of a central government computing service being outsourced. This is held to be a successful partnership due to mutual reliance. The effects of outsourcing in general in the public sector are discussed. These are compared with the potential benefits of outsourcing and the situational framework defined by Earl.

Keywords
Information systems, public administration, outsourcing

1 INTRODUCTION

In this paper the authors describe the first major government outsourcing project in the United Kingdom. The effects on service levels and staff are investigated. The findings are analysed in the context of Earl's framework for outsourcing. This is seen to be an example of successful outsourcing due to a strong strategic partnership between the two organisations.

2 CASE STUDY

This case study is compiled from a series of fourteen interviews carried out in the autumn of 1993. The interviewees were representative of users, former Northern Ireland Civil Service staff and staff who remained within the public sector.
The Central Information Systems Division (CISD) of the Department of Finance and Personnel (DFP) of the Northern Ireland Civil Service was established in 1984 with the following responsibilities:

- the development in conjunction with departments, of an overall information technology strategy;
- the development and operation of common information technology systems;
- the provision of information technology advice and guidance;
- the recruitment, training and career development of information technology staff;
- the provision of a central procurement service for computers and information technology related equipment and
- the provision and maintenance of a central mainframe bureau service (Northern Ireland Audit Office, 1992).

The mainframe bureau service for all NICS departments comprised the running of some 80 applications on 3 ICL mainframes. The applications included payroll, accounts and statistical analysis work. As part of the same strategy an Information Systems Unit was established in each of the 6 Northern Ireland departments (see figure 1). The responsibilities of the ISUs were:

- the planning of departmental information technology needs;
- the development and operation of information technology applications and
- the provision of technical support in pursuit of departmental aims and objectives.

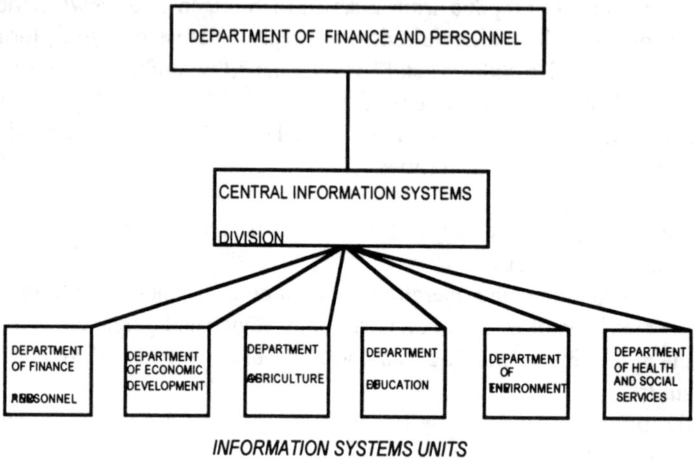

Figure 1 Structure of Central Information Systems Division

The increasing decentralisation of work towards the ISUs combined with a technological shift away from mainframe power to microcomputing systems resulted in a declining workload for CISD. This led to CISD becoming apparently uneconomic with decreasing numbers of applications which in turn meant that the remaining applications were having to bear the increasing overheads. Expenditure on IT in total had increased from £7.5 million in 1984-85 to a peak of £32.01 million in 1989-90. Increasing costs and government policy led senior managers to consider measuring the performance of the bureau service against that of a private sector company in a market testing exercise. Market testing involves ascertaining the value for money of in-house services against tenders from outside organisations (Government purchasing service, 1991). This process took place at CISD before the term market testing was in common currency. The parallel concept of compulsory competitive tendering was launched in local government in 1988. The emphasis in the United Kingdom public sector has been one of increasing efficiency and maximising value for money. Previously, increased efficiency in the public sector was sought through internal investigations of processes for example, under the Rayner efficiency scrutinies. The idea of measuring the performance of public sector services against private sector suppliers was gaining currency. Government policy laid increasing emphasis on efficiency through competition in the market-place.

2.1 The outsourcing process

Beginning in February 1989 a feasibility study was carried out over the subsequent 9 months to ascertain the viability of putting the central computing service out to tender. This aimed to ascertain the level of interest from the Northern Ireland IT industry. It was determined that the tendering process would applicable and in September 1989 the initial invitation to tender was issued and it received 16 responses. From these responses it was reduced to 6 tenders which included the in-house bid. The tenders were subsequently narrowed down to 3 external organisations and final offers were received. In June 1991 the decision was taken to outsource the bureau service with ICL. In the interim period, ICL's facilities management operation was merged with CFM Limited in which ICL had taken a 75% share. It was therefore CFM who signed the contract. The changeover took place in September 1991, to run for 10 years with a review after 5 years. The selection criteria for the outsourcing company took into account a number of factors including value-for-money, quality of service, the ability to take the majority of CISD staff and to ensure a smooth changeover.

The contract was to cover the work of 7 government departments and their executive agencies, some 66 applications in total. Some applications were excluded on grounds of their stage in the development process. The outsourcing contract is estimated to be achieving savings of £1.8 million per annum in a function valued at £6.2 million (H M Treasury, 1991).

The outsourcing deal was initially going to involve 259 staff, but eventually, after the exclusion of some areas, covered 190 staff. In a period of great uncertainty staff felt that the communication process - a system of memos, briefings and presentations was effective. The trade unions were actively involved in the process. The issue of the Transfer of Undertakings legislation did not arise.

2.2 Contract monitoring

The agreement between CFM and NICS consists of a central contract concerned with the overall service and a service level agreement for each of the now 40 individual applications. The contract is managed at three levels - user, departmental and the Business Development Service (BDS) central team. The individual users monitor the service they receive against their service level agreement and verify reports. Departmental representatives check a four-weekly performance report from CFM. The BDS Central Monitoring Group (CMG) is made up of 3 managers whose job it is to monitor the overall contract. They have quarterly meetings with representatives from CFM and departmental representatives to discuss any problems that may have arisen. For those staff who are involved in monitoring the contract a new range of skills is required. In particular the CMG now require improved negotiating skills contract monitoring and accounting skills. Those at departmental level have to pay attention to detail in the examination of the reports.

2.3 CISD staff

The majority of staff who stayed within the NICS have moved to administrative or clerical work outside the IT function. Many of the staff who stayed within the new unit Business Development Service (BDS) were to be engaged in contract monitoring instead of operational activities. BDS resulted from a merger with two other units of the Department and Finance and Personnel, Management Services and the training function - Management Development Centre.

It would appear that those staff who remained within the parent unit underwent the greater amount of change. The environment of the public sector which, prior to the market testing programme had been very stable, had become much more turbulent. This was due to the increased pace of market testing initiatives and the effects of government policy epitomised in New Public Management. IT functions were more frequently included in designations of areas for testing.

2.4 Staff who transferred

CFM selected 110 of the 190 former CISD staff by means of formal recruitment procedures. These staff would appear to have adapted well to the move to the private sector. The stated reasons for transferring were that they wished to stay in their functional speciality. To a greater or lesser extent they were carrying out the same tasks, but for a different employer. They felt that if they had stayed within the NICS they would have been transferred to another function. Equally there was a perception of increased status as they were no longer merely part of a support function, rather they were now part of a company whose business was IT.

Staff who transferred were attracted by the increased emphasis on an individual's performance and responsibility. Not only were they responsible for the work they had originally carried out at CISD but they were given additional duties which have led to an increased variety of work and also increased responsibility.

From the early stages staff have been part of continuous training programmes designed to help them improve their work and to give them a more customer-oriented approach.

2.5 Service delivery

The users interviewed felt that the service levels offered by CISD had been of a high standard. However, the overall quality of service delivered by the outsourcing company is perceived to be even better. This may be due to the customer-oriented approach which has led to reduced response times to queries. The external company is also perceived to be more 'business like' in its approach. Equally it is worth noting that prior to the outsourcing contract many users were unaware of the level of service they were receiving. The documentation of service level agreements has raised user awareness. This has led users to speculate if the savings could have been achieved in house.

This contract is held to be successful by all concerned, users, former CISD staff, both those now in BDS and in CFM. Suggested reasons for the success include a process of good contract management, which is essential for an outsourcing arrangement's viability. Some interviewees commented on the information management problem contract monitoring was itself generating.

There are good working relations between CFM and BDS. Initially CFM actually used part of the CISD/BDS premises as well as employing many of CISD staff. These experienced staff trained in CISD procedures are another contributing factor to the smooth running of the operation. There is a strong bond between the two organisations. Finally the in-depth preparation of the market testing process gave senior managers a deep insight into the workings of the service.

The major negative feature lies in the effect on staff morale of those who remained within the Northern Ireland Civil Service. Having come through one period of radical change, they would appear to be sceptical of future developments.

3 DISCUSSION

In 10 years the information technology function of the NICS has moved from a centralised service to a more federal structure. The central operational level has subsequently been contracted out to an external supplier. The central strategic function has been retained. In this case the vendor organisation is supplying a commodity service. The relationship is operating on both a contractual and co-operative level (Willcocks and Kern, 1997). While outsourcing might be considered a decentralisation measure, it represents a centralisation of operational activities, but monitoring is carried out at departmental level. Strategic planning continues to be the remit of the central group in the existing federal structure (see figure 2). There is a true partnership as each organisation is reliant on the other. NICS relies on CFM (NI) for technical services, this contract was a flagship for the establishment of CFM (NI), so it is committed to client satisfaction beyond their high standard of customer care.

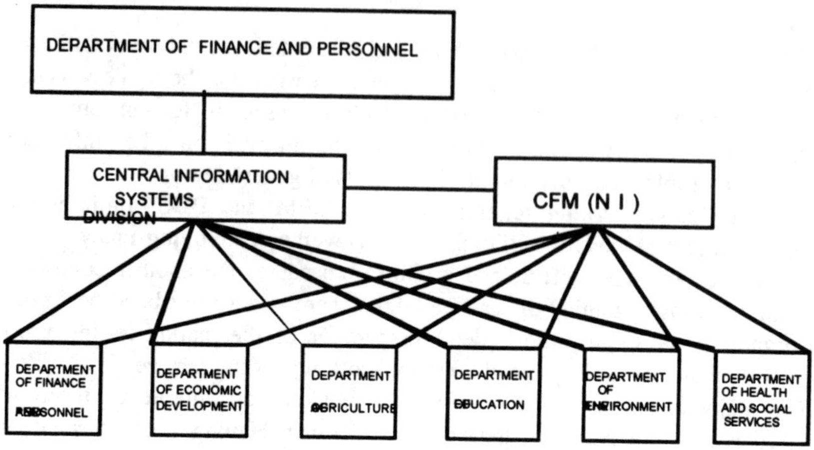

Figure 2 Structure of Central Information Systems Division after outsourcing.

There has been a major depletion in the number of technically expert staff, with the transfer of almost 60% of staff to the private sector. This raises the issue of succession planning for senior staff in the remaining core. The general issue of the impact of the market testing initiatives on staff morale in the public sector cannot be overlooked.

The number of mainframe applications contracted out to the outsourcing company is steadily decreasing, from an initial 66 to 47. The next logical step from the government's point of view would be for the work of the ISUs to be market tested. This may prove more difficult to achieve.

3.1 Benefits of outsourcing

The benefits of outsourcing can now be investigated in the light of this case study. Earl gives the following as the putative benefits of outsourcing:

- cost reduction,
- the opportunity to focus on core business,
- increased quality,
- additional flexibility and
- increased accountability.

In the case of CISD, the cost reductions have been estimated at £1.8 million per annum. More importantly, uncertainty about costs has also now been reduced as costs are agreed in the outsourcing contract. This viewpoint only includes production costs, transaction costs are excluded. Williamson defines transaction costs as the costs of monitoring controlling and managing transactions. As Hirschheim (1993) indicates, managers must consider the total costs, both production and transaction costs, when considering the outsourcing option. The work of the BDS central monitoring team was costed in to the contract. In the drive for efficiency, policy-makers must consider the transaction costs.

The opportunity to concentrate on the core business of the organisation exists for all those not involved in the monitoring process. Some users have found the detail of contract monitoring more time consuming than first anticipated.

Increased quality of service is perceived to have resulted from the fast response times to queries from the outsourcing company as part of its customer-oriented culture. On the one hand, it can be posited that with such a reduction of in-house technical staff, the potential for impartial advice may be limited and the ability to determine service quality may be diminished. On the other hand outsourcing gives access to IT specialists. For the public sector, staff recruitment has traditionally been problematic. CISD had been unable to realise its recruitment targets due to a combination of market forces, where demand for experienced information technology staff had continually outstripped supply, and due to the lengthy recruitment process (Northern Ireland Audit Office 1992).

The opportunity for increased flexibility would appear to be very limited, as the service is bound contractually to one company. There is little prospect of the service returning in its present form to an in-house operation. If another supplier had to be found, the detailed procurement procedures which have already been negotiated would have to be redone. The balance of power weighs heavily in the vendor's favour due to the dependency relationship. There is a trade-off between flexibility and cost containment.

It is evident that clearer lines of accountability do exist which were cited by both users and CFM staff as being beneficial. However clear accountability stems from the contract specification, especially the accuracy and comprehensiveness of service level agreements. It was pointed out that internal service level agreements might have achieved the same result.

There are some benefits which can be realised for the public sector, particularly in the areas of 'fixing' costs and having access to a cadre of specialised staff. Some of the other benefits, notably flexibility, would appear to be unlikely to be realised.

4 FRAMEWORK FOR SOURCING

Earl's framework for making the sourcing decision bears scrutiny in the context of this case study (see figure 3). Above all, CISD gave an example of low risk mature technology, CFM are supplying a commodity to the client organisation. The threat of loss of security of information should be one which is of particular significance to the public sector. Information stewardship lies at the very heart of the role of the public servant. Ascher writing in 1987 commented on the indivisibility of services when examining IT operations, indicating the difficulty of separating IT systems from the work of the organisation. In terms of actual data security, CFM staff are bound by Official Secrets legislation and staff commented that there was increased emphasis on data security as any breaches would have serious contractual implications.

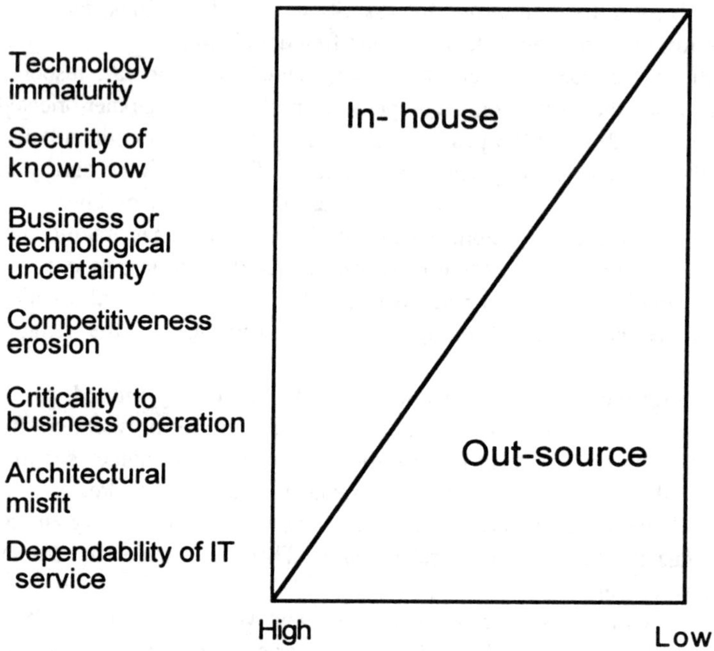

Figure 3 Outsourcing: situational factors (Earl 1991)

The pace of government reforms in the United Kingdom in the past 10 years has made the public sector as prone to uncertainty as many businesses. Major structural changes have occurred in government departments with the separation of the policy making function from the executive agencies under the Next Steps programme. Technological uncertainty for the moment may be low, but the use of optical methods for information storage and retrieval techniques are potentially of relevance to the public sector. The interpretation of erosion of competitiveness concerns the criticality of the information service to the organisation. This is an important consideration for the public sector. Taylor (1992) has put forward the concept of the 'information polity' which recognises the role of information in energising organisations. Outsourcing could have two effects on the information polity. By concentrating attention on information-related issues, outsourcing enhances this state. On the other hand, as a logical extension to Ascher's viewpoint, it may be difficult to separate the information content from the technological means of delivery.

In this case architectural fit was not a problem as the outsourcing company is linked to a proprietary supplier. Information services performance assumes importance if a department consistently underperforms. Earl cites the typical reaction that if 'IS is broke then let's put it out to tender'. A generally and perhaps undeserved perception of poor practice in public sector computing would appear to prevail. For example, in the United Kingdom National Health Service, a perception exists that valuable money is wasted on computers which could be better devoted to direct patient care. This may be explained by public accountability where bodies such as the Audit Office and Public Accounts Committee report on IT failures in the public sector. Similar cases in the private sector escape attention.

Four of the six criteria suggested by Earl have limited applicability to the public sector. As ever, it is in the technological criteria that the transition is smoothest. Assessed against this framework it would seem that outsourcing needs to be considered judiciously. Overall, the underlying rationale behind market testing in IT services in the public sector has been a political one. The absence of the mythical level playing field was commented upon by more than one interviewee. The outsourcing arrangement in this case study has been successful due to an effective partnership between the two organisations. It constitutes a strategic alliance due to the equality of the partners. Other public sector outsourcing arrangements may not enjoy the same level of success.

5 CONCLUSIONS

This earliest example of contracting out of an IT service in the public sector merits examination. The outsourcing contract would appear to be working well due to good relations between the two organisations. The meticulous preparation of those concerned in the in-house bid was of significant benefit in compiling and managing the contract. On comparing the case study against Earl's framework for evaluation, two thirds of the criteria are open to question in the public sector. The wider issues of information stewardship and informatization in public administration may be undermined by such policies as outsourcing.

6 REFERENCES

Ascher, K. (1987) The politics of privatisation. Macmillan, London.

HM Treasury (1991) Competing for quality. London, HMSO.

Earl M J (1991) Outsourcing information services *Public money and management* Autumn 17-21.

Government purchasing service (1991) A guide to market testing in Government. GPS, Belfast.

Lacity, M. C. and Hirschheim, R. (1993) Information systems outsourcing. Wiley, Chichester.

Northern Ireland Audit Office (1992) The management of information technology in government departments in Northern Ireland. London, HMSO .

Taylor J. A. (1992) Information networking in public administration. *International Review of Administrative Sciences,* **58,** 375-389.

Willcocks, L. and Kern , T. (1997) IT outsourcing as strategic partnering: the case of the UK Inland Revenue. *Proceedings of the fifth European Conference on Information Systems*, Cork, **3,** 1470-89.

7 BIOGRAPHY

Anne Davies is a senior lecturer in information management at the School of Management, Queen's University, Belfast. She teaches and researches in the area of public sector information systems particularly in health care. She has published work in the areas of information systems failures and information strategies.

Trevor Campbell is an Information Management graduate who undertook a postgraduate diploma in research methods at Queen' University. He is currently employed as a statistician in the Northern Ireland Civil Service.

12
Corporate Upsizing:The Evolving Role of DSS in Mergers and Acquisitions

A. M. McCosh
The Department of Business Studies,
The University of Edinburgh, William Robertson Building,
50 George Square, Edinburgh EH8 9JY
Tel: +44 131 650 3801 Fax: +44 131 668 3053
e-*mail: a.mccosh@ed.ac.uk*

Abstract

The history of DSS within the mergers and acquisitions movement is reviewed, and the number of changes which have taken place over thirty years is found to have been rather limited. The financial models have changed slightly, but the only major changes have been in database availability. The problem of where to search for the next step is addressed, and the suggestion is offered that the next important DSS area will lie in the softer sciences. Problems of organisation fit, personnel policy, and structure continue to be areas of serious difficulty during merger implementations, and that provides a fertile field for DSS professionals to plough.

Keywords

History, Mergers, Acquisitions, M&A, DSS, Corporate Control

1 INTRODUCTION

Thirty years ago, almost to the day, an article which I co-authored on this subject was published in the journal "Mergers and Acquisitions:- The Journal of Corporate Venture". The summer of 1967 was the high noon of the last-but-two merger wave. The article, entitled "The Use of Computers in Merger Analysis", was the first paper to be published on the subject. It seems reasonable to examine what progress we have made in the last thirty years. Has the Decision Support System concept moved forwards, or backwards? Has it, indeed, moved at all? If it has, which are the areas in which we have made the greatest headway, and which the least? Has the science of corporate upsizing through M&A changed much? I wish I could promise to answer all these questions, but the aspiration of this paper is the more modest one of reviewing a few of the more obvious and salient changes.

First of all, it is appropriate to concede that the largest single change has almost certainly been in the author. In 1967 I had only recently moved from being a doctoral student at Harvard Business School to being an Assistant Professor at Michigan. I was added to the list of authors because John D Glover was far too august a personage to be seen interacting with machinery, while David F Hawkins was far too smart an assistant professor to get involved with doing mathematics and computing when he could hire a doctoral student to do it for him. I have now progressed up the greasy pole of academe to a role faintly analogous to Glover's, though nothing like so august. But I find myself disappointed with our progress. If we were really making a lot of progress, I ought to be just as unable to understand what today's DSS models are doing as Glover was then. But the progress we have made recently has really not been of the transforming kind which was common when the early DSS, primitive though most of them were, came into use.

2 HARDWARE TECHNOLOGY IMPROVEMENTS

The technology, of course, is enormously different. The first few models were written on an IBM 1401, an IBM 7090, and (later) and IBM 360/65. There were no micro-computers available. The nearest thing to a micro was a Digital Equipment Corporation PDP-8, but user access to that was so severely rationed that the project had to be moved back on to the IBM machines to get the paper done on time. Data were loaded by punched cards, as were the programmes, and we were only slowly adding hard disks to the systems to enable data files to be kept on line. These disks were very expensive, and space on them was stringently rationed. The chief bureaucrat of computing at Michigan at the time allocated a lot of space to full professors, a modest amount to associate professors, a tiny amount to assistant professors, and a minuscule amount to doctoral students, even though the actual usage and need was almost exactly the other way round. It took, I think, about five years to get that sorted out. Even in the major companies which eventually picked up the idea of computerised merger and acquisition analysis, the technology was totally mainframe based, and there were tight controls on who was allowed to use the machinery and for what purposes. The idea of using the computer for confidential work, so confidential that the computer technicians and managers were not to be allowed to see any of it, was totally revolutionary, and required the personal intervention of the chairman of the board of directors in at least three of the companies I was working with at that time.

There was virtually no communications capability in 1967. By the time we wrote the second paper, in 1969, the technology had advanced so that we were able to connect to a mainframe through a teleprinter terminal machine, very like the telex machines of that time, using an audio modem and a conventional phone line. I can still recall the exhilarating thrill of life in the fast lane, the first time I was able to transmit at 4800 baud. A whole corporate data file could be loaded to disk in a mere twenty minutes or so.

The improvements in the hardware side of the technology are clear and unequivocal.

3 SOFTWARE TECHNOLOGY IMPROVEMENTS

On the software front, too, the technology has undoubtedly moved, though it is not quite so obvious that the movement has been forwards. Most of the early programmes were written in FORTRAN 2, then FORTRAN 4. By 1969 we were working under timesharing and using, for the most part, Dartmouth Basic Language. It has become fashionable now to regard these as dinosaurs, and various new devices are offered as the modern way to go about the task of writing a programme. Structured programming and object orientated programming, C, C+, C++, C+++ and the rest are all touted as improvements. I am afraid that they simply are not. They do the same things as the old languages, and the student DSS submissions that have come to me over the thirty year period are still characterised by the same kinds of mistakes in 1996 as I was getting in 1966. I do not teach programming, but rely on the students having taken a course from one of the specialists. We really have made very little progress on this front of general high-level languages:- all we have achieved is diversity.

I will readily admit that the introduction of spreadsheets, starting with Visicalc in 1977 and moving forward to Lotus and Excel now are very important and useful innovations. For certain kinds of DSS, the spreadsheet approach is a real and important advantage which was not available in the early years. I will further concede that the automatic macro facility which is available in some software packages is a substantial benefit in the right hands. This facility enables a spreadsheet user to initiate a sequence of calculations by pressing the keys in the right order, and having these recorded for later automatic use. When you examine the results of this process, former users of Dartmouth Basic have absolutely no trouble in reading it. The Microsoft Visual Basic is so like the old Dartmouth Basic that I have to hope they are paying adequate royalties for it.

I am, therefore, willing to concede that some modest progress has been made on the software side of technology in the context of corporate upsizing DSS applications. Most of the changes that have taken place are in graphics, which is almost totally useless for the kinds of work which merger analysis involves.

4 DATA SERVICES

The most complete change that has occurred in the field of corporate upsizing DSS and M&A in general is in the availability of computerised data sets. In 1966, useful card services were available, giving financial and other history for every company on the New York, American, London, and Frankfurt exchanges. I am reasonably confident that similar services were available for the other exchanges too. The developer of an M&A DSS had all the data he could possibly wish for. The nature and form of it, however, left a lot to be desired. The data had to be transcribed, reformatted, and stored in a specially designed file that the M&A analysis programme could be programmed to read. This was a very tiresome business. For most M&A work, it was necessary for something like eighty or ninety numbers to be copied across for each company that was being worked on. In a typical situation, while the search for merger partners was proceeding, there would be twenty or thirty companies. Some of these data were relatively stable, changing only once a quarter or even once a year. Others, however, especially share price data, had to be changed daily. Because of the extremely confidential nature of the work, it was not possible to delegate this tedious data transcription to a secretary, who would certainly have done the job better and more efficiently than I did.

It was therefore a great and welcome relief when computerised data files with download facilities came on the market. Compustat, Datastream, Microexstat, and other services enabled the data to be fed directly from the supplier's files into a spreadsheet, where they could be rearranged for later loading into the merger model.

It is perhaps a bit ironic that the same flexibility and ease of use of the data files from the service agencies had the secondary effect of eliminating some of the competitive advantage which DSSs for M&A had previously provided. With the arrival of the datafile and the transfer programmes, every public company could easily obtain the services of a DSS. All the investment banks and merchant banks had at least one such model in operation by 1980, and the competitive advantage battlefield shifted away from having a DSS for merger analysis to having the best DSS for merger analysis. This, of course, was less easy for the client companies to differentiate. A good merger analysis system and a mediocre merger analysis system look pretty similar until you dig into the works.

The availability of computerised data sets is, perhaps, the most significant of all the changes that have occurred in corporate upsizing DSS in the thirty years.

5 RELATIVE ABSENCE OF CHANGES IN THE ECONOMIC MODELS OF THE MERGER

I will discuss the content of the typical merger model in a later section, but first it is necessary to consider what changes have taken place in this part of the process. I should preface this section of the paper with the caution that many of the investment and merchant banks regard their M&A DSS as a major competitive advantage, and I have therefore only direct access to a small proportion of the total. In some instances, it has been possible to see the results of another M&A DSS because it is being used by the other side in a negotiation, and it is therefore sometimes possible to infer what the model was doing. At the same time, it would be as well to recognise that this is an anecdotal report on the changes, not a comprehensive survey.

The basic changes that I have seen in the M&A DSS have been remarkably few. There have been certain specific changes, such as the automatic importation of data, and sometimes the graphical presentation of the consequences of the merger. The fundamentals of the analysis has hardly changed at all in the thirty years. The basic reasons for merging have not changed, of course, so I suppose I should not be surprised that the economic analysis has stayed the same and therefore that the DSS is still much the same.

The changes that have taken place are more to do with the instrument used to pay for the acquisition. In 1967, there was a strong fashion for mergers to be financed by convertible preference shares. By the mid-1980s, there was a fashion for using high-yielding fixed interest non-investment grade securities, which was the official name for junk bonds. In the 1990s, the relatively low levels of interest rates has made it sensible to think in terms of a cash merger. During this time period, there have also been changes in the laws governing mergers and acquisitions, and changes in the regulations issued by the stock exchanges. While some of these changes have caused quite a fuss when they were happening, it must really be admitted that the market for control of corporations is pretty much the same as it has always been. A few things have become taxable that were not before, and a few things that were taxable have ceased to be taxable. That can certainly change the decision as to whether a merger makes sense or not, but the economic model used to study the situation is essentially unaltered.

The changes to the economic models used to study the feasibility of merger proposals have been relatively modest, and are mainly matters of presentation or of incorporating changes to the tax laws or the stock exchange rules, all of which have been minor.

6 THE GENERAL NATURE OF THE M&A DECISION: [A] OBJECTIVES

The main objective which the companies taking part in a merger or acquisition are seeking to fulfil is to make their shareholders richer and to make the managers richer by giving them a bigger empire. A secondary objective, held by the smaller companies, may be to arrange to be taken over because the family which owns it has nobody in the new generation who can carry on the managerial task. In the case of a hostile bid, the objective of the managers of the target company is to avoid being taken over, usually because they will probably be fired the day after the acquisition is consummated.

Studies of the success and failure of mergers have been somewhat negative about the whole process. Generally, when a merger or acquisition takes place, the shareholders of the company which is purchased do rather well, and the managers of the acquirer do well (because they have a bigger empire and that usually brings more pay), while the managers of the acquired company usually get kicked out. The history is a bit mixed as to whether the shareholders of the acquirer do well or badly. This depends on many factors, one of which is whether the acquiring managers pay too much for the company being acquired, and this particular topic is therefore of great interest, and is the principal focus of most of the M&A DSS models.

Michael Jensen of Harvard has estimated the gains to US shareholders of companies which have been taken over. These average out at over forty billion dollars a year for the dodecade ending 1988. The gains to the shareholders of the buying companies has averaged four billion. These large sums could be compared with the dividends paid to the entire US shareholding public during this same twelve year time period, which amount to about $86 billions annually.

The financial objective of the merger is usually to enhance the earnings per share of the parent company by buying an earnings stream (which was formerly the smaller company's) and issuing shares for it. If you issue few enough shares, the total earnings of the combine divided by the new total number of shares will be a higher number than the result you had before, dividing the parents earnings by the previous total number of shares. In order to get away with this manoeuvre, you have to have previously arranged that your share price is rather high, so that the shareholders of the smaller company are willing to accept a smallish number of them in exchange for their company. This action on their part may not be a dim as it sounds. The alternatives available to the shareholders of the small company, other than selling out to a big one, may be relatively few. This is often the only way the shareholders can get rid of a group of useless managers, who happen to have a sizeable shareholding.

At the same time, it is true that earnings growth is a principal reason for mergers to happen. It is often the case that the large company can put more funds behind a good idea than the smaller company, and this may enable it to take a leading position in a new market than the small company could ever achieve on its own. Jensen thinks that growth is a bad reason for mergers, but his examples are all related to very big firms, to which this important reason does not apply.

There is near unanimity now that the idea of diversification as a reason for merging is bad. Sam Hayes is especially forthright in his criticism of the merger wave of the 1960's in which companies bought other companies <u>because</u> they were different from anything else the large company did. This diversification was supposed to enable the good times in one industry to offset any bad times in another, and a general improvement in overall results was supposed to follow. This did not work. The senior bosses did not understand all the companies for which they were responsible, made very bad decisions, and became vulnerable to break-up bids in the next merger wave of the 1980s.

There are many other objectives which managers can seek to fulfil by means of a merger. A full discussion can be found in any of the text books on the topic, such as Brealey, Myers and Marcus. For the moment, it is enough to note that earnings growth is one major goal, that diversification is definitely out of fashion, and that capital gains to the shareholder groups are very effective instruments for implementation.

7 THE NATURE OF THE M&A DECISION:- [B]IMPLEMENTATION AND ANALYSIS

Although the objectives are numerous, they are at least fairly clear. When it comes to the task of making the merger work, the situation is very much less clear, and the results have been quite poor, by almost any definition of good and poor that one cares to select.

In the first place, there is the inadequacy of the analysis of the way in which the merged enterprises were going to be managed after the merger. In Emmons and Perry's paper, reporting a roundtable discussion in 1997 of this general area, specialists from all subject areas complained about the amateurish ways in which some very important issues had been handled. They quote KH Wruck as being concerned about acquirers imposing a bureaucratic system on a freeform enterprise, and then wondering why it was no longer creative. They quote L Paine's concern about the mismatch of personnel policies, especially when a thuggish business managed purely for shareholder value takes over another which had emphasised employee development. RL Nolan was worried about the failure to think through the coalescence of the various corporate information and computing networks, while Michael Beer was even more worried about the failure to cope with the need for some kind of joint strategic understanding, even if it was one which was much more heavily influenced by the parent than by the new subsidiary. Please note that these deficiencies were being reported in 1997 as current problems, not as historic issues which are now behind us.

They certainly are not new ideas. The principal arguments were set forth at length through the analysis of a survey in Kitching's paper of 1967, entitled "Why Do Mergers Miscarry?". Having surveyed twenty-five large acquirers, some of whom had made a dozen purchases, he was able to report that "concentric marketing" mergers were failing disproportionately often, and his definition of that phrase makes it clear that the problems lay in the organisational and interpersonal concerns addressed by Wruck and Paine 30 years on. Kitching also identified the need for a manager of change to take a clear and cohesive managerial line in directing the total business, after listening to both teams. This has much in common with Beer's comment about the early need for a joint strategic document. It would appear that we are making quite a few of the same errors now as we were then.

It must be acknowledged that the merger wave of the 1980s was largely a successful one, in bringing concentration and focus to the task of large company management. Most of the 1990s mergers which are proving successful are building on this strong foundation. Usually, they are devoted to the fulfilment of a strategic goal, which cannot be handled easily by organic growth methods.

8 THE FINANCIAL MODELS

We shall return to the topic of implementation when we consider the way forward for DSS in Mergers. First, it is necessary to consider what the more financially orientated DSS models were and are doing, before we look at the problem of what these models' successors should be doing in the future.

As was suggested above, the original models (some of which are still in use) were designed to ensure financial viability. The assumption was made that the more sociological and strategic issues would be dealt with by other means. It was not seen as the financial modeler's job to address these issues.

The models were designed to work out what a fair price for a given subsidiary would be, and what form that payment ought to take. The usual route was to decide how much the parent company wanted to pay as a premium over the present market price of the shares, and then to try a variety of packages that could achieve that. The packages would range from 100% cash to 100% shares, with, possibly, a number of variants in the form of convertible preferred shares, or bonds, or preference shares. The selection of the particular package would be a matter for the preferences of the shareholders of the company being acquired, some of whom might be very cash hungry (and willing to pay the taxes now) while others were content to accept paper in exchange (and postpone the taxes for a future period).

In the model below, the exchange that is being explored is an exchange of shares only, where the larger firm "Parent" is seeking to buy the smaller firm "Small" by issuing Parent shares in exchange for the shares of the small company.

	Parent	Small
Number of shares	8000	2000
Share Price	16	16
Earnings total	5000	1850
Growth expected	8	4
Dividend/share	4	1

In the above example, Parent might offer to buy Small by offering six Parent shares for every five Small shares. If this were the offer, and it were to be accepted, the situation could be shown to be as follows

	Before Merger	After Merger
Parent Earnings per share	0.625	0.659 *
Small Earnings per Small share	0.925	0.79 **
Small Dividend/share	0.01	0.05
Capital owned by Small	16	19.2
Dividend, Parent	.04	0.042

* ((5000+1850)/(8000+(6/5)(2000)))
** 0.659 * 6/5

In this situation, the Parent has increased its earnings per share, and slightly increased its dividend by means of the merger. The shareholders of Small have made a capital gain of 20% from 16 to 19.2, and have increased their dividend income by 400% from a penny to five pence. They have given up some earnings per share (down 14.6%) in order to obtain these two benefits. Both companies were very stingy indeed in terms of dividends. The shareholders of Small may, however, have been glad to escape from the very confining Small dividend situation to the still confining but at least larger Parent.

It is not appropriate in this paper to go into the intricacies of merger and acquisition models in any detail. In every case that I have seen, the mission is to work out the financial consequences of the merger proposal. The decision to offer six for five, in the above example, would be arrived at by the parent managers using their M&A DSS, and would be evaluated on receipt by the Small managers using theirs. The models would be calibrated to deal with taxation, with dividends, with capital values, with growth rates, and with the more complex kinds of merger. These will be mergers in which the instruments on offer are not just shares, but might include cash, preference shares, junk bonds, or all four of these.

The underlying equations in use in merger models which I have seen used recently are really very similar to the ones which were in use thirty years ago. They have had to be somewhat more sophisticated because of the changes in the legal system governing M&A, but the basic task remains essentially the same.

9 THE SITUATION NOW FOR DSS IN M&A

Have we really made a lot of progress? In a sense, of course, the answer has to be yes. There are very few mergers nowadays in which a DSS is not employed to work out the terms and conditions under which the merger will be agreed. We are using much fancier hardware. We have access to infinitely more convenient databases. We have made some slight progress in terms of the development of our software tools.

In another sense, however, the answer could be "not much". The actual models we are using are the same as the primitive ones of thirty years ago, with various legally required adjustments. Also, since everyone is using the DSS approach, there is less competitive advantage to be gained from the use of them. The costs of developing and updating these DSS models is very considerable however, and the firms that have them feel they must spend to keep themselves in a state of at least competitive equality, if they cannot attain competitive advantage.

We could perhaps compare the use of DSS in M&A to the use of ATMs in the banking industry. For a few years, the banks that had ATMs gained a competitive advantage from having them. Nowadays, almost all banks have them, and the banks that do not have them are suffering a severe competitive disadvantage from their absence. But all the banks are incurring very large costs to keep their ATMs up to date.

It could be argued that decision support systems for corporate upsizing through merger and acquisition have suffered the fate of so many bright ideas of bygone times. Perhaps they have become a commodity?

10 A POSSIBLE WAY FORWARD

As a professional in the DSS area, I find the thought of being a commodity rather too depressing. I am confident that there are many things we can still do within the field of M&A to make sure that the DSS concept continues to be of service. Not just a commodity service, either, but a differentiating service which makes a real economic and social difference to the M&A problems which businesses confront. What, then, might such a differentiating service look like? I take it as given that we will continue to produce financial and quantitative DSS models of the kind discussed earlier.

The clue to our next move lies in the critical comments which were listed in the middle part of the paper. The mergers are still failing, either absolutely or compared to what had been hoped. The reasons they are failing are known, and have been known for years. The organisational styles are not only different but seriously incompatible. The information systems and computer systems are not only different but seriously incompatible. The policy of the businesses are seriously different, with one emphasising people, a second emphasising shareholder value, a third emphasising product quality and a fourth emphasising cohesion of distribution channels.

There are no databases that deal with these issues. There are anecdotes and a number of studies of corporate style. There is no real "cookbook" with instruction for the novice to follow so that he can get the merger to come out the way he wanted it to be. We may have reduced the financial aspects to a formula or a near-formula, but on organisational, systems, and orientation issues, we are still in the jungle.

That must be the area where we will make our big contribution. If the job was easy, nobody would pay us much to do it. We need to devise databases, questionnaires, and other data devices to allow the classification of enterprises, in terms of organisational style, information systems approach, and policy emphasis. A few of these datasets, or at least the components from which to build them, already exist. We need to glean the academic fields to find the change management routes that work when various kinds of incompatible entity are being brought together. Is there, we must ask, a subtle way of managing this aggregation of firms, or is brute force the only hope? And having asked the question, we need to equip ourselves with a bundle of at least historical answers, and ideally theory-founded ones as well.

Then we need to package these histories into case studies which are rich in detail and description, and use some kind of text analysis process to isolate the similarities and differences between them. From there we can move to a comparison between them and the particular pair of companies we are trying to assist now. Some of this material exists already, but it will need substantial expansion and significant reorientation if it is to be a resource for the next generation of DSS for M&A

The major new policy issues for DSS in M&A will lie on the corner, where strategy, behavioural sciences, and information technology meet. The way forward in DSS for M&A may well turn out to be even more fun than it was way back in '66.

11 REFERENCES

Brealey, R.A., Myers, S.C. and Marcus, A.J. (1995) Fundamentals of Corporate Finance. McGraw Hill, New York.

Emmons, G. and Perry, N.O. (June 1997) Blockbuster Deals:- M&As Make a Comeback. *Harvard Business School Bulletin*, , Boston, Mass. p52-59.

Glover, J.D., Hawkins, D.F. and McCosh, A.M. (Summer 1967) Computers in Merger Analysis. *Mergers and Acquisitions* **2,** 17-32.

Hawkins, D.F., McCosh, A.M. and Lampe, J.C. (1969) Time Shared Merger Analysis. *Mergers and Acquisitions*, **4,** 11-19.

Hayes, S. (1997) Blockbuster Deals Make a Comeback. *Harvard Business School Bulletin*

Jensen, M.C. (1996) Mergers and Acquisitions, in *Corporate Finance* (eds. Ross, Westerfield, and Jaffe) 4th edition, Irwin, Chicago.

Kitching, J. (1967) Why do Mergers Miscarry? *Harvard Business Review* Boston Mass, p84-101.

12 BIOGRAPHY

Andrew McCosh has been a member of IFIP since 1984. He was professor of management accounting at Manchester Business School from 1971-1985, and Dean of the Faculty for part of that time. He was professor of finance at the University of Edinburgh from 1986-1995, and Head of Business Finance, Accountancy and Economics for part of that time. He has published forty papers and seven books on systems and on finance.

13
The competitiveness of the Hungarian managers

Z. Z. Paprika
Budapest University of Economic Sciences
Budapest V. Veres Pálné st. 36.
H-1053, HUNGARY
Telephone: +36 1 1183 037, facsimile: +36 1 1172 959
e-mail: paprika@mercur.bke.hu

Abstract

Apart from leadership styles, decision-making is influenced by the quality, education, experience, personality and skills of managers. This study reflects the level of skills/abilities of the managers included in our statistical samples. In other words, this paper would like to reveal whether the Hungarian managers have had the proper attitudes/skills to implement the change of the economic system or not.

Keywords

Management skills/abilities, decision making style, economic transition

1 GENERAL INTRODUCTION TO THE RESEARCH PROJECT

When our research group joined the research program "In Global Competition - Microeconomics Factors of Competitiveness of the Hungarian Economy" conducted by the Business Economics Department of BUES (Budapest University of Economic Sciences) at the end of 1995, we expressed our professional opinion - i.e., the method of making business decisions in the microsphere is one of the strategic factors of any market economy - in an institutional format by forming the Decision Making sub-project.[1]

We need to define clearly how the persons playing part in the economy make business decisions in order to describe precisely the real business world, to evaluate its effectiveness, to compare it with the competitors. The Decision Making sub-project within the research programme defined the competitiveness of companies as

---

[1] Members of the Decision Making sub-project are as follows: István Bartók, Norbert Becser, Ferenc Dénes, Szabolcs Gergely, Péter Nagy, Tibor Tamás, Zita Zoltay Paprika.

the simultaneous abilities to operate and to change. Consequently, a competitive company is stabile and flexible at the same time and it tries to maximise its long-term profit by transforming the available resources, while it is expected to adapt itself to the norms of the society and to the rapid changes of the environment.

Due to the fact that the first step and the most direct manifestation of adaptation is the decision-making of the management, our research aimed to provide a picture of the current decision-making practice of the Hungarian microsphere, based on a thorough theoretical background and on a large empirical study. Moreover, we intended to improve the quality of decision-making by drawing consequences and offering suggestions.

Our research concentrated on the executives. From the executives' point of view we dealt with the lower levels of decision making as well. In other words, we studied the issues of strategic decision making. Accordingly, the success and competitiveness of companies have a component that can be defined as the quality of management decision-making; the comprehensive research of this component - similarly to the general analysis of competitiveness - has been done for the first time in Hungary. Since strategic decision-making is the essence of the management function, it is understandable that our research focused on this issue. In our opinion, this topic is especially important nowadays: due to the historical and economic changes, Hungarian companies have to make more strategic decisions than usually under rapidly changing, uncertain and complex circumstances.

The authors Adam Angyal and Sándor Kovács describe leadership in terms of four factors. These are as follows:

- It is an activity that needs special expertise.
- It is a collective term of problem-solving activities.
- It gives answers to outer expectations (role-play).
- It is a part of the political power system.

We focused on the second factor, according to the definition that first and foremost leadership is problem-solving and decision-making (Angyal -Kovács 1996).

One of our hypothesis was that there should be a correlation between the quality of strategic decision making and the competitiveness of companies. We also supposed that the Hungarian managers intended to make rational decisions, which may not be the most fruitful strategy in a turbulent economy. According to our previous experiences, the decision-making hierarchy of the Hungarian companies was rather centralised. In state-owned companies, this can be explained in terms of their historical roots; in partly or entirely foreign-owned companies the initial mistrust and the slow learning-curve cause this centralisation. Leadership style shows itself both in preparing decisions and making decisions. For this reason we identified different leadership styles and wanted to analyse them in terms of decision-making attitudes. We expected that as a consequence of the presence of multinational companies, foreign investments and of education, the Anglo-Saxon and German management patterns had become dominant in Hungary.

We put the emphasis on in-depth interviews of top executives. We tried to contact the most important Hungarian companies by using the *Figyelõ Top 200* list and tried to interview the CEOs/top executives. We prepared a structured draft for these interviews and did not vary it in order to receive comparable answers. We considered the large British "Bradford studies" research programme to be the most important precedent of our research (The Bradford studies are described in Hickson *et. al.,* 1986).

The Bradford Studies programme was launched at the beginning of the 1970s. Its aim was to provide an in-depth analysis of executive decision making that was more comprehensive than any other previous analysis. The studies finished in the mid-eighties and the programme's researchers created and analysed a really significant database that includes 150 decision-making cases from 30 English organisations.

The launching of the Hungarian comprehensive research program "In Global Competition" in 1995 was a great opportunity to us to adapt the methods of the British researchers to the Hungarian circumstances and to start a similar research program. We had 6 months between May 1996 and October 1996 to complete the field research. During this period we interviewed 50 executives of 42 Hungarian and 8 Spanish companies (the Spanish companies formed the control-group).[2]

In order to gather the information precisely, always two of us made the in-depth interviews. The interviews lasted between 1.5 and 2 hours and were based on the draft tested by our work group.

Repeating the 15 year-long Bedford studies in 6 months resulted in significant differences in the methodology. The greatest disadvantage of our method was that it did not ensure the thorough control/checking of the data we gathered. The researchers of the Bedford studies controlled several times the creditability of the data provided by the executives of the 30 companies. Our efforts to check the data was limited by the lack of time, so our primary aim was to test the largest sample we could possibly reach in 6 months. Only one third of the executives we got in touch with were willing to welcome us and there were many of them who found it difficult to give an interview that lasted 1.5 to 2 hours. As a result, we could not even have thought of organising control-meetings or enhancing the intensity of data-collection. Our data can not be regarded to be objective.

Our interviews answer the following questions: what was the opinion of the executives about the issues raised by us; how did they perceive the decision-making process in their company; how did they evaluate the management in summer-fall 1996? We can have only impressions of how these answers reflect reality. Although our draft included several control questions that were capable of revealing

---

[2] José Sempere and Rafael Moner (Universidad de Valencia) took part in interviewing the Spanish executives

the inconsistency of the different answers of a given executive, these control questions could not solve the aforementioned problem.

On the other hand, the standardised methodology of our field research was our advantage. The Bradford Studies changed their method of information gathering more than once during the 15 years of the programme, whereas the Decision Making sub-project of the research program "In Global Competition" used the same methodology throughout without any modifications. Another strength of our research was that, except on one occasion , top executives gave us interviews. This is very important when we analyse strategic decisions. Thus it is worth mentioning here the composition of our sample as one of the main strengths of our research.

Typically, large companies answered our questions. 61% of them employ more than 1000 employees. The remaining 40% represent the companies with 50-100, 100-300, 300-500 and 500-1000 employees in even proportions.

36% of the companies did not have a state-owned predecessor. The remaining 64% were either directed by a "company board" or by the government. 53% of the companies are currently free from state ownership. Only 5% of them are totally owned by the state.

Foreign companies have more than 50% ownership in roughly 30% of the companies (15% of the companies are totally owned by foreign companies). Foreign banks and foreign private persons have only an insignificant proportion of ownership.

Hungarian private persons have more than 50% ownership in roughly 20% of the companies (12% of the companies are totally owned by Hungarian private persons). 10% of the companies are totally owned by their management.
The companies can be regarded as "half-opened", since only 10% of them export more than half of their output but 29% of them import more than half of their output (the proportion of import exceeds 90% in 6% of the companies).

More than 60% of the companies could increase their inland sales during the last 3 years. On the other hand, 11% of them suffered more than a 10% decrease in sales.

During the same period, 34% of the companies said that they had significantly increased profits after tax and 20% of them had increased the return on sales as well. On the other hand, 27% of the companies said that their profits after taxes had decreased and 28% of them said that the return on sales had decreased.

We know that the chosen 42 Hungarian companies may not be a representative sample of Hungarian Companies. But we did try to provide a colourful, comprehensive and informative sample and we feel we have been successful in doing so. Our intention was to have a sample that reflects the strengths, the weaknesses and the transitional nature of the Hungarian economy, from both the industries and the ownership structures point of view. Different representatives of various industries (e.g. a totally foreign-owned car-making company, a totally state-owned commercial bank, a recently privatised electricity utility) are included in the sample. The idea was that, apart from revealing the nature of strategic decision making in the various industries, we should be able to draw general conclusions about the methods of decision making within the Hungarian economy in transition.

Although our research focused on the in-depth interviews, the central questionnaire of the research program "In Global Competition" also played an important role in terms of controlling our results of management skills and decision-making attitudes. The statistical population of the central questionnaire was formed by those companies that

- have more than 50 employees
- are independent legal entities
- use double-entry book-keeping
- already existed before 1992

10% of these companies were chosen to be in the basic sample of the central questionnaire in order to be representative of Hungarian companies in terms of

- industries
- regions
- number of employees
- ownership structure, based on the owners of subscribed capital

Taking the aforementioned 4 factors into consideration, 593 companies were chosen to be in the basic sample. Companies listed in the *1995 Figyelõ TOP 200* were added; in the end we asked 665 companies to co-operate. 325 of them accepted our request,which can be regarded as a high percentage of positive responses.

2 PERSONAL CHARACTERISTICS OF DECISION MAKING

The level of decision making and thus the competitiveness of the company is influenced by the abilities, skills, methods and techniques of the decision makers. We analysed these factors in detail and compared the results of the Hungarian sample with the results of the analysis of the Spanish companies.

2.1 Management skills

To survey the strengths and weaknesses of the management of Hungarian companies, we used the patterns of previous international projects. As a result, we made a list of 11 factors that we thought included all the relevant skills and abilities of decision making. The list includes the skills that represent the traditional as well as the dynamic, entrepreneurial leadership style. We used it

(a) to identify the challenges the managers have to face

(b) to evaluate the preparedness of the managers.

We applied different methods during the in-depth interviews and the questionnaire respectively, but this did not the comparison of the results difficult. Furthermore, it provided an additional opportunity to control the stability of the results.

We tried to break the usual "I ask - you answer" pattern during the in-depth interviews by asking the managers about management (that is, self-evaluation) in a different way. Before the interviews, we wrote down the 11 skills onto separate cards. We started the interviews by asking the managers to rank these cards in terms of importance. This ranking reflected what the interviewed person generally expected or demanded from the Hungarian managers. Once we had obtained the ideal ranking, we asked the interviewee about the strengths and weaknesses of his or her own management. The third ranking proved to be the hardest task in many cases: namely, to rank the cards according to the interviewee's own strengths and weaknesses.

Figure 1 shows the ranking of the ideal management skills in order of importance (the less the attached number, the more important the given skill is). It includes both the Hungarian and Spanish executives' opinions.

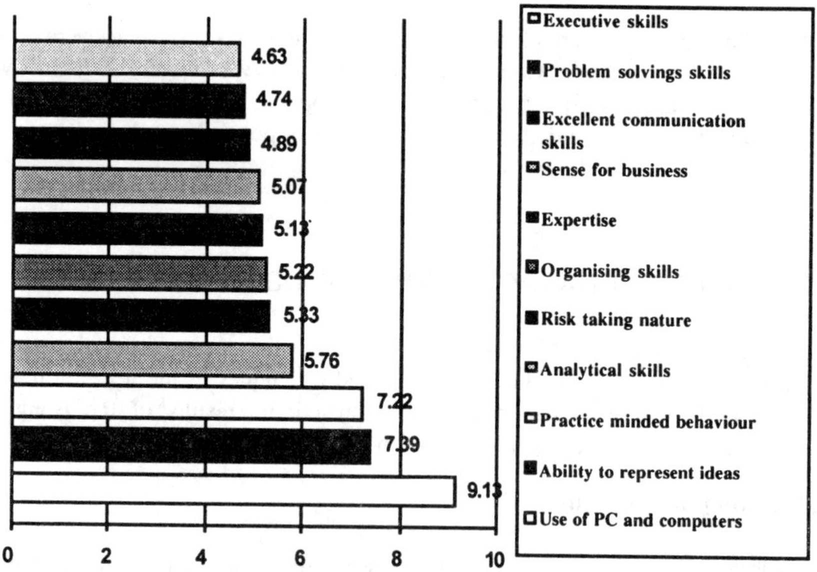

Figure 1 Ranking of the ideal management skills

Table 1 Challenges the managers have to face in Hungary and in Spain

Management skills	*Hungarian companies*	*Δ*	*Spanish companies*
1. excellent communication skills	4.87	-0.13	5.00
2. expertise	5.39	1.52	3.87
3. executive skills	4.79	0.92	3.87
4. problem solving skills	4.47	-1.53	6.00
5. ability to represent ideas	7.44	0.32	7.12
6. organising skills	5.31	0.58	4.75
7. sense for business	5.16	0.54	4.62
8. use of PC and computers	9.15	0.15	9.00
9. analytical skills	5.76	0.01	5.75
10. practice minded behaviour	7.31	0.58	6.75
11. risk taking nature	4.50	-4.75	9.25

It may not be surprising that the expectations are different in the Hungarian and in the Spanish sample. Of course, a lower average score indicates that the given skill is more important than those with higher averages. The rankings also indicate that certain skills are more needed in one country than in the another.

The third column of Table 1 shows these differences. Negative differences occur when the Hungarian managers consider a given skill to be more important then the Spanish managers. It is quite obvious that the evaluation of risk-taking nature is absolutely different in Hungary and in Spain. The Hungarians ranked it second, the Spanish ranked it in the last place. This indicates that even at the end of the current period of transition of the economy, the Hungarian managers think that their (economic) environment is uncertain, unpredictable, and full of potential negative surprises. Uncertainty and forced decision-making is reflected in the second biggest negative difference, namely, that the Hungarian managers think that problem-solving skills are inevitable. As far as the positive differences are concerned, the Spanish managers regard traditional leadership skills (e.g. expertise, organising skills, executive skills) to be more important than do the Hungarians. In other words, the ideal Spanish manager is more traditional than the Hungarian one.

Table 2 shows the preferences of the Hungarian and Spanish managers (in descending importance). According to the Hungarians, the main task of the executive is to solve problems, which is perceived as a continuous - and exhausting - activity. Hungarian managers have to select issues quite often, have to decide which problem must be dealt with first. This requires the ability to realise the essential problems. Executive and communication skills could support the executives to resist lower levels of management in the case of pushing decision-making "upwards".

Table 2 Ranking of the ideal management skills in the Hungarian and Spanish sample

Hungarian companies	Spanish companies
problem solving skills	executive skills
risk taking nature	expertise
executive skills	sense for business
excellent communication skills	organising skills
sense for business	excellent communication skills
organising skills	analytical skills
expertise	problem solving skills
analytical skills	practice minded behaviour
practice minded behaviour	ability to represent ideas
ability to represent ideas	use of PC and computers
use of PC and computers	risk taking nature

It is worth while to compare these evaluations with the results of the Egon Zehnder International "Corporate Governance" conference questionnaire. The researchers of the aforementioned program asked the following questions:

(a) Ideally what viewpoints should play a decisive role in the selection of executives?

(b) What viewpoints play a decisive role in practice?

The results showed that the expectations and the reality did differ from each other significantly. Functional, industrial knowledge and personal leadership skills are regarded more important in practice than they should be. On the other hand, international experience and certain personal skills (e.g. long-term strategic thinking) are not so important in practice as they should be (Egon Zehnder International, 1995).

The preferences of the Spanish managers reflected a different attitude. According to the Spanish managers, the companies should be organised on a basis of expertise and executive skills, and they can be made successful with the help of business sense. It is clear that the Spanish managers think in terms of a more self confident model.

Table 3 illustrates the answers regarding the strengths, weaknesses (and neutral factors) of the managers' own companies. In this table the numbers indicate how many votes a given skill received from the managers.

Table 3. The strengths and weaknesses of company management in the Hungarian and Spanish models.

Management skills	*Hungary*			*Spain*		
	S	*N*	*W*	*S*	*N*	*W*
1. excellent communication skills	18	14	10	5	1	1
2. expertise	27	12	3	6	1	1
3. executive skills	12	16	14	5	2	1
4. problem solving skills	23	13	6	5	1	2
5. ability to represent ideas	11	18	13	3	1	4
6. organising skills	13	18	11	6	1	1
7. sense for business	22	13	7	7	0	1
8. use of PC and computers	7	18	17	2	1	5
9. analytical skills	18	14	10	4	1	3
10. practice minded behaviour	26	14	2	4	1	3
11. risk taking nature	16	8	18	3	1	4

It is worth mentioning that, on aggregate, more than one third of the Hungarian managers considered the skills to be neutral, which can be interpreted in different ways:

- The company management possess these skills at an average level, so they are neither strengths nor weaknesses (good-intended interpretation).
- The management is "uneven" (quote from the CEO of a commercial company), that is, there are significant differences between the skills of the executives, which creates problems at top level.
- The managers simply do not know each others' skills in such detail as was presented on the list of 11 components (pessimistic interpretation).

The Hungarian managers considered practice-minded behaviour and expertise to be the most positive factors of the company management (see the first column of Table 4). The fourth place of good sense of business is promising, since the transition to a market economy is to be completed in Hungary.

The lack of a risk-taking nature and of the ability to represent ideas are serious weaknesses in an economic environment that is full of challenges. The low level of PC skills is a serious weakness as well. While our list did not include this, many managers of multinational as well as state-owned companies regarded the lack of knowledge of foreign languages as a serious problem, too. The importance of honesty and reliability were mentioned many times, too; although these are not skills, they influence decision-making and are very valuable when the economy is infected with crime.

The Spanish interviewees gave more definite answers since the proportion of their neutral answers did not reach 20%.

Sense for business ensures a competitive edge in the Spanish economy, especially when it is supported by expertise and organising skills. The low level or lack of risk-taking nature and of the ability to represent ideas can be explained by the fact that we asked the executives of companies that were stable with good market positions and which had been on the market for a long time.

Table 4 includes the rankings of the skills of the company management and the self-evaluation of the Hungarian managers. We weighted the values with the numbers of votes and calculated an average value so as to produce the rankings.

The most obvious finding is the low position of PC skills in both lists. The ranking of risk-taking nature and expertise are significantly different in the two lists. The Hungarian managers said that they themselves were more adventurous risk-takers than were the company management. Pragmatic skills also dominate the self-evaluation list but the importance of expertise is less here than that shown in the first column of Table 4.

Table 4. The real ranking of the management skills in the Hungarian sample.

Evaluation of the company management	*Self-evaluation of the interviewees*
practice minded behaviour	organising skills
expertise	problem solving skills
problem solving skills	risk taking nature
sense for business	analytical skills
analytical skills	practice minded behaviour
excellent communication skills	sense for business
organising skills	excellent communication skills
executive skills	expertise
risk taking nature	ability to represent ideas
ability to represent ideas	executive skills
use of PC and computers	use of PC and computers

As far as the self-evaluation list of the Spanish managers is concerned, first place was given to organising skills (similarly to the Hungarian ranking). Another similarity is that the Spanish managers also regard the level of their own expertise to be lower then that of the company management.

On the other hand, they regarded their own PC skills to be better than the PC skills of the general company management.

At this point we should emphasise that our findings regarding the skills of the Hungarian company management reinforced the results we gained by asking 325 executives in the research program “In Global Competition”. In that survey the managers had to evaluate on a five point scale the same skills we used in the in-depth interviews as well.

Table 5 Rankings of the management skills by the managers in the central survey (325 managers) and by the managers of in-depth interviews (42 managers).

Evaluation of the company management	*Evaluation of the company management*
practice minded behaviour (4,15)	practice minded behaviour
expertise (3,99)	expertise
problem solving skills (3,78)	problem solving skills
sense for business (3,71)	sense for business
excellent communication skills (3,61)	analytical skills
organising skills (3,61)	excellent communication skills
ability to represent ideas (3,60)	organising skills
executive skills (3,54)	executive skills
risk taking nature (3,47)	risk taking nature
analytical skills (3,46)	ability to represent ideas
use of PC and computers (2,93)	use of PC and computers

The two sets of rankings are very similar to each other, which is very important in terms of the reliability of the results. The following skills are the leading ones in both lists: practice-minded behaviour, expertise, problem-solving skills, sense for business. The skills suggest that the management has adapted itself to the changing environment: it is pragmatic, skilful, but lacks the risk-taking nature and the ability to represent ideas which are needed for an offensive leadership style.

A factor analysis, based on the answers of the sample of 325 managers, produced very interesting results: The factors are clear and characteristic. The first factor was determined by the variables that represented the classical management skills. The management literature includes many lists of the main managerial functions. We quote now the function list of Gulick and Urwick who belong to the Taylorian "scientific management" school (Kieser, 1996):

List of managerial functions:

- planning
- organising
- human resource management
- leading
- co-ordinating
- reporting
- making the budget

Table 6. Rotated factor-matrix of the analysis.

	1st factor	*2nd factor*	*3rd factor*
Excellent communication skills	.78221	.24244	.12568
Expertise	.77275	.18489	.22429
Executive skills	.73281	.19635	.38378
Problem solving skills	.61450	.53391	.08078
Organising skills	.54468	.42091	.23879
Risk taking nature	.10739	.75073	.27546
Practice minded behaviour	.25971	.68298	-.00516
Ability to represent ideas	.46715	.63019	.06879
Sense for business	.22134	.60477	.35215
Use of PC and computers	.18202	.06141	.87592
Analytical skills	.29435	.33653	.66987

It is easy to realise that, according to this list, the successful manager has excellent communication skills, expertise, organising and problem-solving skills. In summary, the first factor includes the needs of the scientific management. We should emphasise, though, that nowadays the traditional management school has lost its original significance.
The modern trends consider supporting other employees and ensuring the proper environment (executive role) to be the main task of the management, rather than the "leadership" role.

The second factor is dominated by the skills that can be connected to the (market) environment. Risk-taking nature and the sense for business obviously influence the business performance on the market and these skills ensure a competitive edge in the period of the birth of a market economy. Pragmatism and the ability to represent ideas can be very fruitful for companies pursuing either a reactive or proactive strategy. In other words, the second factor includes the skills of a dynamic, clever manager.

The third factor illustrates the analytical skills of the managers from two different aspects. The first aspect is a conditional one: do the managers possess the required PC skills? The other aspect measures the level of analytical skills. Although it is trivial to connect these two aspects, their influence on each other is rather interesting in practice: those managers who have PC skills use analyses for supporting and preparing decisions more often.

2.2 Leadership styles from the decision-making point of view.

From now on we will focus on the Hungarian in depth interviews when analysing the preparedness of the decision makers. The dimensions of the analysis were as follows: the ideal ranking of the studied management skills and the different decision making attitudes. We identified four attitudes: optimising, political, satisfactory (bounded rationality), intuitive. The factor analysis of the two dimensions above revealed which management skills are connected to which decision making attitudes. Without naming the six factors gained by the analysis, we briefly introduce the ideal executive patterns in the given factors.

The decision makers following the optimising and satisfactory approach have very good PC skills. The decision makers mixing the political and intuitive approach have very good executive skills. The open-minded, pragmatic decision maker has a good sense for business as well. The innovator type of decision makers can be described as having expertise, good problem-solving skills and the ability to represent ideas. The decision makers with outstanding organising skills have a more risk-taking nature, too. And there are decision makers whose main strength is good analytical skill. In order to find out which approaches were typical of the managers in the sample, we made a cluster analysis in which we separated 3 groups. To describe them we used the method of averages, the results of which we publish now by groups.

The signs in the tables mean the following:

+ the frequency of the skill is above the average
- the frequency of the skill is below the average
0 average

Our survey consisted of three elements:

- First we asked the managers what they thought were the necessary management skills under the current economic circumstances in general.
- Then we asked them what was their opinion about the required skills of their own company management .
- Finally we asked them what were their own skills.

To identify the groups we used names of the fauna - we hope these harmless associations make our results more understandable.

The managers in the first group can be identified as having an average preparedness combined with valuable routine and intuitive leadership. Unfortunately, they are not prepared to face new kinds of challenges, since they are below the average in terms of sense for business and risk-taking nature. Moreover, problems may arise because of the weak ability to represent ideas as well. At the same time, these managers lost their spirit, they turned inwards neglecting the modern market-driven requirements (just look at their evaluation of the traditional management skills, especially expertise in the first column).

Many of these managers have been professionals for decades, they have survived transitions already. Others belong to the younger generation and have became leaders recently. The companies they represent were significant state-owned companies in the past that have been privatised. Foreign ownership, significant inland bank and local government ownership are dominant in them. Their inland sales are significant, their activities aimed mainly at inland markets. They have even business profits. It is worth mentioning that these managers can be described by the theory of bounded rationality (Simon, 1992). They also face more internal problems than average, but still have the energy to look for problems productively, which is a proof of their toughness.

Table 7 First group (20 persons): The mules

Management skills	*Ideal*	*Management*	*Self evaluation*
1. excellent communication skills	-	0	-
2. expertise	–	+	0
3. executive skills	-	0(+)	0
4. problem solving skills	–	0	+
5. ability to represent ideas	–	-(0)	–
6. organising skills	0	-	-
7. sense for business	–	-	0
8. use of PC and computers	-	0	-(0)
9. analytical skills	++	+	-
10. practice minded behaviour	+	++	0
11. risk taking nature	0	-	+

The second group includes the most dynamic, most open-minded managers. They considered almost all skills to be important (except the traditional ones, e.g. executive skills, organising skills), thus setting up a high standard. Their strengths are as follows: thorough theoretical background, communication skills, sense for business and risk-taking nature. These managers are self-confident: they think that they are better than the other members of their own company management in terms of representing ideas, sense for business, PC skills, analytical skills and problem-solving skills. They are not afraid of challenges and are aware of the fact that the greatest competitive edge can be reached by a willingness to take risks.

Unfortunately this is the smallest group. Managers of export-oriented, privatised/multinational companies belong to this group. They are proactive. The profits of their companies are a little bit higher than the average. Different types of companies - a metal-processing company, an industrial component producing company, a commercial bank - are included in the group. The managers represent the forty-year old generation; they are maximalist, rational and logical thinkers

Table 8. 2nd group (7 persons) : The tigers

Management skills	*Ideal*	*Management*	*Self evaluation*
1. excellent communication skills	++	++	++
2. expertise	0	0	-
3. executive skills	-	+	-
4. problem solving skills	++	++	0
5. ability to represent ideas	++	-(0)	++
6. organising skills	–	-	–
7. sense for business	++	+	++
8. use of PC and computers	++	0	++
9. analytical skills	—	–	++
10. practice minded behaviour	–	-	++
11. risk taking nature	+++	++	++

The third group represents the traditional management approach. These managers lack certain skills (e.g. expertise, executive skills, PC skills) but have already improved their ability to represent ideas, their organising skills and sense for business. It is worrying that they underestimate the importance of practice-minded behaviour and a risk taking nature. These managers considered executive skills to be the most important management skill that combined with expertise and excellent communication skills identifies the ideal traditional leadership style. The companies represented in this group are not the biggest ones. They are export-oriented, with significant ownership proposition of the state, which is "burdened" by the "colourful" privatisation that resulted in different other owners (foreign private person, foreign financial institution, inland private person, management buy-out). The business results of the companies are good but they are threatened by outer factors. The problem solving method of the managers of these companies is rather intuitive.

Table 9 Third group (15 persons): The elephants.

Management skills	*Ideal*	*Management*	*Self evaluation*
1. excellent communication skills	+	-	-
2. expertise	++	-	+
3. executive skills	+++	-(0)	+
4. problem solving skills	+	0	-
5. ability to represent ideas	+	+	-
6. organising skills	+	+	+
7. sense for business	+	++	+
8. use of PC and computers	0	-	-
9. analytical skills	0	+	+
10. practice minded behaviour	-	–	-
11. risk taking nature	-	+	-

Of the three groups, the tigers are the most promising in terms of competitiveness. They are prepared and skilful enough to face the challenges of the current economic environment. The mules can also produce balanced results using their toughness, routine, and not-worse-than-the average skills. The elephants have a longer way to go but the orientation of their improvement is promising. Supplementing the analysis of the Hungarian sample we can mention that the eight Spanish companies were divided into the aforementioned three groups as follows: four were mules, two were tigers, two were elephants. This indicates that not only the Hungarian company management are changing: the management of the Spanish control-group were changing as well.

3 REFERENCES

Angyal, Á. and Kovács, S. (1996) Management sub-project research study *"In Global Competition" research program*, Department of Business Economics Budapest University of Economic Sciences.

Bazerman, M. H. (1990) Judgements in Managerial Decision Making. John Wiley&Sons, New York.

Dénes, F. and Paprika, Z. (1996) Survey of Hungarian managers, Ph.D. dissertation, Budapest University of Economic Sciences Ph.D. Program.

Egon Zehnder International (1995) Corporate Governance. Manuscript.
Guillen, Mayro F. (1994) Models of Management. The University of Chicago Press, Chicago.
Harrison, E. F. (1996) A process perspective on strategic decision making, *Management Decision* **34, 1**.
Heller, F (1992) Decision Making and Leadership. Cambridge University Press
Hickson, D., Butler, R., Cray, D., Mallory, G. and Wilson, D. (1986) Top Decisions: Strategic Decision Making in Organizations. Basil Blackwell, Oxford.
Hoványi, G (1996) Competitiveness of companies: new circumstances, new concepts. *Vezetéstudomány*, **5.**
Kieser, A. (1996) Organizational theories. KJK, Budapest.
Paprika, Z (1996) Research study of the decision making sub project. *"In Global Competition" research program*, Department of Business Economics, Budapest University of Economic Sciences.
Paprika, Z. (1997) The characteristics of strategic decision making in the Hungarian microsphere. *"In Global Competition" research program*, Department of Business Economics, Budapest University of Economic Sciences.
Pettigrew, A. and Whipp, R. (1991) Managing Change for Competitive Success. Basil Blackwell, Oxford.
Schoemaker, P. J. H. (1993) Strategic Decision in Organisations: Rational and Behavioural Views, *Journal of Management Studies*, **30.**
Simon, H. (1992) Economics, Bounded Rationality and the Cognitive Revolution. Edward Elgar Publishing Limited.
Wallace, John B. (1991) Developing better managers: creating change through effective training. Kogan Page, London.

4 BIOGRAPHY

Dr. Zita Zoltay Paprika is an assistant professor at the Business Economics Department of Budapest University of Economic Sciences. She teaches decision making theory and decision making methodology at undergraduate, graduate and post-graduate levels. She is in charge of the minor organised for graduate students which is called "Managerial Decision Making". She also permanently works as a consultant, during which activity she has been a project manager on several occasions. From 1991 to 1994 she was the Hungarian co-ordinator of the TEMPUS BEAMS (Business Economics and Management Support) JEP-2360 Project financed by the European Union. She is also the manager of the Decision Making sub-project of the "In Global Competition" research program conducted by the Business Economics Department of BUES.

14

Organisational Culture and Modes of Conflict Behaviour

S. Ayestarán, C. Martínez-Taboada and J. Arróspide
Department of Social Psychology
University of the Basque Country
Apartado 1249
20080 San Sebastián, Spain
Tel.: 34 43 310600 Fax: 34 43 311055
e-mail: pspayets©ss.ehu.es

L. Garcia
Department of Social Psychology
London School of Economics
Houghton Street, London WC2A 2AE, UK.
Tel. 44 171 955 7695/7767 Fax: 44 171 955 7565
e-mail:l.garcia@Lse.ac.uk

Abstract

The different ways of handling a conflict have traditionally been considered as behavioural characteristics of the individual. In this paper, we endeavour to analyse the different ways of handling a conflict in relation to the culture of the organisations. We analyse the culture with three dimensions: high versus low identification of the members with the objectives of the organisation; high versus low power distance; closed versus open system. Combining these three dimensions we elaborate different patterns of organisational culture favouring different forms of conflict behaviour. Departing from these suppositions we accomplished an intervention in a sanitary organisation with the general hypothesis that the culture of this organisation responded to the definition of Pattern 4: *high power distance + closed system + low identification*. This cultural pattern had to strengthen the behaviour of passive competition, based on resistance and control of the programme which the Basque Public Health Service wanted to impose.

Keywords

Conflict, culture, closed-system, open-system, identification, power.

1 INTRODUCTION

Nowadays it is acknowledged that conflicts, in themselves, are neither constructive or destructive. They are simply the expression of an unresolved problem that causes tension between the individuals or groups making up an organisation. However conflicts, when appropriately managed, can add substantial value to organisations. Conflict can be the medium by which problems are recognised and overcome (Simosi, 1997). Therefore the important thing is not to avoid the appearance of conflicts, but to learn how to manage them. Furthermore an underlying, non-explicit conflict is more difficult to handle than a conflict that is openly expressed.

In organisational settings, employees who discuss conflict disclose information, challenge assumptions, dig into issues, and, as a consequence, are able to make more informed decisions. This is what Tjosvold (1991) calls 'positive conflict'. Through this type of conflict, managers and employees can take a long-term view, anticipate and exploit changes, and keep in touch with each other as well as with customers, suppliers, specialists, and investors. The management of conflict can be indeed a fundamental competitive advantage for the organisation since it helps organisations to develop new strategies.

Organisations certainly need such advantages. We live in a world that it is in constant change. in order to cope with such a reality and 'survive', our organisations have to adapt to that situation by changing themselves. Companies and individuals and groups within those companies confront ongoing change and uncertainty. They need to be poised to appreciate emerging opportunities, circumvent pitfalls and threats, and realise competitive advantages. And one of the key issues in handling this type of change is successful management of conflict situation within the organisational setting.

2 ORGANISATIONS AND A TAXONOMY FOR MANAGING CONFLICT

Contemporary organisations are networks of independent units, having 'groups' as their building blocks. For that reason, relations among the individual components of the organisation are complex; they are characterised by a mixture of co-operation and competition. People compete against each other for power and scarce resources but, in the meanwhile, they rely on each other in order to accomplish their tasks, while emotional ties are formed among them (Masterbroek, 1987). Owing to the necessary interdependency among organisational units, effective organising cannot take place, unless such interdependencies are managed effectively and a balance is reached between co-operation and mutual dependency on the one hand, and rivalry and autonomy on the other hand.

Within such an environment, social interactions among organisational members are complex, since they reflect a fundamental incompatibility (Boulding, 1963): the simultaneous need of competition and co-operation. Consequently as organisations develop and increase size and diversity, different problems emerge. The members of the organisation are likely to have different perspectives about these problems and the conflicts experienced can range from the competition over different resources and struggles for power, to failure to coordinate efforts to achieve a concrete goal or in the way the personal relationships are handled.

Even when the members of the organisation have common interests and agree basically about the goals to be achieved the conflict may arise among them. In any kind of conflict situation people's attempts to manage it will reflect the set of shared assumptions and practices that are in use in a particular organisational context (Garcia and Simosi, 1995).

Moreover, human behaviour in any organisation is of a complex nature, being the product of the interaction between the organisational role expectations and the different personalities of individuals working there (DeCosta, 1991). In every organisation, the formal and informal procedures in terms of rules, norms, beliefs etc., which govern the daily activities if its members and serve to achieve organisational goals, will shape the ways the conflict situations will be handled (Argyris and Schon, 1978). Thus, people working in a specific organisation adhere to the conflict norms in use in that organisation.

Traditionally, the ways of handling conflict (Blake and Mouton, 1964) have been considered mainly as individual behavioural characteristics based, on the one hand, the empirical base of the classical distinction between groups centred on task processes and groups centred on socio-emotional relations (Bales, 1950) and ,on the other hand, the conceptualisation of conflict management based on the following two aspects: (1)Interest in results that favour one's own self; (2) Interest in results that favour the other party.

Combining these two aspects, Thomas and Kilman defined 5 ways of handling conflict: *Competition, Collaboration, Compromise, Avoidance, Accommodation.* We explore these briefly below:

- *Competition:* when, in situations of conflict, the individual tends to maintain his or her interests at the cost of others.
- *Collaboration:* when, in situations of conflict, the individual tends to find halfway solutions that satisfy both parties. Thus, when he or she tries to ensure that "everyone is happy".
- *Compromise:* when, in situations of conflict, the individual tends to find halfway solutions that satisfy neither him /herself nor the others. Thus, when s/he tries to fairly distribute the costs of the conflict among the members of the group.
- *Accommodation:* when ,in situations of conflict, the individual tends to give in to the other person's interests.

- *Avoidance:* when in situations of conflict the individual has a greater tendency to try and resolve the problems him or herself.

Recently, authors like Van de Vliert and Euwema(1994) have questioned this manner of approaching the management of a conflict. The reason is apparent: in both the original conceptualisation of Blake and Mouton's and in their subsequent taxonomy of ways of conflict, management the focus is solely on the intentions or inclinations of the each of the subjects. There are a great many factors which play an important role between the intentions of a person and his or her actual behaviour, i.e., the rules of managing the conflict imposed by the group and the role adopted by each individual in the group, as well as factors internal to the person, i.e. the level of self-esteem of the person and earlier training in the handling of a conflict etc. Thus, the behaviour of the individual in situations of conflict doesn't necessarily coincide with his/her previously espoused intentions. This is why Van de Vliert and Euwema prefer to use descriptive aspects closer to behaviour in the handling of a conflict. These aspects are *Agreeable/Disagreeable* and *Active/Passive* (Van de Vliert and Euwema, 1994).The operational definitions of these two aspects are based on Bales' Symlog:

- *Agreeable:* shows agreement; reduces tensions; shows solidarity.
- *Disagreeable:* shows disagreement; shows tension; shows antagonism.
- *Active:* offers information; offers suggestions; offers opinions; offers guidance.
- *Passive:* asks for information; asks for suggestions; asks for an opinion; asks for guidance.

Figure 1 Refined characterisation of modes of conflict behaviour in terms of agreeableness and activeness (Van de Vliert and Euwema, 1994).

COOPERATION			
Passive		Active	
Nonconfrontation		Negotiation	
Disagreeable	Agreeable	Disagreeable	Agreeable
Avoidance	**Accommodation**	**Compromise**	**Collaboration**

COMPETITION			
Passive		Active	
Indirect Fighting		Direct Fighting	
Agreeable	Disagreeable	Agreeable	Disagreeable
Process Controlling	**Resistance**	**Issue Fighting**	**Outcome Fighting**

In this taxonomy we must pay attention to three aspects. Cooperative behaviour includes a certain amount of competition: disagreeable behaviour, such as avoidance and compromise, mean that cooperation is being sought, but without eliminating competitive feelings. On the other hand, accommodation and the solving of problems demonstrate more harmonious cooperation. In competition, disagreeable behaviour, such as control of the group process and issue fighting mean that there is less competition than when disagreeable resistance and outcome fighting behaviour are used.

This taxonomy of ways of managing a conflict demands that, when observing this behaviour, consideration be given both to the actions and to the emotional state of the members of the group. There is also a fourth aspect we need to take into account when considering or analysing conflict in organisational settings. This is the context in which that conflict is trying to be managed: the "cultural context" of the organisation.

We do not regard organisational members as being acted upon by the work environment. Instead, we just advocate that their own motivations and cognitions necessarily operate in a social context (Condor and Brown, 1988). To understand this, we have to view communicative interactions among organisational members as a process of enactment of a shared reality (Morgan, 1986). Organisational life consists of a set of assumptions and expectations towards one another, which determine both formal and informal interactions within the organisational setting (Garcia and Humphreys, 1995). Such a shared reality serves as a means of communication among organisational members. Issues such as organisational structure, job descriptions, policies and operating procedures have interpretative function, since they enable organisational members to shape the organisational reality (Morgan, 1986).

3 CONFLICT MANAGEMENT WITHIN A CULTURAL FRAMEWORK

Various ways of management of conflict have traditionally been considered just as the behavioural characteristics of the individual (McDougall, 1920). In this work, we endeavour to analyse the different ways of managing conflict in relation to the wider social context where those conflict situations occur, i.e., in relation to the culture of the organisation (Turner, 1987).

Usually, the members of an organisation belong to several and overlapping cultural frames of reference where organisational reality, as such, is only one part of the daily life. As members of a particular social group, class, region or country we bring into the organisation different cultural influences. From this point of view it could be difficult to explore the influence the culture of the organisation has in the different ways the individuals manage organisation-related conflicts. However if we take into account that the organisation is in itself the "nexus" where those broader, societal, "feeder" cultural frames of reference come together, the consequence is that although many external cultural influences permeate the organisation's boundary, each organisation has a particular combination of cultural influences which mixes and interacts within a given organisational boundary.

It is true that any kind of organisation, just like any living being, needs to define its social identity in order to establish the limits of where it belongs and to mark the differences between "them" and "us". The members of the organisation define their identity by specifying the characteristics that distinguish them from other groups. They tend to define themselves as "unique" or "different" or "special" in contrast to other groups or organisations . The "identity" of the organisation and the group becomes strengthened by established rituals of admittance and behavioural rules which those wishing to belong to the group must follow. This does not mean that we consider the group or the organisation as a closed system: quite the contrary, we are aware that the boundaries of any organisation tend to be permeable and in a sense arbitrary, thus quite open. This type of boundary allows us to consider, nevertheless, some degree of "uniqueness", because boundaries are about space demarcation even though the space within a boundary is versatile, multiple and mobile. At the same time they have the unique quality of preserving differences and identities whereas allowing interchange or "contamination".

However , when an organisation or group is too deeply concerned with defining and strengthening its identity, due to uncertainty, change or perceived threats etc., it has the tendency to fall back on itself and develop self-defence mechanisms which eventually convert the group into a closed social system (Ayestarán, 1996). These behaviour-regulating mechanisms of the group members are as follows:

- The group becomes the only group reference for its members. The membranes of the group become impermeable to outside information.
- Interpersonal interaction is reduced in order to control the risk of conflict within the group.
- Conflictive behaviour in relation to outside groups is reinforced and cognitive processes of favouritism within the group is bolstered. The figure of the prototype who ends up assuming the role of charismatic leader is strengthened.
- The "black sheep" mechanism is set in motion, so that members seen as the cause of the group's problems are pushed aside or expelled.
- Functional opposition between personal identity and social identity is accentuated, thus calling for behaviour which is coherent with the social identity of the members and condemns the strengthening of personal self-esteem.

All of these mechanisms have one sole purpose: to control the individual interests of the members of the group and to achieve a unity of action revolving around the objectives of that action. The result is that the group does not allow its members to demonstrate direct confrontational behaviour in conflict management; instead, it favours compliant behaviour, avoidance and indirect confrontation. This can become a progressively dysfunctional defence as the group isolates itself from understanding the process which triggered the defence mechanism and therefore distancing itself from a constructive participation individually and/or collectively in it.

This is the context in which individual/group conflict arises, the purpose of which is to strengthen autonomy of the individual with regard to the group, thus bringing about a cultural and structural change in the latter.

4 SOCIAL INTERACTION AND THE DEVELOPMENT OF A NEW CULTURAL FRAMEWORK WITHIN THE ORGANISATION

This type of individual/group conflict can be overcome in two ways:

a) By changing the prototype of the group, thereby implying a purely structural change - the access to power of a new subgroup arranged around a new prototype. The group continues with the same identity and hierarchical structure that it had before the conflict. The group leader changes but the culture of the group remains the same as before. Changes of this kind often occur in political parties, religious institutions and professional groups.

b) By changing the group culture. For this to happen, the group encourages interaction and direct confrontation between its members, the negotiation of cognitive perspectives and personal interests in relation to the group objectives, the solving of problems and the integration of individual objectives into the new group objectives. Here, the change is both structural and cultural, and involves:

- Questioning the earlier definition of the group. Questioning allows the group to work out a new definition for itself that is more compatible with the demands of the cultural, economic and social environment.
- A change in the power structure, that is to say, a closer relationship between the leader and the members making up the group.
- Greater participation by all members in defining the objectives of the group.
- Restructuring the activities of the group, placing greater importance on its objective interdependence as far as tasks are concerned.
- The group no longer being the only reference group for its members. They can take references from other groups.
- An increase in internal group conflict. The conflicts are interpersonal and affect the values of the group as well as its objectives and the rules governing its internal interactions.
- A reduction in intergroup conflict and the creation of new conditions for intergroup collaboration.

In a sense, this type of socio-cognitive conflict and the change that follows it, involves two tendencies: one that aims at maintaining existing frameworks and agreement , and the other that aims at changing them by imparting an original form to things and ideas. This will serve the double purpose of offering a familiar and secure background to connect the new ideas and events while, at the same time, offering the necessary foreground where individuals, through their reflective awareness, will be able to make choices, manipulate and even innovate their conditions, paving the ground for a new intergroup collaboration.

5 DIALECTIC IDENTIFICATION/INTERACTION

Any group of human beings must maintain its identity, while, however, responding to the demands of the environment and allowing for the personal growth of its members. When the pole of identity is stressed, the group favours non-confrontational behaviour and indirect confrontation between its members. Group cohesion then takes the shape of identification with group objectives and rules. This kind of cohesion is not good when it comes to managing differences between individuals and tends to unify their thoughts and actions (groupthink), thereby implying a loss of creativity and initiative, as well as the group's capacity to respond to the demands of the environment. The chances increase that poor decisions will be made and the group becomes a closed social system.

The change of cultural frameworks within the group implies greater interaction between its members, and transforms a potential conflict between the individuals and the group into a conflict between its members. Individual interests take on greater relevance and competition puts cooperation and the very existence of the group into danger.

6 A SYSTEMIC PERSPECTIVE OF THE GROUP

Until now, the systems theory has produced little relevant research in the area of groups and organisations, and it can be said that no new knowledge concerning intra- and inter-group dynamics has been presented. However, the systemic perspective permits better integration of our knowledge to the area of groups. We believe that there are two important concepts regarding the overcoming of individual/group opposition and the relation of intragroup dynamics to intergroup dynamics.

The open or closed group systems refer to the way in which groups handle their internal differences, deviations from their rules and intra-group conflicts.

- The group as a closed system involves: circular stable internal relations; stable balance; the maintenance of identity; self-referential relations; a reduction in internal fluctuations; control of the environment from inside the system; the absence of reciprocal relations with other systems; the hierarchical organisation of relations between systems. It also implies a reduction in constructive interpersonal interaction and the avoidance of conflict.

- The group as an open system involves: dynamic and unstable internal relations; unstable balance; structuring at a higher level of balance; reciprocal relations between systems; an increase in fluctuations; influence of the environment on the system; inter-systemic interaction; a lack of hierarchically-organized inter-systemic relations.

Applying these concepts to social systems helps us to learn about the role played by both intra- and inter-group conflict in the construction of social reality and its evolution towards more complex forms of operation.

Isomorphism between the different subsystems means that the dynamics of development and conflict are similar for the individual, group and inter-group subsystem. This means that any changes introduced to one of the subsystems will affect the dynamics of the other subsystems.

7 THE INFLUENCE OF CULTURE ON MODES OF CONFLICT BEHAVIOUR

Depending on the psycho-social model of the group, we can define group culture on the basis of three variables:

- High/low power distance: High power distance reduces social interaction inside the organisation. Low power distance increases social interaction.
- High/low group identification: High group identification reduces individual autonomy. Low group identification increases individual autonomy.
- Closed system/open system: Closed systems reduce intragroup conflict and increase intergroup conflict. Open systems increase intragroup conflict.

In the following diagrams, we demonstrate the influence of group culture on decision taking.

- Pattern 1: *low power distance + closed system + high identification:* Conflict avoiding behaviour and the maintenance of group harmony.
- Pattern 2: *low power distance + closed system + low identification:* Conflict avoiding behaviour and the reduction of interpersonal interaction.
- Pattern 3: *high power distance + closed system + high identification:* Accommodating conflict behaviour.
- Pattern 4: *high power distance + closed system + low identification*: Process controlling and resisting conflict behaviour.
- Pattern 5: *high power distance + open system + high identification:* Compromising conflict behaviour.
- Pattern 6: *high power distance + open system + low identification:* Issue fighting conflict behaviour.
- Pattern 7*: low power distance + open system + high identification:* problem solving conflict behaviour.
- Pattern 8: *low power distance + open system + low identification:* outcome fighting conflict behaviour.

The highest standard of conflict behaviour occurs when group culture is defined in terms of low power distance, the group functions as an open system, and there is high identification with the group by its members.

8 APPLICATION OF THE MODEL TO PSYCHOSOCIAL INTERVENTION.

Below we present an intervention carried out by Cristina Martínez-Taboada in the Basque Public Health Service to illustrate the utility of the model presented for the intervention.

8.1 Request

The request for intervention on behalf of the Nursing Department of the Basque Public Health Service came as a result of the persistent failure to implement a mother/child care programme supposedly to be operated by the midwives belonging to the outpatients network. Paradoxically, the programme sought to introduce the very bases for development, evaluation and systematic functioning that the midwives had themselves long been clamouring for. The request for intervention involved:

- Talking to the midwives group to see if resistance to the new programme could be diminished
- Generating a group dynamic to analyse the difficulties in the implementation of the programme.
- Finding possible solutions to these difficulties.

8.2 Hypotheses

We started from the general hypothesis that the culture of this group responded to the definition of Pattern 4: HIGH POWER DISTANCE + CLOSED SYSTEM + LOW IDENTIFICATION. This cultural pattern had to strengthen the behaviour of passive competition, based on resistance and control of the programme which the Basque Public Health Service wanted to impose.

- An analysis of the situation confirmed our initial hypothesis: The culture of the group, in a closed system, resists change.
- This resistance manifests itself in the failure to implement the new programme.
- The programme is not seen as meeting the group's demands, but on the contrary as an imposition from above.

8.3 Objectives of the intervention.

Based on the suppositions we have just set out, the intervention was planned to achieve the following objectives:

- To set up a group dynamic that would permit the group to become aware of its internal manner of functioning and of the repercussion of this manner of functioning on its relations with other groups in the Institution. The objective was to succeed in making the group receptive to information from other groups and, in this way, to relate to these groups' positions. This is what we understand by "converting a closed system into an open system".
- To underline the differences of opinion and of existing positions within the same group, without its members being able to express these differences. This manner of functioning indicates to what point the group of midwives was reproducing the hierarchical culture of the Health Institution.
- To analyse, as objectively as possible, the positive and negative aspects of the programme imposed by the health authorities, trying to assess the programme itself, while putting the influence of the conflict with the authorities to one side. The purpose was to achieve greater identification of the midwives with the objectives of the mother/child care programme and bring them closer to the objectives of the Health Institution.

8.4 The intervention process.

The intervention began by acknowledging the professional and personal interests shared by the group, and which formed the basis of its motivation, looking at the goals, expectations and working conditions of each group member. Our attention soon focused on the common denominator of the sociostructural conditions: the hierarchic set-up of the Institution, in going over the relation between the group and superiors - and looking at the many ways in which different individuals had contributed towards impeding the new programme- the hitherto stable defensive balance began to give way.

This process enabled the group members to question their own attitude towards the programme, and to recognise the psychosocial factors which gave its implementation a somewhat menacing aura.

Of these factors, the following were found to be fundamental to the intervention:

- the programme was seen as a means by which superiors sought to further their own interests;
- therefore any hindrance of the programme thwarted such interests;
- professional difficulties were always blamed on superiors;
- therefore the midwives' group itself was never to blame.

Rising awareness of these psychosocial factors gave group members an increased ability to take a personal stand with regard to both the job and the programme, and the degree of intragroup conflict became apparent. Conflict between the different levels of hierarchy assumed a lesser role. The participants became more able to view the programme as a group task, to examine it dispassionately and subsequently take a decision. This process was greatly helped by the Institution's decision to consult the group of midwives. The group could negotiate certain aspects such as the materials to be used.

8.5 Changes obtained

- The midwives contributed to the implementation of the programme.
- Commonly accepted methods of evaluating the systemisation of the programme were established.
- The programme was implemented in Gipuzkoa and subsequently, using the same intervention design, in the rest of the Basque Autonomous Community.

9 CONCLUSION

The objective of the intervention was to change the behaviour of the midwives as regards their conflict with the health authorities. It was specifically an attempt to pass from a style of resistance and control of the process to an open confrontation and to a behaviour based on compromise and negotiation.

This change of behaviour was achieved thanks to the cultural change which had previously been achieved with the group. The intervention was directed at achieving this cultural change. The cultural change implied:

- Transformation of the internal dynamic of the group of midwives, making it more open to outside information and offering it the possibility to demonstrate the discrepancies between its members.
- Reduction in the degree of hierarchical organisation of the Institution by creating channels of dialogue and negotiation between the group of midwives and the Management of the Basque Public Health Service.
- Separation of the assessment of the task from the negative emotions associated with conflict with the authorities, thereby facilitating greater identification with the objectives of the programme and of the Health Institution.

10 REFERENCES

Argyris, C. and Schon, D. (1978) Organisational Learning: A Theory of Action Perspective. Addison-Wesley, Reading, Mass.

Ayestarán, S. (1996) El grupo como construcción social. Barcelona, Ediciones Plural.

Bales, R. F. (1950) Interaction process analysis: a method for the study of small groups. Addison Wesley, Cambridge, Mass.

Blake, R. R. and Mouton, J. S. (1964) The Managerial Grid. Gulf, Houston.

Boulding, K. (1963) Conflict and Defence. Harper and Row, New York.

Condor, S. and Brown, R. (1988) Psychological processes, in *The Social Psychology of Intergroup Conflict* (eds. W. Stroebe, A. W. Kruglanski et al.). Springer-Verlag, New York.

DeCosta, J. (1993). Conflict Management and the Learning Organisation: A Case Study. PhD Thesis. The Fielding Institute, California, USA.

Garcia, L. and Humphreys, P. (1995) Major Organisational change and its Impact in culture, in *People, Technology and Productivity: New Visions and Strategies for the Next Century*. National Productivity Centre, Turkey.

Garcia, L. and Simosi, M. (1995) Managing Undergoing Cultural Change in Organisations .Unpublished presentation for the IX European Congress in Social Psychology. Athens, Greece.

Mastenbroek, W.F. (1987) Conflict Management and Organisation Development. Holland: Wiley.

McDougall, W. (1920) The Group Mind. Putnam, New York

Morgan, G. (1986) Images of Organisation. Sage, London.

Simosi, M. (1997) The Processing of Conflict in Organisational Groups: A Case Study in a Greek Industrial Company. PhD Thesis. Social Psychology Department, The London School of Economics. London, U.K.

Tjosvold, D. (1991) The Conflict-Positive Organisation. Addison-Wesley, London.

Turner, J. C. (1987) Rediscovering the Social Group: A Self-Categorisation Theory, Basil Blackwell, Oxford.

Van de Vliert, E. and Euwema, M. C. (1994) Agreeableness and Activeness as Components of Conflict Behaviours. *Journal of Personality and Social Psychology*, **66**, 674-687.

10 BIOGRAPHIES

Sabino Ayestarán, Cristina Martínez-Taboada and Juanjo Arrospide form a team of professors in Social Psychology in the University of the Basque Country in Spain. Their research interests are related to the Psychology of groups and the Psychology of the organisations. In their theoretical research, they have developed a psycho-social model of group that tries to integrate Self-Categorisation Theory and Social Interaction Theory with support from Systems Theory. In this context, they have devoted many projects to the analysis of the conflicts, in the interpersonal level as well as in the organisational and political level.

Lucia Garcia is a researcher in the Social Psychology Department at the London School of Economics (LSE), working on organisational change and its impact on the culture of organisations. She also teaches Organisational Psychology and Qualitative Research Methods for the Methodology Institute at LSE. She has participated in a number of research projects in Latin America and Eastern Europe regarding organisational transformation in those countries. Currently she is a research officer on the WHO Healthy Cities Evaluation Project.

15

Systems logic for problem formulation and choice

E. L. Nappelbaum
Russian Institute for Systems Analysis
9 Pr 60 Let Octabryja, Moscow 117312, Russia
Tel/Fax +7 095 282 4275
e-mail: ernapp@aha.ru

Abstract

This paper provides a critique of the traditional practice of developing decision analysis and decision support techniques founded on a linear model of choice to frame the decision problem and its "solution".

Decision problem representation methods generally represent the problem in terms of some or all of the following five components: *Alternatives or options*, that is, different moulds in which the world around us will be cast as the result of our decision; the *scope* of these alternatives, which outlines the boundaries of the problem as conceived by the decision maker; the decision-makers' *preferences*, reflecting their attitudes and values as well as their understandings of the interests they have in the problem they are trying to tackle; the *logic of choice*, that is, the argumentation process through which we are capable of interrelating all the other components to arrive at the final decision; *Instrumental intentions* of the choice, combining both the reasons about how we are planning to exploit the results and the ideas of how choice is to be implemented.

In the conventional linear analysis, the first two components represent the "objective reality" of the choice, while the third (and to a certain extent the fourth) component introduce the subjective dimension of it. "objective reality" and subjective preferences are inputs to the choice procedure, which completes the analysis, and so instrumental intentions are often neglected.

Instead, a *circular model of choice* is proposed, in which the representation of all the above components can be balanced, and in which the knowledge and subjectivity of all the participants involved in the decision making and implementation process may be considered.

Keywords

Decision making, linear model of choice, circular model of choice, systems logic, problem formulation

1 INTRODUCTION

If one chooses to look in a detached and objective manner at the field of science, often called cognitive or behavioural sciences, the latest attempts to study a variety of issues related to human action, creativity, problem-solving and decision-making (to mention just a few), one cannot fail but notice a certain trivialization of these issues. One can hardly avoid a feeling of uneasiness when one encounters the cases of equating rationality of choice with transitivity of preferences, equating learning with con-traction of the option set (either in the deterministic or in the probabilistic setting), equating goal-seeking behaviour with search of the optimal point (be it local or global) in a space of attributes, equating creativity with search in a maze and equating decision-making with folding of partial evaluations in a multi-attribute space. Other instances of the same kind are over abundant and can be found not only in papers which attempt some degree of formalization of the issues related to intelligent behaviour but also in works aimed at a more philosophical and comprehensive mastering of the subject. Perhaps, this is most vividly demonstrated in the field of artificial intelligence (AI) where most of the discussions, aimed originally at a deeper under-standing of major underlying issues, typically boil down to the exposition of some new scheme which is not up to all the intricacies of the arguments leading to its advent.

It is possibly even more surprising that, despite the uneasiness mentioned above, we time and again witness how these oversimplified generalisations lead to some important practical results and devices, to a better grasp of the same issues that have been construed in a rather caricatured way.

One of the possible explanations of this apparent paradox can be found in the general idea that the underlying principles of any purposeful (or, at least, any cognitive) behaviour should be very simple as if by definition and that it is only the complexity of the environment over which this behaviour unfolds itself that makes the outward manifestations of this behaviour so intricate and messy. Such a stance has been argued quite persuasively by H. Simon (1967, 1969) among others, and is the core of some recent theorising (e.g., the mutual-causality theory of Maruyama, 1963). Nevertheless, the uneasy feeling mentioned above does not vanish and, indeed, it comes to grow even stronger with each attempt to extend the scope of application of some particular explanatory scheme which was locally proven to be quite successful.

The situation reminds one quite distinctly of the early 'untransferability" of the first tools of artificial intelligence where each new successful solution had a very strong *ad-hoc* flavour and did not lend itself to easy generalisation and dissemination as a general instrument of tacking Al problems (see, for example, Boden, 1977).
Moreover, sometimes the mere possibility of explaining complex behaviour on the basis of a relatively simple generative rule appears to be insufficient for admitting

it as the explanation. Furthermore, external compatibility of the explanation with observed behaviour by no means guarantees the validity of the explanation.[1]

In this paper, I would like to go beyond merely expressing the afore mentioned doubts and argue that, whenever something can be explained within a framework based on relatively simple underlying principles, it would not be a very gross exaggeration to state that the particular mechanics of the scheme are nearly irrelevant and that there may exist a number of similar explanatory schemes that will do nearly equally well. In other words, I would like to argue that, in each explanatory scheme used to analyse intelligent behaviour and, indeed, to design a more intelligent behaviour, there is always more than what meets the eye and what is put generally forward as the main vehicle of the logic of the analysis and design. The following specific examples may help clarify this claim.

One of the most developed area of AI is pattern recognition (in fact, it is so well developed and advanced that recently we have started actually to regard it as a field apart). A lot of effort has been spent in this area to refine various algorithms for classification, discrimination and learning based on various underlying assumptions. In their practical applications, however, techniques employing such algorithms all score either almost equally well or not at all. This statement, of course, is not entirely accurate as some problems will always exist which adapt especially well to the language of one specific approach (especially if the languages of the problem descriptions are structured dissimilarly) and it is precisely those problems that the authors of a particular technique refer to when they wish to demonstrate the superiority of their brainchild. In most of the other cases, however, it has proved nearly always possible to reformulate the original problem in such terms that, within the given pattern representation, a different technique will perform nearly as well as the original one.

In the light of such evidence, it is quite easy to start musing about whether it is really the implementation technique to which the success has to be attributed rather than to the chosen language of the pattern representation. By the same token, we cannot fail to notice that the vast variety of econometric models used to predict the next year's GNP and the like fare nearly equally well, independently of the many differences in their underlying assumptions and independently of the particular choice of the logic of extrapolation. At the same time, all of these econometric models fail rather dismally whenever some structural change happens in reality calling for a parallel change in the structure of their source data. Finally, the entire history of decision-making methodology has proven times and again that, whenever we have found an appropriate language to represent our options, nearly any reasonable scheme of analysis of multi-attribute decisions will do and that, in the absence of the proper understanding of the real content of the options, no such

[1] Some really deep analysis of the difficulties which may be encountered along this way can be found in Humphreys and Berkeley (1985).

device will be of any help. Given this brief discussion, I am quite sure that the reader will have no difficulty in providing some more examples on his own.

In the suspicions formulated above, I am ready to claim that, whenever a problem that requires a lot of thinking and creativity, when it is dealt with in an ordinary manner, and when it can be tackled by a relatively simple means within a theoretical framework, the success of its solution should be attributed mainly to a fortunate and judicious way of representing the problem rather than to the formal logic of manipulation of this representation.

2 REPRESENTATIONS AND THE LOGIC OF CHOICE

There is nothing new, of course, in this highlighting of the crucial importance of adequate representation. Recently, the problem of representation has been constantly in the very focus of scientific attention (see e.g. Bobrow and Collins, 1968; Fodor, 1981, Schank, 1986) and many interesting and valuable ideas have come to their fruition in this way. [2] The representation problem, however, is dealt with as if *it* were a separate issue, as if it were actually possible to look first for an adequate representation, and only after that, choose one to try finding an appropriate way of solving the problem thus represented. One of the main contentions of the present paper is that this kind of decomposition of problem solving activity is possibly a major source of trivialization and that, in reality (that is, in really creative thinking and problem-solving), the process of choosing the proper representation just can not be divorced from both problem formulation and problem solving.

In order to argue this viewpoint I would like to consider first our basic understanding of the logic of choice, the possibility of its application to the selection of an adequate representation for a problem and its inner relation with the problems of cognition on the basis of the general ideas suggested in Emelyanov and Nappelbaum *(1985)*. Independent of the level of our contemplation of a decision problem, be it purely theoretical or imminently practical, and independent of what particular kind of thought we are trying to follow in organising these thoughts, be it the logic suggested by Jeffrey *(1965)*, or the methodology put forward by white *(1975)*, or the ideas of Simon (1960), we always represent the problem in terms of the following four major components:

---

[2] Nonetheless, we can notice some traces of trivialization in this particular area of study as well. For instance, the formalisms of the frames which are currently in existence appear to be much more limited, restrictive and impoverished in comparison to the general considerations used to erect the foundation for them (see Minsky, 1975).

- *Alternatives* or *options:* that is, different moulds in which the world around us will be cast as the result of our decision;
- The *scope* of these alternatives, which outlines the boundaries of the problem as conceived by the decision-maker;
- The decision-makers' *preferences* reflecting their attitudes and values as well as their understandings of the interests they have in the problem they are trying to tackle;
- The *logic of choice,* that is, the argumentation process through which we are capable of interrelating all the other components to arrive at the final decision (i.e., to choose the preferred alternative).

The first two of these components represent, as it were, the objective reality of the choice while the third and, to a certain extent, the fourth introduce the subjective dimension of it (see Figure 1). Indeed, it is in the first two components in which all the information about the objective possibilities and the objective constraints relevant to the problem under consideration are embodied while the third component introduces subjective personal attitudes towards various facets of the different worlds which should emerge as a result of the choice. As to the logic of choice it embodies, this comes essentially from the methodology of traditional science where it prevails. Indeed, the logic of choice, as depicted in Figure 1, independently of the algorithm of evaluation and of folding of partial criteria, can be interpreted as a result of a conjoint measurement (Krantz et al, 1971) of the utility of options performed by humans seen as instruments. An equally valid alternative interpretation explicates options as instruments, while the choice becomes a conjoint measurement of the attitudes of humans. This latter interpretation is especially useful in the context of revealed preference analysis.

In this sense, the only, rather limited, place for creative reasoning in the choice process is in the folding of partial criteria and in finding appropriate trade-offs between gains and losses achieved on various dimensions of the option characterisation. And there is nothing accidental in the fact that such a profound thinker as Simon (1969) was quite adamant at stating that there is no special need for a separate logic of choice as it is patently sufficient to analyse the consequences of various choices and to select those which seem to be more appealing.

The situation, however, is by no means that simple. First of all, the first three components of the problem characterisation are mutually inter-dependent. Indeed, the options which we see fit to consider are not just names or labels but rather manifestly incomplete representations of the reality, bundles of attributes which we consider to be essential for ultimate evaluation, and, as such, the choice of a representation for the options depends on the choice of the preferences. Conversely, with different representations of the options, we perceive these options differently, and, consequently, apply different criteria in their comparison.

At first glance, it may seem that the scope of alternatives to consider is independent of both the choice of representation and the preferences. Meanwhile, it is only rarely that this set of alternatives turns out to be the result of a formal combinatorics in the attribute space and, indeed, examination of the rejected combinations quite often reveals semantic relations which only rarely find their proper expression in the representations chosen.[3] Moreover, it seems patently unsatisfactory to reduce the reasoning about one's choice to a mere folding of partial evaluations of alternatives in terms of partial preferences seen as projections of some "global preference" to be revealed (see Emelyanov and Nappelbaum, 1977). In order to demonstrate this to one's own satisfaction it is sufficient to try to explain in these terms the human capability of changing one's opinion, or reframing, or the phenomena of external persuasion. Indeed, it seems to be extremely difficult to explain all these discontinuities in the process of reasoning, and all these instances of illumination and revelation in terms of gradual updating of the parameters of the criterion folding mechanisms. It is even more difficult to imagine in what terms one may argue about the nature of the mechanism itself.[4]

Some argue, of course, that the formulation of the choice problem is always preceded by its holistic perception and this is a Gestalt perception (Mandler and Mandler, 1964) which is focusing our attention to the relevant representation and a proper choice of preferences.[5] This brings us to consider another, fifth, component of the choice problem formulation which is only too often misguidedly neglected when contemplating a choice situation:

- *Instrumental intentions* of the choice, combining both the reasons about how we are planning to exploit the results of the choice and the ideas of how the choice is to be implemented.

One of the first attempts to attract our attention to this aspect of the comprehension of the choice situation can be found in Lancaster (1966). The need for such a component becomes quite clear if we return to the original intention of the paper which is to reason about the choice of representation. Indeed, it would be difficult even to start thinking about a proper way of representing something before having a rather clear idea about what we are going to do with this representation, both

---

[3] The information gained through such an examination is, actually, capitalised upon in many creative techniques such as morphology analysis Koberg and Bagnail, 1974) or synectics (Cordon, 1961).

[4] It is interesting to note that though it is precisely this objective which is claimed in the title of the book by van Grich (1987), the content of the hook attacks very different and much more interesting topics.

[5] A more detailed analysis of such a shift in the focus of our attention with regard to a problem of choice can be found in Humphreys and Berkeley (1983).

meaningfully and formally. Moreover, it is precisely this choice of intentions that relates the problem of choice of the representation to the problem of choice of a substantive alternative.

In addition, I would like to draw the reader's attention to the diversity of various problems of choice (of representation, of preferences, of the logic of choice, of intentions, of the set of alternatives etc.) we are forced to consider when we attempt to analyse the finer points of the choice procedure.

Elsewhere Emelyanov and Nappelbaum, 1985)1 have argued that a natural way of avoiding the tenets of interdependencies of the various components mentioned above (as well as the infinite replicative proliferation of the choice problems of both lower and higher levels) is to abandon completely the implicative linear logic underlying the approach shown in Figure 1 and to start analysing the problem in the light of an entirely different "circular" logic based on the ideas of balance.

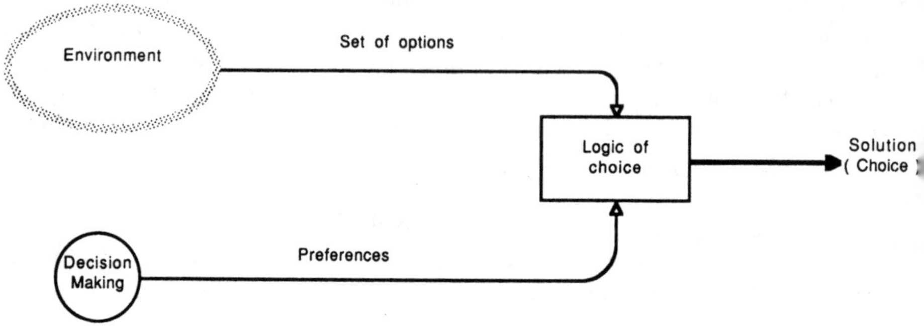

Figure 1 The linear logic of choice

The idea of balance as an underlying principle governing human behaviour is by no means new either in psychology (Heider, 1946) or in cybernetics (Pask, 1975). It was strongly advocated by the proponents of cognitive dissonance (Festinger, 1957) though this school of thought has failed, in my opinion, to bring it to its natural conclusions through trying to temper it with the ideas of maximisation which is foreign to the principle of balance (something is either balanced or not and so it is rather strange to speak of the *degree* to which it is balanced).

Within the general framework I propose here, the idea of utility maximisation is rejected totally as a foundation of choice or, for that matter, of any form of intelligent purposeful behaviour. Within this framework, in the process of choice, we do not choose only an option but, rather, choose, concurrently and interdependently, *all* the five components of the problem formulation outlined above and select the option which in the light of this formulation we will consider as the choice. In doing so, we shift our attention from the problems of utility measurement to the problems of construction of the *languages* in which we are going to describe our options (as well as discriminate between them), the *values* (or preferences) we see as relevant, and our *intentions* of actions (both for implementation and utilisation) as well as the *set of alternatives* to consider and the *logic of choice* to apply. I have tried to capture this change of the logic of choice in graphical terms through changing from the scheme of Figure 1 to that of Figure 2.

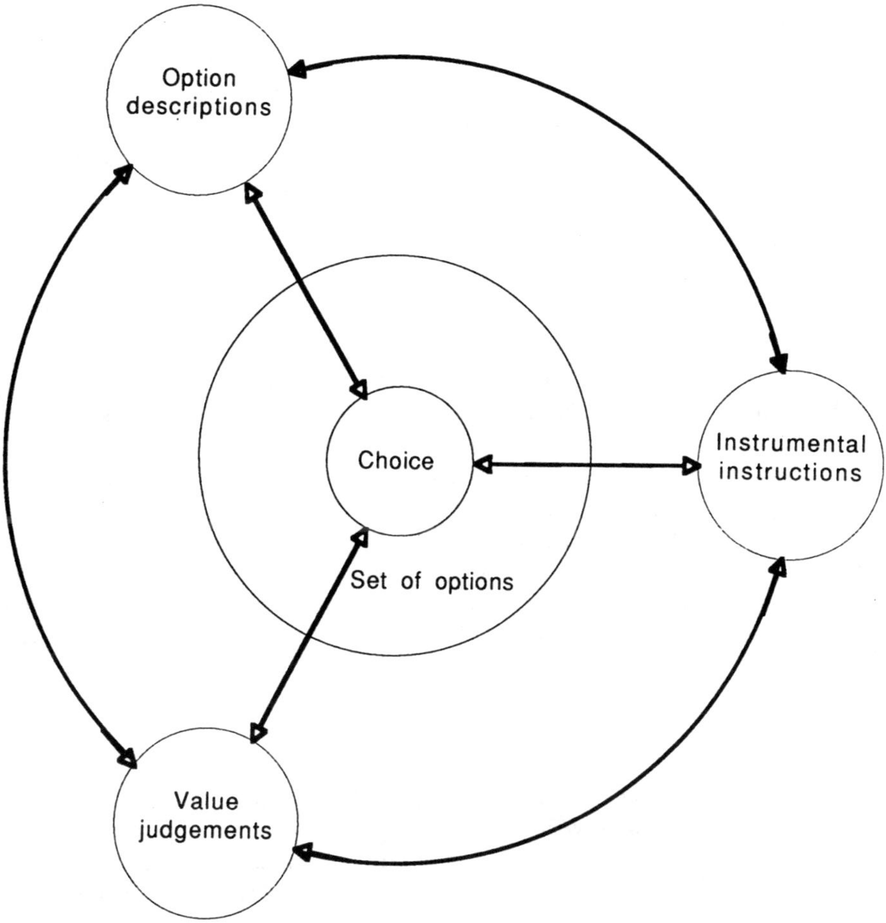

Figure 2 The circular logic of choice

The scheme sketched in Figure 2 places a heavy emphasis on the dynamics of construction of various representations or languages (very much in the sense of Pask's, *1975*, conversation theory) which proceeds until we reach the balance consisting in an obvious self-sufficiency of data (that is, when the data conveyed by a representation of each particular kind shown in a circle in Figure 2 are both sufficient and necessary for applying representations of the remaining kinds) and in an inner consistency which requires that the original dilemma of choice disappears altogether as, under the constructed representation, one of the options now dominates all the rest quite clearly.

In actual terms this means that we look for or, rather, design such an overall representation of the choice situation (with declarative, instrumental and the value components as well as with the choice boundary indicated) that makes the problem of choice disappear altogether in the sense of removing completely all the doubts (or cognitive dissonance) produced by the previous embaras du choix. The problem of choice, therefore, turns out to be reduced to the problem of problem-solving, that is, to the problem of finding a representation which balances out in the sense explained above. Such a change of the general perspective leads to several important conclusions about how we deal with the problems of choice in general.

First of all, due to the need for inner consistency, the resulting (holistic) representation should be, by necessity, a very compact one. A more complicated version of representation would introduce unavoidable cognitive dissonance, contradictory evaluations such that the representation loses its holistic, Gestalt nature.

Even with the simplest kind of representation it is not always possible to achieve the balance we seek. Hence, many a time the balance is reached through liberal use of "default" elements of representation for which the true information is either lacking or substituted for by something we wistfully wish to happen even against the strongest evidence.

The suggested compactness of the holistic representation along with its balanced nature makes it quite easy to mould the inner reasoning it is built around into a variety of seemingly different forms of implicative deductive kind. Hence, there exists a variety of different soft methods of systems analysis (Checkland, 1981) or, by the same token, of methods dealing with decision-making, forecasting, knowledge integration etc. In reality, however, they are all just a rationalisation of an ad hoc circular representation logic ("successful" or otherwise).

The latter consideration can provide an explanation of the seeming simplicity of intelligent behaviour as well as of the trivialization of some crucial and profound notions. As soon as we have been really successful in capturing the essence of a situation (as expressed by our capability to design a holistic representation of it), we can mould the underlying reasoning within a simple framework, while some of the features of this logic (such as transitivity of preferences, independence of attributes, minimisation of the descriptive space, etc.). Any attempt to characterise this intelligence, rationality or creativity in these terms thus merely reflects our intention of working within this logic rather than really uncovering some property of the intellect, of rationality or of creativity.

Because of the compactness dictated by the inner consistency principle, the balance achieved is rather fragile and temporal but, at the same time, it is essentially attribute-tight and isolated in the sense that has been brought to our attention by the ideas of autopoiesis (Maturana and Varela, 1979). But, by the same token, this implies that, for the same actual situation, it is always possible to design several competing representations. Thus, the depth of our comprehension of the situation depends crucially on the number of representations one may design for it, rather than on the comprehensiveness of any of these representations (this latter criterion is self-contradictory in any case).

These representations are conceptually discrete in the sense that one cannot move from one to the other in an evolutionary manner (e.g., by modifying gradually the weight one may place on an attribute). They are also conceptually incomparable because they exist in different psychological worlds where even the same variables may have different interpretations. Any simple merger of these worlds is impossible precisely because of the organisationally closed semantic and pragmatic constriction of the balanced representation which constitutes each of them.

This cognitive closure not only involves the dimensions that enter explicitly in the representation but also explicitly presupposes a certain understanding (or a cognitive commitment) that all the remaining dimensions do not threaten the integrity of this closure. Any change of the situation may, in principle, invalidate this assumption and, hence, such a representation may be a very poor candidate for transitive chaining. This may explain the well-known phenomenon whereby an originally quite interesting and meaningful statement of a problem may become quite artificial and even nonsensical with further attempts at its generalisation and development.

The possibility of having several incomparable and equally valid representations of the same actual situation calls for considering the problem of choice at another level, that is, of choosing one of these representations (small worlds). As I have pointed out earlier, this problem of choosing the appropriate representation cannot be solved through a mere merger of all the relevant representations.

This new problem should be treated exactly in the same terms in which we tackled the original one: we have to design for it an entirely different representation, with its own options, its own declarative language, its own higher-level values, and its instrumental intentions (see Figure 3 for a schematic explication of the interlevel logic dependencies). As such, it addresses a completely different scope of reality with the languages designed for the original choice being singularly inappropriate for this new level of contemplation.

At first glance, it may seem that these last propositions bring us firmly back to the difficulties related to the phenomena of proliferation of problems of choice. The situation, however, is not equivalent to that of Figure 1. Indeed, to be able to create a higher level of the choice uncertainty, one has to design several representations of the basis of choice between several viewpoints embodied in the separate representations of the original level. This, however, calls for additional efforts and the margin left by previous decisions which have committed us to some higher-level logic may be rather limited.

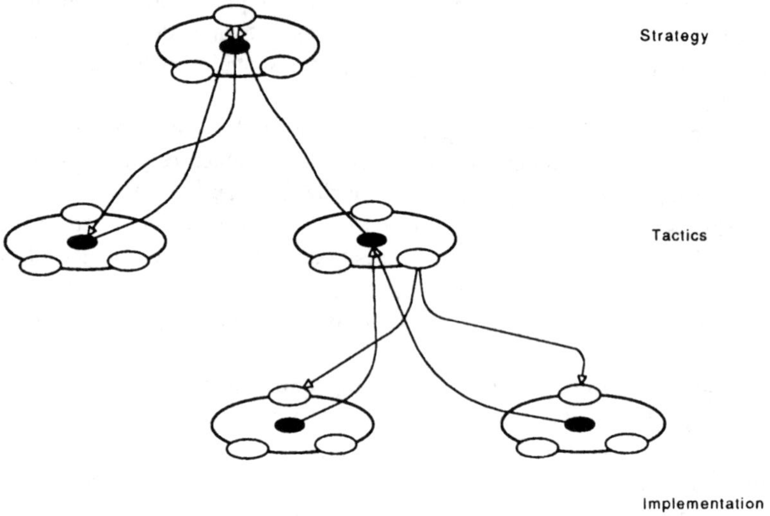

Figure 3 Interlevel dependencies in the circular logic of choice.

Another restricting factor may be associated with the reasons of implementation of the chosen option. The shift of attention to various individual actions involved in implementation must be followed by re-focusing our perception of the situation, by the design of a new representation in terms of which something which originally looked to be the solution may now appear not to be so.

Similar considerations of the economics of design of holistic representations make us understand some aspects of the dual role played by stereotyping in cognition and thinking. On the one hand, stereotyping is a highly useful device helping us to economise on the representation design and to organise incoming information in a more efficient fashion (this aspect has been discussed elsewhere, e.g. in Pospelov, 1981, with respect to the frame ideas). But, on the other hand, it makes our thinking less flexible and less open to new ideas, it creates conceptual blocks to be discarded, and it makes us blind not only to some (possibly crucial) details which fall outside the stereotyped perception, but also to some fundamental assumptions underlying the semantic framework of the stereotype (Mason and Mitroff, 1981). The same considerations may give us some answers to the questions formulated in the beginning of this paper. Indeed, it is the design of a new balanced representation, and thus the achievement of a new cognitive closure (be it self-made or suggested by somebody else) that may lead us to a change of mind, to reframing.

3 SYSTEMS ANALYSIS AND ORGANIZATION OF KNOWLEDGE

An attentive reader may have possibly noticed that, though I have started to discuss the logic of choice, my last comments apply equally well (and, indeed, were intended to apply) in more general settings. This is fully in line with my general contention that, actually, any problem of choice reduces itself, in the final analysis, to a problem-solving kind, while the solution of any problem of the latter type depends crucially on the appropriate choice of the problem representation.

In problem-solving terms, Figure 2 can be interpreted (see Figure 4) as a representation of the logic of problem formulation with *declarative* (description of the problem search space), *instrumental* (description of the operators or transformations in the problem search space), and *value* (definition of a solution or of an instrument for identifying one) components which must be self-sufficient and properly balanced (in the sense that they suggest a solution) since, in the final analysis, only the existence of a solution makes the problem formulation appropriate.

Figure 4 The circular logic of problem formulation

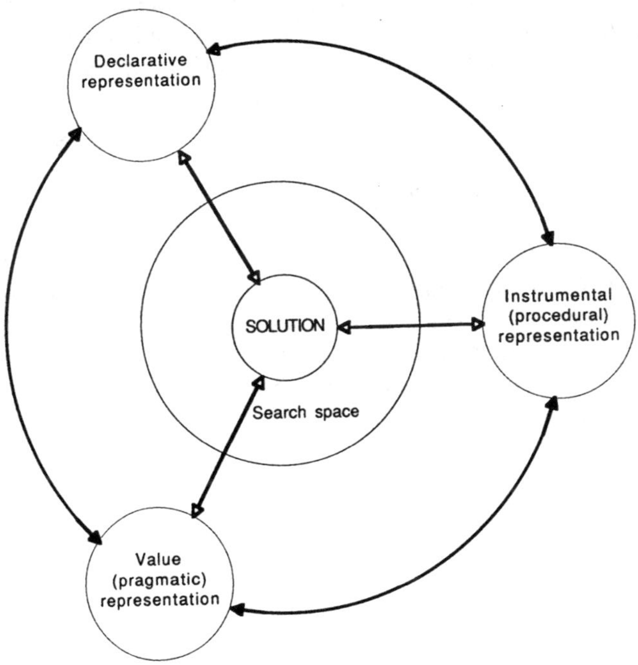

In this sense, there is actually none of the customary time distance that separates the formulation of the problem from the instance of arriving at its solution. The problem is not really formulated (at least, we cannot be sure of it) till it is solved and vice versa. The validity of this statement is rather evident when we deal with what are called soft or ill-structured problems but it is also equally true in much more rigorous, well-structured settings. As Lakatos (1963) has brilliantly demonstrated, even in the limiting case of a mathematical problem, we always start with a premonition of a specific solution; we know it, though possibly mistakenly, and only after that, we start to argue it or rationalise it. of course, in the course of the latter process, we may well find a need for changing the solution and for qualifying or modifying the original formulation and for rejecting either or both of them.

In reporting the problem solution, however, we rarely (if at all) describe or even refer to the process through which we originally arrived at the solution. Moreover, we present it as if the solution were originally divorced from the problem formulation and has come to us as a total surprise. Note that in the case of the most well-structured type of knowledge, i.e. in mathematics, it is customary to present the problem statement and the problem solution simultaneously and on the same footing in the form of a theorem.[6]

All the processes related to the formulation of a problem and to the simultaneous discovery of a solution, were for a very long time thought to be outside the realm of science. It is only recently that we have started to consider these processes as subject-matter of scientific research, of professional skill acquisition (e.g., within Operations Research groups, independent consulting etc.), and of special-purpose techniques and devices. They have come to be an important part of the systems analysis methodology (the chronology of development along these lines are well covered in Checkland, 1981). They are also quite prominent in various creativity enhancement techniques (de Bono, 1970; Adams, 1979), and they lie at the core of many Al research projects, though in a heavily camouflaged form.

This burst of interest is not so difficult to understand. The increased pace of development as well as the higher complexity of the processes we have to deal with have prompted a strong demand for speedy problem-solving to cope with the realities of modern times. While quite a few of these problems are standard, at least from the structural viewpoint (hence the emergence of Operations Research as a problem solving discipline), many of these problems are in principle unique, well-adapted only to the current environment and have to be handled without delay, thus

---

[6] The same standard does not, however, apply to the companion problem of finding the proof. Here, *both* the problem formulation and the way of arriving at the proof are left hidden from the audience.

allowing little time for an illuminating insight to produce itself from an unstructured contemplation of the problematique.

Though to-day we know of several competing standard techniques or even methodologies for problem formulation or conceptualisation, most of them do not do real justice to the multi-faceted nature of the process. The majority start by considering a particular, strictly defined, component of the problem representation and try to unfold it into a fully-fledged conceptualisation in a kind of implicative fashion. True, many if not all of them provide for some feedback but this is only a poor relation of the circular balancing logic we wish to advocate. At the stage where feedback is involved, the conceptualisation will already have gone sufficiently far to prefocus our attention on a particular framework, and so the feedback comes in useful only as an instrument of fine tuning rather than for reconceptualization of the problem.

Within the framework proposed here, it is essential to see that there are many entry points into the process of conceptualisation, and none of them may claim the privileged role. We may enter the problem from a prospective declarative representation (i.e., by initially choosing the description of the space where we shall develop our options), or from an analysis of the instrumental possibilities we have (i.e., from a set of actions we see as relevant and feasible with respect to the problematique), or from the angle of the value components (i.e., by stating our objectives and goals), or from a detailed analysis of a particular option we have in mind (e.g., by asking ourselves why we are dissatisfied with the status quo), or, indeed, from a detailed analysis of the scope of the options, leading to the better understanding of hidden assumptions manifest in implicit constraints. And, of course, the actual entry point may be a combination of those mentioned above.

Independently of the entry point we have chosen, however, it is essential that our cognitive logic of conceptualisation is inherently flexible enough not to keep us within the same frame that was premeditated by the entry representation. Choice of a particular entry point should not mean that we are doomed to stay forever within its domain. It is precisely in this feature that many of the current conceptualisation techniques are lacking.

What we really need is a comprehensive battery of methodologies and techniques that will allow us to analyse the inherent structure of an existing stereotype, to reveal the hidden assumptions which underly it, to burst and disintegrate it and to use the debris as entry points into entirely new creative cognitive closures. To be able to achieve all this we need, of course, an underlying theory and a set of appropriate meta-principles. In other words, we need a developed understanding of the principles of knowledge organisation that make it possible for human beings to solve problems efficiently and creatively, to make decisions and, in general, to interact intelligently with the world in which they live. In my view, it is precisely this objective that systems analysis and design, operations research, decision-making methodology, design methodology and many other similar fields are trying to achieve, though this idea is present in most of these fields in an implicit and subconscious form.

Systems research, it seems, has achieved a closer grasp of the topic than have any of the others as it is much more flexible in its choice of entry points and adopts fewer assumptions which make some components of original formulation of the problem unalterable. We also hope that the general scheme of organisation of knowledge into an integrated atomic whole presented earlier may serve as a foundation of this new science of the knowledge organisation into system is understood to be specific forms of knowledge organisation especially suitable for intelligent interaction with the environment (Emelyanov and Nappelbaum, 1985).

In order to be in line with our own conception we have to accept the possibility of another organisation of knowledge that constitutes the entire problem domain of systems research. Indeed, in a sense, this paper is trying to present a cognitive closure for development of systems methodology and methods with the current dissatisfaction with their explication taken as the problematique which we are quite aware but do not really know what to do with. The only feature that puts our thesis apart is that it is self-contained, that is, the whole approach can be derived from the same principles it applies to the analysis of situations within systems practice and systems theory.

Moreover, many of the principles that have been proclaimed by many other explications only as imperative desiderata, as some meta-axioms, come here as natural conclusions. Some of these have been considered elsewhere (e.g. in Emelyanov and Nappelbaum, 1985). Here I would like to dwell a bit on a general belief that systems analysis offers a kit of tools especially suited for handling new kinds of problems: those which are described as ill-structured.

Although I fully sympathise with many intentions and assumptions that lie behind this claim, I am afraid that its actual wording is rather unfortunate and may be rather misguiding. First of all, by contrasting ill-structured and well-structured problems we are hiding the fact that in every human activity, however well-structured it may be, we always start with an extremely ill-structured problem and always end up by solving a well-structured problem derived from and substituted for the original ill-structured one. But in order to be able to substantiate this contention we first have to consider what kind of a structure we have in mind when we speak about ill- or well-structured problems.

Generally, ill-structuredness is seen in terms of the inherent fallibility of the original formulation of the problem which reflects a high level of cognitive complexity of the environment we are trying to cope with. Ackoff and Emery (1974) speak of the messiness of such problems. Pospelov and Pushkin *(1975)* point to the differences between the language of description of the world we deal with and the language in which we describe our objectives and our goals. Larichev (1979) sees the problem as a patchy, partial way of describing our criteria of comparison. Mason and Mitroff (1981) give a comprehensive list of weaknesses and stress that, in an ill-structured problem, not only there is no means of distinguishing a solution but also there is no hope of achieving one that will remove the problem altogether. Within the framework of this paper, all this can be seen as an original imbalance of the problem presentation to be used as issue for ultimate removal from the problem formulation. This is, however, only partially true.

It seems to be true that in every ill-structured problem the main criterion of balancing (i.e., that of internal consistency) is not met. The original formulation *either* points to a variety of apparent solutions which we do not know how to distinguish between *or* apparently offers no guidelines for searching for a solution. In a sense, both of these cases amount to the same thing: the impossibility to implement something which we would see as a solution.

Indeed, even the most blatantly ill-structured problem (e.g., "I am quite unhappy about the present state of the things and I have to do something to improve it") is actually perfectly balanced. It is obviously self-sufficient and internally consistent as it points to an obvious and immediate solution: "Do something efficient". The problem, however, is that this "solution" does not tell us anything about how we can implement it. And, as soon as we try to get some better understanding of the state of things and of the ways to improve it (i.e., as soon as we start asking ourselves what we are dissatisfied with, what we can do, how we will distinguish an improvement etc.), we will also need to change all the other components of the problem statement to preserve the balance which was so easily achieved originally.

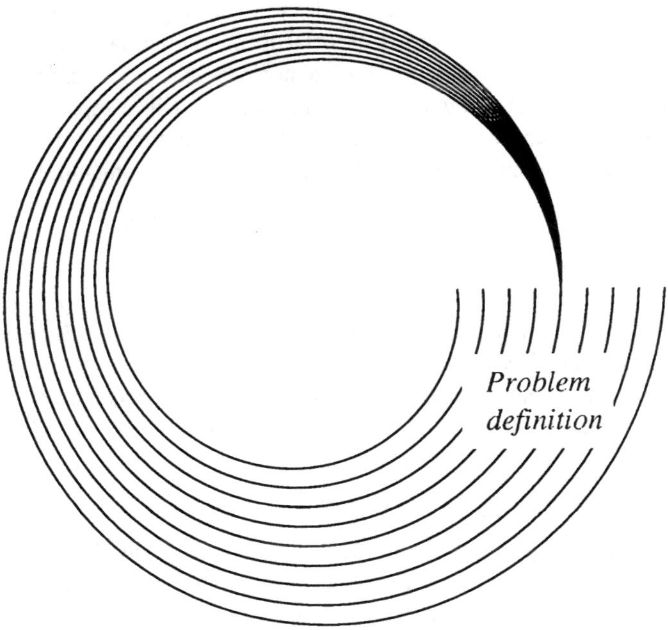

Figure 5 The problem definition cycle

In reality, this means that we are forced to reformat our problem in a way that will make it narrower, more pointed, till an implementable solution emerges as the sole natural consequence of the new formulation. I have tried to express this idea graphically in Figure 5 which focuses on the fact that, as a result of a Systems analysis of a problem, we return to the same stage from which we have started, that is, to the problem formulation, though now this is sharpened by what we have gained in the course of our analysis.

Unfortunately, however, only in a few cases are we likely to do this by invoking some meaningful consideration. More often than not we do it by an implicit (and sometimes even unrecognised) substitution of the original problem by another one obtained either through an arbitrary prefocusing on some "obvious" way of dealing with the problem, or through the introduction of some "meta-criteria" of rationality imposing rather arbitrary constraints on possible solutions[7]

In reality, all these meta-considerations are not actually the inherent features of a solution but, rather, result from the problem analyst's desire to make his or her life a bit easier. Their adoption in any practical case should be conditional on checking that the assumptions which underly their construction are met in the case in question. In many cases however this is not done as they are not considered by the problem analyst to be important enough to be verified regardless of the cost incurred in meeting them. As a result, intransitivities detected within the problem representation constrained by the meta criteria may be viewed as originating through "subjective error" in developing the problem representation. This ignores their real value as pointers towards aspects of the situation which control the problem definition, which are not representable within the current constrained representation, but which should play an important part in a representation which was closed in a more appropriate way (Berkeley and Humphreys, 1982).

In terms of the framework presented in this paper, such unnatural ways of narrowing the problem statement constitutes just another instance of default reasoning in achieving a balanced representation of the *second-order* problem, i.e., of designing a balanced representation of the original meaningful problem. In this respect, it would be useful to recall that, within the framework we discuss here, the ultimate choice of a representation (and hence of a solution) depends very much on implicit constraints placed both *from above* by the considerations of a higher "ethical" level, and *from below* by considerations of implementability of the instrumental intentions proclaimed in the representation. In a sense, all this has to

---

[7] The whole philosophy of optimality is a vivid demonstration of such an approach and it had a telling effect on many fields of research that may possibly never have used the word "optimality" in their professional language; the same comments apply to the ideas of transitivity or independence in the choice theory etc.

be considered concurrently with the present level" representations and, in this sense, the diagram in Figure 6 is more appropriate than that in Figure 5.

Because of the limitations on the size of this paper it is not possible to develop this last ideas any further here. I will note only that, in line with the framework of Figure 6, the principles of balancing should encompass not only a single holistic representation but rather the entire branching chain of those stressing once again the inseparability of analytical, design and implementation components of a problem.

This brings also to the fore the temporal aspect of the problem designing exercise. First of all, the greater the number of levels we are trying to include in our analysis/design problem solving the greater the time scope of our analysis both in terms of the time required to solve the problem and the time horizon of the designed scenario. Meanwhile, we should be equally aware of the inherently provisional nature of the balance we have managed to achieve. Therefore, it is always necessary to look for a proper trade-off between the depth of the analysis and the temporary nature of the framework one has adopted for this particular purpose, that is, to find the borderline between determination and obstinacy. The system of values we adopt within this framework, and redesign again and again, is the most powerful tool we have for coping with this problem. Most of the heuristics considered in Newell and Simon (1972). can be explained in these terms as well.

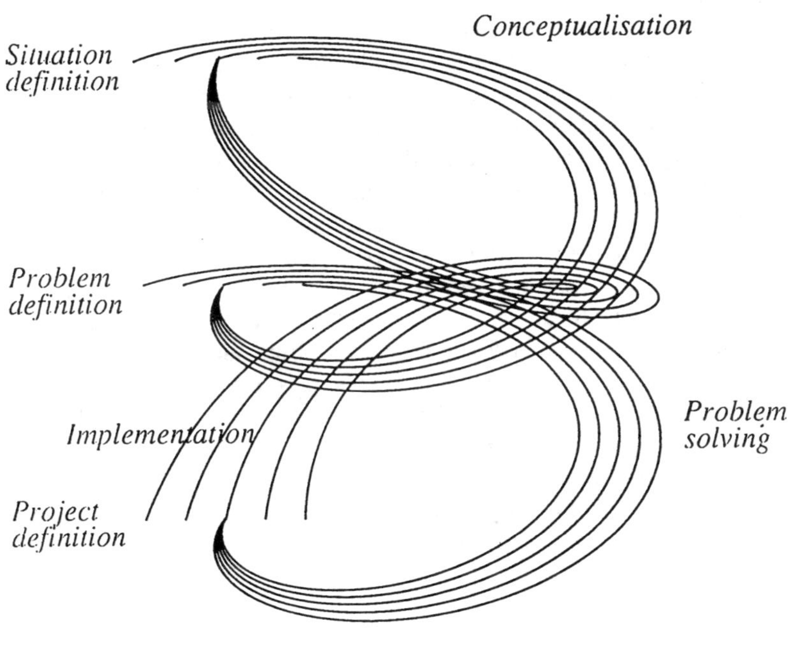

Figure 6 Situation, problem and implementation definition cycles

On the other hand, this intrinsic need for "multi-levelness" of the presentation may be an answer to another conceptual difficulty with the existing methodologies for problem solving and decision making. I refer here to the fact that problem solving and decision making offer an obviously discrete-time vision of the world according to which both the problem and the choice make the time freeze, as it were, and disrupt the natural continuous flow of events. In one sense, this halting nature of problem solving or decision making is highly significant as it indicates that the time is ripe for posing, contemplation and rethinking. But, by the same token, it disrupts all the natural ties that exist between the problem and the processes that have led to its creation and cut it out of the natural texture of life. The line of thought I am advocating makes the future much less visible and provides for the connection between the events that have led to the perception of the problem to be explicitly accounted for.

These considerations of various facets of the temporal aspects of the presented framework seem to be a nice and fitting point to wind up the present discussion. Some of the multi-layer representations developed in the course of thinking out the way of solving some particular problem may turn out to be robust and persistent enough to be applicable for many other problems to come. In this case, they give rise to a new theory of an appropriate scale, while the reasons underlying its creation become almost immaterial as the theory progresses to its full maturity and while the corresponding research activity ceases to belong to the systems realm. Unfortunately (or, possibly, fortunately), most of the systems designed in this manner cannot claim the same robustness and long-term nature. They remain valid only for a limited period of time and, also, for rather unique circumstances.

It would be also useful to note that the multi-layer representation construed here comprises not only what has been retained in it explicitly but also what has been discarded. In this sense, all the rest of the systems analysis protocol should be kept at the back of our mind and be constantly used for systems monitoring, i.e., for checking the validity of the provisionally adopted vision against the new influx of evidence in terms of both what has been adopted and what has been discarded.

The same arguments should be applied to the theory at hand. Of course, I would be very pleased to see it as an enduring framework. But I am equally aware of the fact that it is very much preconditioned by the past developments in systems thinking and that its implementational depth is not yet as deep as one might desire. Therefore, it would be rather premature of me to forecast its viability and generality. But, even if its life-span is doomed to be short lived, I do hope that it may be a source of some new insights and as another option to be kept in mind and to provide a reference to check against in further developments of systems methodology.

4 ACKNOWLEDGEMENTS

I feel impelled to express my gratitude to Dr. V. Antonuk, Academician S. Emelyanov, Academician J. Gvishiani, Dr. P. Humphreys, Dr. E. Mirskii and Dr. D. Pospelov, with whom I have had the opportunity to discuss these matters at length and whose comments were to me of great help and inspiration. I would also like to thank D. Tsoubelis for his work in developing the mathematical graphics programs which drew figures 5 and 6.

5 REFERENCES

Ackoff, R. L. and Emery, F. (1974) On Purposeful Systems. Aldine-Atherton, Chicago.

Adams, J. L. (1979) Conceptual Blockbusting. Norton, New York.

Berkeley, D. and Humphreys, P. C. (1982) Structuring Decision Problems and the "bias heuristic". *Acta Psychologica,* **50,** 201-252.

Bobrow, D. G. and Collins, A. (1968) Representation avid Understanding: Studies in Cognitive Science. Academic Press, New York:.

Boden, M. (1977) Artificial Intelligence and Natural Man. Basic Books, New York.

de Bono, E. (1970) Lateral Thinking: A Textbook of Creativity. Ward Lock, London.

Checkland, P. (1981) Systems Thinking, Systems Practice. Wiley, Chichester.

Emelyanov, S. V. and Nappelbaum, E. L. (1977) Logic of Rational Choice, in: The State-of-the-Art Report in Science and Technology. *Engineering Cybernetics.* VINITI Publications, Moscow. (in Russian).

Emelyanov, S. V. and Nappelbaum, E. L. *(1985)* Systems, Purposefulness and Cognition, in *Systems Research II.. Methodological Problems* (ed. J. M. Gvishiani). Pergamon Press, Oxford.

Festinger, L. A. (1957) A Theory of Cognitive Dissonance. Row & Peterson, Evanston.

Fodor, J. A. (1981) Representations. MIT Press, Cambridge, Mass.

van Gigch, J. P. (1987) Decision Making about Decision Making. Abacus Press, Cambridge, Mass.

Gordon, W. J. (1961) Synectics. Harper and Row, New York.

Heider, F. (1946) Attitudes and Cognitive Organization. *Journal of Psychology,* **21**, 107-112.

Humphreys, P.C. and Berkeley , D. (1983). Problem Structuring Calculi and Levels of Knowledge Representation in Decision Making, in *Decision Making under Uncertainty* (ed. R. W. Scholz) North Holland, Amsterdam.

Humphreys, P.C. and Berkeley, D. (1985) Handling uncertainty: levels of analysis of decision problems, in *Behavioural Decision Making: Theory and Analysis.* (ed. G. N. Wright) Plenum, New York.

Jeffreys, R. (1965) The Logic of Decisions. McGraw Hill, New York.

Koberg, D. and Bagnall, J (1974) The Universal Traveller. A Soft-Systems Guidebook to Creativity, Problem-Solving and the Process of Design. William Kaufman, Los Altos, California.

Krantz, D. H., Luce, R. D., Suppes, P. and Tversky, A. (1971) Foundations of Measurement: Additive and Polynomial Representations. Academic Press, New York.

Lakatos, I. (1963-4) Proofs and Refutations. *British Journal of Philosophy* (in four parts).

Lancaster, K. J. (1966) A New Approach to Consumer Theory. *Journal of Political Economy,* ***74*** (1).

Larichev, 0.1. (1979) *Science and Art of Decision Making.* Nauka, Moscow. (in Russian).

Mandler, J. M. and Mandler, G. (1964) Thinking: From Association to Gestalt. Wiley, New York.

Maryuama, M. (1963) Generating Complex Patterns by Means of Simple Rules of Interaction. *Methods,* **14**,17-26.

Mason, R. and Mitroff, I. (1981) Challenging Strategic Planning Assumptions. Wiley, New York.

Maturana, H. and Varela, F. (1979) *Autopoiesis and Cognition.* Riedel, Boston.

Minsky, M. (1975) A Framework for Representing Knowledge, in *The Psychology of Computer Vision* (ed. P. H. Winston) McGraw Hill, New York.

Newell, A. and Simon, H. A. (1972) Human Problem Solving. Prentice Hall, Englewood Cliffs.

Pask, 0. (1975) Conversation, Cognition and Learning. Elsevier, Amsterdam.

Pospelov, D. A. and Pushkin, V. N. (1975). Intelligence and Automata. Soviet Radio, Moscow. (in Russian).

Pospelov, D. A. (1981) Logic-Linguistic Models in Control Systems. Energoizdat, Moscow. (in Russian).

Schank, R. C. (1986) Explanation Patterns. Erlbaum, Hillsdale, N. J.

Simon, H. A. (1960) The New Science of Management Decisions. Harper and Row, New York.

Simon, H. A. (1967) Motivational and Emotional Control of Cognition. *Psychological Review,* **74**, 29-39.

Simon, H. A. (1969) The Science of Artificial. MIT Press, Cambridge, Mass.

White, D. J. (1975) Decision Methodology. Wiley, Chichester.

6 BIOGRAPHY

Eric L. Nappelbaum is Vice Chancellor at the Moscow School for Business of Political Science and Law and Research Director at the Moscow Institute of System Analysis, faculty of Operational Research. He studied Physics and Computer Sciences at the Moscow State University and did his PhD on Control Problems at the Moscow Physical Technical Institute. Dr Eric L. Nappelbaum is member of All Russian Academy of Science , Department of Operational Research and IT Strategy. Dr Eric Nappelbaum has published more than 40 international papers. He is Visiting Professor at the London School of Economics and Political Science and at the International Management Centre in Budapest. The research interests of Dr Nappelbaum include Organisational Transformation, System Analysis and System Logic.

INDEX OF CONTRIBUTORS

KEYWORD INDEX